ETHICS, POLITICS,
AND HUMAN NATURE

ETHICS, POLITICS, AND HUMAN NATURE

Edited by

Ellen Frankel Paul, Fred D. Miller, Jr., and Jeffrey Paul

BASIL BLACKWELL

Copyright © Social Philosophy & Policy 1991

ISBN 0-631-17885-6

First published 1991

Basil Blackwell Ltd
108 Cowley Road, Oxford, OX4 1JF, UK

Basil Blackwell Inc.
3 Cambridge Center,
Cambridge, MA 02142, USA

British Library Cataloguing in Publication Data
Ethics. politics, and human nature.
1. Man. Nature.
I. Paul, Ellen Frankel II. Miller, Fred D. (Fred Dycus)
III. Paul, Jeffrey
128.4

ISBN 0-631-17885-6

Library of Congress Cataloguing-in-Publication Data
Ethics, politics, and human nature/edited by Ellen Frankel Paul,
Fred D. Miller, Jr., and Jeffrey Paul.
p.   cm.
Includes bibliographical references.
ISBN 0-631-17304-8
1. Punishment–Philosophy.   2. Criminal law–Philosophy.
I. Paul, Ellen Frankel II. Miller, Fred D. (Fred Dycus)
III. Paul, Jeffrey
HV8675.E83 1990
364.6–dc20
[90-299]

Typeset in 10 on 12 pt Ehrhardt
by SB Datagraphics Ltd, Colchester
Printed in Great Britain by Whitstable Litho, Kent.

CONTENTS

INTRODUCTION

"'Tis evident, that all the sciences have a relation, greater or less to human nature; and that however wide any of them may seem to run from it, they still return back by one passage or another." So observed David Hume, in the introduction to *A Treatise of Human Nature*, published in 1739. This collection of essays returns again to the topic of human nature in order to consider its relevance for fundamental questions in ethics, political philosophy, and public policy. How should we understand the rights, obligations, and virtues of human beings? What is the proper relationship between the individual and society? Should politics obey human nature or try to change it?

Th The contributors to this volume begin with a critical review of traditional views of human nature: on one view, found in classical philosophy, human beings are naturally or essentially part of greater wholes such as society, the state, or the universe; on another, favored by early modern philosophers like Hume, morality is grounded in natural human passions or sympathies; and a third view, popularized by Rousseau, discerns within human nature a fundamental ambivalence or antipathy towards society. In recent years a new theory called sociobiology has appeared, claiming that the science of biology and the theory of evolution have an essential place in the explanation of human social behavior. The central essays in this volume consider what light biology may shed upon the traditional controversies of ethics and politics. The concluding essays address issues which have become unavoidable as a result of technological and social advances: should human beings presume to change human nature itself, and what moral standards should be used in evaluating such a perilous undertaking?

"Natural Virtues, Natural Vices," by Annette C. Baier, is an examination of David Hume's *Treatise of Human Nature*. Hume claimed to base his moral findings on his conclusions about human nature, yet it was Hume who proffered the devastating criticism of previous moral analyses: that they illegitimately moved from "is" to "ought." Baier discusses that notorious passage in the *Treatise*, and finds that it does not rule out some sort of non-deductive inference from facts about human nature and human preferences to conclusions about moral virtues. Hume's own claim that some virtues are "natural" — that is, that they tend naturally to occur in normal people — is precariously balanced by his recognition of our equally "natural" sexist and nationalist vices, which are encouraged by some of our social artifices. The ambivalence in his theory corresponds to the ambivalence of its subject matter: our attitudes and reflective preferences.

David Gauthier, in "*Le promeneur solitaire*: Rousseau and the Emergence of the Post-Social Self," analyzes the social nature of mankind in the work of Rousseau, who began his autobiographical writings with the claim that they "may be used as the first comparative work in the study of man, which is certainly yet to be begun." Whereas in his social thought Rousseau traced mankind's passage from solitude to society, in his autobiographical writings he traced his own passage from society to solitude. *Les Reveries du promeneur solitaire* shows the last stages of this progression, in which the self-portrait reveals what Gauthier calls the "post-social self." The portrait is unique, yet exemplary; Rousseau is the first to live in a post-social condition. Gauthier's examination of Rousseau's depiction of his own life uncovers the roles of love and of language in the undermining of Rousseau's acceptance of solitude.

Michael Ruse's essay offers a comparative examination of theories of human nature in the work of Aristotle, Kant, and Hume. Additionally, however, it is the first in a group of essays that deal with the emerging discipline of sociobiology. This discipline is predicated on the idea that important insights about man's social nature can be derived from the science of biology. Ruse argues in "Evolutionary Ethics and the Search for Predecessors: Kant, Hume, and All the Way Back to Aristotle?" that the key to morality lies in our genes. Natural selection has made us altruistic, he writes, and it has given us the feeling that morality is in some sense objective. Ruse finds some support for his claims in prior moral philosophy, but (as expected) there are some points of difference. A major area of tension lies in the Aristotelian notion of "human flourishing," something which today's commentators argue lies beyond the grasp of biology. Ruse concludes, however, that continued empirical research may solve such problems.

Alex Rosenberg, who writes on "The Biological Justification of Ethics: A Best-Case Scenario," identifies several projects which evolutionary theorists who are bent on assimilating ethics to biology might explore. Rosenberg argues that only one of the projects he discusses is possible — justifying morality to the egoist by explaining its emergence as having adaptational qualities — and that one just barely. Rosenberg goes on to sketch a best-case scenario for the fruition of this project, and identifies some central obstacles that such an explanation would have to overcome.

Richard A. Epstein's contribution to this volume details "The Varieties of Self-Interest." His essay explores the relationship between the diverse forms of self-interest and their implications for the appropriate structures of government. Epstein's explanation of how the interplay of natural individual differences creates social results that tend to approach the preferences of the individuals in question paves the way for his discussion of what social organizations would tend to form if natural differences are given play, and what sort of measures we might use to assess competing forms of social order. His analysis suggests that the biological bases of our behavior should not be ignored and ought to supplement explanations from social determinants.

In "The Origins of Morality: An Essay in Philosophical Anthropology," Andrew Oldenquist proposes an integrated causal and analytical explanation of morality. He proposes a "bridge theory" to unite biological and cultural explanations with moral phenomena. His theory rests on the notion that a moral belief is identical to a desire or aversion given certain conditions such as having a willingness to universalize, a disposition to use moral words, and a reason with general appeal. Oldenquist derives moral facts from our evolved human nature, which includes innate sociality and various reinforcements and inhibitions caused by culture. He calls the inquiry into these matters "philosophical anthropology." His attempt to derive a common, cross-cultural morality and show how it illuminates particular aspects of our lives is bolstered by his discussion of such universal phenomena as loyalty, regard for children, and rationality. He defends this notion of common morality against criticisms that it is reductionist or a form of biological determinism.

Christina Sommers's essay opens a series of discussions of human nature and contemporary controversies. In "The Feminist Revelation," Sommers explores the current explosion of academic writings on feminism. Although there are a number of different groups which are self-identifiedly feminist, she divides them into two main categories: "liberal feminists" and "gender feminists." Liberal feminists strive for equal opportunity and equality before the law; they do not find people's preferences, the traditional family, or other social institutions inherently oppressive and targets for elimination. Gender feminists, however, call for radical reconstruction of society. Sommers suggests that the gender feminists who denigrate heterosexuality and the conventional family are inherently authoritarian. The gender feminists' vision is so all-encompassing that its adherents tend to ignore dissenting voices.

Zbigniew Rau's contribution to this volume rests on a distinction between theories of potential as against actual human nature. In "Human Nature, Social Engineering, and the Reemergence of Civil Society," Rau argues that theorists who call for supplanting actual political systems with revolutionary ones based on their speculations about potential human nature are playing a dangerous game. Rau examines Marxist-Leninist attempts to do precisely this. During the first decade of the Soviet state, leading theorists explicitly stated their desire to remake human nature by subjecting it to radically altered social institutions. Rau analyzes the work of Alexander Zinoviev, Czeslaw Milosz, and the Czechoslovakian school of independent political writers for indications of why this grand enterprise failed. Rau finds that the reemergence of civil society in Eastern Europe is the principal evidence for the failure of Marxism-Leninism to create the "new man." This failure, despite the most vigilant effort ever made to control all of social life from the center, indicates that there is an irreparable flaw in political theories that attempt to fashion human nature to the desires of a human designer.

Another method of transforming human nature — germline genetic engineering — has aroused considerable concern among ethicists. H. Tristram Engelhardt, Jr. argues, in "Human Nature Genetically Revisited," that much of this concern may be overstated or misplaced. There ought to be no general moral proscription against the use of genetic engineering as a therapy or as a means of enhancing particular human capacities. Limitations on genetic engineering are justified only on prudential grounds; that is, one ought to avoid interventions that are likely to cause more harm than benefit to the individual involved.

A conception of human nature lies at the root of all political philosophizing. As the contrariety of viewpoints expressed in these essays indicates, we are far from settling the basic controversies over human nature that have haunted Western thought at least since the era of the Greeks.

ACKNOWLEDGMENTS

The editors wish to acknowledge several individuals at the Social Philosophy and Policy Center, Bowling Green State University, who provided invaluable assistance in the preparation of this volume. They include Mary Dilsaver, Terrie Weaver, Terry Telfer and Kim Kohut.

We wish to thank Executive Manager Kory Tilgner, for his tireless administrative support; Publication Specialist Tamara Sharp, for her patient attention to detail; and Managing Editor Dan Greenberg, for editorial assistance above and beyond the call of duty.

CONTRIBUTORS

Jonathan Barnes is a Fellow of Balliol College and Professor of Ancient Philosophy in the University of Oxford. He has held visiting posts at various universities in North America and Europe. His main professional interest is in ancient philosophy. His most recent publication is *The Toils of Scepticism* (Cambridge University Press, 1990).

Annette Baier is a Professor of Philosophy at the University of Pittsburgh. She has previously taught at Carnegie-Mellon University, the University of Sydney, the University of Auckland, and the University of Aberdeen. She studied at the University of Otago and Oxford University. She has published many articles in the philosophy of mind, ethics, and the history of philosophy, some of which are collected in her recent book, *Postures of the Mind* (University of Minnesota Press, 1985; Methuen Press, 1986). She is working on a book about David Hume.

David Gauthier is Distinguished Service Professor of Philosophy at the University of Pittsburgh. His most recent books are *Morals by Agreement*, in which he develops a rational, contractarian theory of morality, and *Moral Dealing*, a collection of his essays on the history of contractarian thought and on justice, rationality, and ideology. Previously, he wrote *The Logic of Leviathan*, a study of the moral and political thought of Thomas Hobbes. His current research interests are in understanding Rousseau as a critic of modern society, and in refining the maximizing conception of practical rationality.

Michael Ruse is Professor of Philosophy and Zoology at the University of Guelph. His research interests lie in the history and philosophy of biology, especially evolutionary theory. He is the author of a numnber of books, including *The Darwinian Revolution: Science Red in Tooth & Claw* (University of Chicago, 1979), *Taking Darwin Seriously: A Naturalistic Approach to Philosophy* (Basil Blackwell, 1986), and *Homosexuality: A Philosophical Inquiry* (Basil Blackwell, 1988). He is now working on a study of the concept of progress in biology. Ruse is a Fellow of the American Association for the Advancement of Science and of the Royal Society of Canada.

Alex Rosenberg is Professor of Philosophy at the University of California, Riverside. He is the author of *Microeconomic Laws, Sociobiology and the Preemption of Social Science, The Structure of Biological Science, Philosophy of Social Science*, and co-author of *Hume and the Problem of Causation*, as well as papers on ethics, biology, and economics in *Social Philosophy & Policy*. He has held Guggenheim, American Council of Learned Societies, and National Science Foundation fellowships.

Richard A. Epstein is James Parker Hall Distinguished Service Professor of Law at the University of Chicago, where he has taught since 1972. He has been the editor of the *Journal of Legal Studies* since 1981, and a member of the American Academy of Arts and Sciences since 1985. His books include *Takings: Private Property and Eminent Domain* (1985), *Cases and Materials on Torts* (4th ed., with C. Gregory and H. Kalven, Jr., 1984), and *Modern Products Liability Law* (1980). He has taught courses in civil procedure, contract, land development, property, torts (including defamation and privacy), jurisprudence, legal history, Roman law, and workers' compensation. He has written extensively in these areas, as well as in those of constitutional and labor law. Before joining the University of Chicago faculty, he taught at the University of Southern California Law School from 1968 to 1972. He is a graduate of Columbia College, Oxford University (Juris.), and the Yale Law School.

Andrew Oldenquist has been a member of the Ohio State University Philosophy Department since 1962 and an Associate of OSU's Mershon Center since 1981. He has written on ethical theory, action theory, theories of alienation, applied ethics, social and political philosophy, and the philosophy of education. His recent books include *Normative Behavior* (1983), *The Non-Suicidal Society* (1986), *Society and the Invidivual* (coedited with Richard Garner, 1989), and a forthcoming volume, *Alienation, Community, and Work* (coedited with Menachem Rosner). While at Munich University, he will work on a new book that integrates philosophical, biological, and cultural accounts of the origins and nature of morality.

Christina Sommers is an Associate Professor of Philosophy at Clark University. She has published several articles in the area of moral philosophy. She is the editor of *Right and Wrong* and the coeditor of *Vice and Virtue in Everyday Life*.

Zbigniew Rau teaches at the University of Texas at Austin, where he specializes in the politics of the Soviet Union and Eastern Europe. He was educated at the University of Lodz and received his Ph.D. from the Polish University in England. From 1985 to 1988, he was a Visiting Fellow Commoner at Trinity College, Cambridge University. Rau is currently completing the first Polish edition of Locke's *Two Treatises of Government* as well as a book entitled *Contractarianism versus Holism : The Argument of Locke's Two Treatises of Government*. He has written several articles for *Political Studies* which present a liberal interpretation of the emergence and growth of civil society in Eastern Europe.

H. Tristram Engelhardt, Jr. holds an M.D. with honors from Tulane University School of Medicine (1972) and a Ph.D. from the University of Texas at Austin (1969). Dr. Engelhardt is a Professor in the Departments of Medicine and Community Medicine, and Member of the Center for Ethics, Medicine, and Public Issues, Baylor College of Medicine. He is editor of the *Journal of Medicine and Philosophy* and coeditor of the *Philosophy and Medicine* book series. He has authored over one hundred and forty articles, in addition to numerous book reviews and other publications. His most recent book is *The Foundations of Bioethics* (Oxford, 1986).

PARTIAL WHOLES*

By Jonathan Barnes

Individualists like to think of themselves as atoms, their trajectories causally dependent on collisions with other similar entities but their essence resolutely independent and autonomous. They are whole and entire in themselves: they are not elements or adjuncts of some greater whole. Collectivists take an opposite view. Their oddities and accidents may be individual and independent, their movements and machinations largely self-determined, but in their essence they are necessarily bound to others – for all are adjuncts and elements of a larger whole.

In this essay I discuss one version of the collectivist philosophy, a version which has (I suspect) been as popular and as widely supported as any philosophy of human nature. In Section I, the constituent ideas are expounded, largely by way of citation from Alexander Pope. In Section II, the anthropological aspect of Pope's philosophy is subjected to scrutiny; and in Section III, the axiological side of the theory is examined. I hope to show that the collectivist view, in its Popean form, is untenable. But I hope, too, to display its power and its potency.

I. The Moral Philosophy of Alexander Pope

What if the foot, ordain'd the dust to tread,
Or hand to toil, aspir'd to be the head?
What if the head, the eye, or ear repin'd
To serve mere engines to the ruling Mind?
Just as absurd for any part to claim
To be another, in this general frame:
Just as absurd, to mourn the tasks or pains
The great directing MIND of ALL ordains.
All are but parts of one stupendous whole,
Whose body Nature is, and God the soul.

Thus Pope, at the end of the first Epistle of the *Essay on Man*.[1] The thought is this: each of us, like any other natural object, is a part of the universe; it is folly to deny the fact – and folly to wish it changed; for our good is determined and our moral comportment should be governed by our partial status in the universal All.

* This is a lightly revised version of the paper which I presented to the Social Philosophy and Policy Center's "Ethics, Politics, and Human Nature" conference. I am grateful to my audience for several helpful suggestions, and to Ellen Frankel Paul for a sheaf of valuable comments.
[1] I 259–68: I quote from the Twickenham edition, edited by Maynard Mack: *The Poems of Alexander Pope* III i (London: Methuen, 1950).

The universe, devised and managed by God, forms a "vast chain of being."[2] Man is in the middle, and in the chain

> Nothing is foreign: Parts relate to whole.[3]

But each of us is not only a part but also a "system" or a whole. That we are parts does not entail that we are not also wholes; and men – unlike atoms – are what were once called 'partial wholes',[4] parts of a greater whole which are themselves wholes with parts of their own. Moreover, that we are parts of the universe does not entail that we are not also parts of lesser systems, which in their turn are parts of the universe. In particular, we are also parts of a social system. For the natural world is a strictly hierarchical system –

> ORDER is heav'n's first law; and this confest,
> Some are, and must be, greater than the rest[5]

– and the social world matches the natural world in its structure. Heaven's first law, both in its natural and in its social form, is of the last importance; for

> if each system in gradation roll,
> Alike essential to th' amazing whole;
> The least confusion but in one, not all
> That system only, but the whole must fall.[6]

A part cannot "contain the whole."[7] Hence our knowledge of the world is limited –

> 'Tis but a part we see, and not a whole.[8]

Yet despite our myopic vision, we may be brought to see that God did not make the world with the good of its parts in view. Rather,

> He fram'd a Whole, the Whole to bless.[9]

---

[2] *ibid.,* I 237. Compare I 237–258: it is the "scale" (i.e. the *scala naturae*) at I 208, and the "chain of Love" at III 7–26.

[3] *ibid.,* III 21.

[4] See Jonathan Barnes, "Bits and Pieces", ed. J. Barnes and M. Mignucci, *Matter and Metaphysics* (Naples: Bibliopolis, 1988), pp. 223–94.

[5] *Essay,* IV 49–50.

[6] *ibid.,* I 247–50.

[7] *ibid.,* I 32.

[8] *ibid.,* I 60. Some commentators stress the *Essay*'s insistence on the presumptuousness and frailty of human reason, and make Pope into something of a skeptic (see esp. Maynard Mack, *Alexander Pope : A Life* (New Haven/London: Yale University Press, 1985), pp. 527–30). But despite the doleful and the scornful passages, Pope cannot be called a consistent skeptic. According to one critic, skepticism "is indeed trumpeted by Pope at the beginning of the second epistle but is merely disregarded elsewhere" (A. D. Nuttall, *Pope's Essay on Man* (London: Allen and Unwin, 1984), p. 50).

[9] *Essay,* III 111.

For

> While Man exclaims, "See all things for my use!"
> "See man for mine!" replies a pamper'd goose;
> And just as short of Reason he must fall,
> Who thinks all made for one, not one for all.[10]

More generally.

> Remember, Man, "the Universal Cause
> Acts not by partial, but by gen'ral laws;"[11]
> And makes what Happiness we justly call
> Subsist not in the good of one, but all.[12]

Thus your myopia will be cured by philosophical speculation, which will assure you that

> All Nature is but Art, unknown to thee;
> All Chance, Direction, which thou canst not see;
> All Discord, Harmony, not understood;
> All partial Evil, universal Good:
> And, spite of Pride, in erring Reason's spite,
> One truth is clear, "Whatever is, is RIGHT."[13]

Later, it is true, Pope's cosmic optimism is qualified in an apparently significant way:

> God sends not ill; if rightly understood,
> Or partial Ill is universal Good,
> Or Chance admits, or Nature lets it fall,
> Short and but rare, 'till Man improv'd it all.[14]

---

[10] *ibid.*, III 45–48.

[11] The aphorism in quotation marks is repeated from *ibid.*, I 145–6 – where, however, it is put in the mouth of an imagined anthropocentric *objector* to Pope. Yet there is no doubt that at IV 35–36, Pope is speaking *in propria persona*. For an attempt to explain the dislocation see Nuttall, pp. 145–46 (but note that elsewhere Nuttall is prepared to find "stark inconsistency" in Pope, p. 98).

[12] *Essay*, IV 35–38.

[13] *ibid.*, I 288–94.

[14] *ibid.*, IV 113–16. The lines are obscure. At IV 115 the printed editions give "Or Change admits": this is not easy to read (at least, my own ear finds it extraordinarily difficult to construe "Change" as the *subject* of "admits"), and it offers a puzzlingly weak thought (how is Change contrasted with Nature?). "The thought stammers woefully," says Nuttall (p. 157). "Chance" is an obvious emendation: in fact Pope's earlier version had "Or Chance escape" at this place (see the *apparatus* to the Twickenham edition); and I suppose that "Change" is a printer's error. Even so, the quatrain remains hard. I paraphrase it as follows: "Any ill which befalls a part of the universe either (i) is in the end for the good of the whole (and hence not really an ill for the part), or else (ii) is the result either (a) of coincidence or (b) of an exception to the generally valid natural laws. In the case of (ii), ills will be rare and will not last for long; or rather, they were rare and short-lived until men, by their free action, made them common and persistent." (The word "improv'd" either is ironical or else bears the now obsolete sense of "increased.") – Note that the earlier version of the *Essay* had a distich in place of the quatrain:

Not quite everything that is is right. Yet the general tenor of the *Essay* is Panglossian. What happens happens for the good of the whole. And what is good for the whole must be good for the parts – for where else might partial goodness be found? Evidently, then, we should strive to discover our own part in the universal whole – our nature, our position, our function. And having discovered our part, we must punningly play it –

> Honour and shame from no Condition rise;
> Act well your part, there all the honour lies.[15]

Epistle II of the *Essay* elaborates "the proper study of Mankind"[16] and pursues its inquiry into specifically human nature, the essence of which is constituted by the twin principles of self-love and reason. The inquiry suggests that self-love is and ought to be the dominant principle (for "Nature's road must ever be prefer'd"[17]); and it emerges that reason should be subordinate to instinct. The beasts fare well when they follow nature –

> Say, where full Instinct is th' unerring guide,
> What Pope or Council can they need beside?[18]

nor should men aspire to more:

> And Reason raise o'er Instinct as you can,
> In this 'tis God directs, in that 'tis Man.[19]

The development of Pope's views on human nature is not free from confusion and incoherence; nor is it always clear that our status as parts of the universe is guiding his thought. But the chain of being is rarely forgotten for long, and it is our partial nature which shows us the road to happiness. For happiness will come to the man

---

> God sends not Ill, 'tis Nature lets it fall
> Or Chance escape, and Man improves it all.

The change in wording is slight, in sense enormous. From which a cynic may infer that Pope was less concerned with what he said than with how he said it. Compare the notorious case of I 6, where Pope originally wrote

> A mighty Maze of Walks without a Plan,

and later changed the line to read

> A mighty Maze, but not without a Plan.

See Nuttall, pp. 54–55, for a hopeless attempt to acquit Pope of frivolity.

[15] *Essay*, IV 193–94.
[16] *ibid.*, II 2.
[17] *ibid.*, II 161.
[18] *ibid.*, III 83–84.
[19] *ibid.*, III 97–98.

who takes no private road,
But looks thro' Nature, up to Nature's God;
Pursues that Chain which links th' immense design,
Joins heav'n and earth, and mortal and divine;
Sees that no being any bliss can know,
But touches some above, and some below;
Learns, from this union of the rising Whole,
The first, last purpose of the human soul;
And knows where Faith, Law, Morals, all began,
All end, in LOVE of GOD, and LOVE of MAN.[20]

For although the Whole is made for the good of the Whole, the general good determines the good of the parts – *our* good.

Man, like the gen'rous vine, supported lives;
The strength he gains is from th' embrace he gives.
On their own Axis as the Planets run,
Yet make at once their circle round the Sun:
So two consistent motions act the Soul;
And one regards Itself, and one the Whole.
        Thus God and Nature link'd the gen'ral frame,
And bade Self-love and Social be the same.[21]

It is philosophy – in the generous sense of the term – which teaches us all this. By nature, we love first ourselves, and then others:

God loves from Whole to Part: but human soul
Must rise from Individual to the Whole.[22]

Our rise leads us through the circles of propinquity, until the whole of creation is embraced in our transformed self-love:

Self-love but serves the virtuous mind to wake,
As the small pebble stirs the peaceful lake;
The centre mov'd, a circle strait succeeds,
Another still, and still another spreads
Friend, parent, neighbour, first it will embrace,
His country next, and next all human race,
Wide and more wide, th' o'erflowings of the mind
Take ev'ry creature in, of ev'ry kind.[23]

[20] *ibid.*, IV 331–40.
[21] *ibid.*, III 311–18.
[22] *ibid.*, IV 361–62.
[23] *ibid.*, IV 363–70.

Such is the scheme. It rests ultimately upon a teleological principle, which is implicit throughout the *Essay* and which Pope states explicitly in his prefatory "Design":

> Having proposed to write some pieces on Human Life and Manners, such as (to use my lord Bacon's expression) *come home to Men's Business and Bosoms*, I thought it more satisfactory to begin with considering *Man* in the abstract, his *Nature* and his *State*: since to prove any moral duty, to enforce any moral precept, or to examine the perfection or imperfection of any creature whatsoever, it is necessary first to know what *condition* and *relation* it is placed in, and what is the proper *end* and *purpose* of its *being*.

In sum, Pope's moral philosophy amounts to something like this. In order to determine our moral duties, we must first determine our function and place in the world. Philosophy shows that we are each a part of a greater whole – we are ourselves systems which are parts of systems which, ultimately, are parts of the whole universe. The parts are united by the strongest links of mutual support. The whole is ordered for the good of the whole. Recognizing this, we must ourselves learn to strive for the good of the whole, transcending our individual interests. It may at first seem repugnant to do this, but it is also natural. And once we have done it, we shall realize that, so harmonious is the universal system, our own individual good is achieved precisely when we subordinate ourselves to the universal good.

I call this Pope's moral philosophy. And so it is. But the label might mislead. First, and evidently, it is only a part of the moral philosophy elaborated in the *Essay on Man*, which itself is only a part of the grand project of ethical philosophizing which Pope conceived but never carried out.[24] Secondly – and more importantly – the philosophy was not invented or put together by Pope. On the contrary, he strove only to write "what oft was thought, but ne'er so well expressed": the contentions of the *Essay* can be found in a dozen duller treatises. I have cited Pope not because he is idiosyncratic but because he gives stunning and brilliant expression to a commonly accepted view.

The *Essay* was published in 1733/4. It was an immediate success, running through numerous editions and being translated into some twenty European languages.[25] It was successful not – or not only – because of its poetical genius, but rather – or especially – because of its moral and philosophical content. It inspired the young Immanuel Kant.[26] It impressed Voltaire, who announced that "Pope's *Essay on Man* seems to me the finest, the most useful, and the most sublime didactic poem ever written in any language."[27] Although there were some dissenting

---

[24] On this see, e.g., Nuttall, pp. 46–47.

[25] See, e.g., Mack, p. 541–42. Pope himself refers to seven translations in a letter of November 1743, in which he politely declines Christopher Smart's offer to translate the whole of the *Essay* into Latin (see G. Sherburn (ed.), *The Correspondence of Alexander Pope*, vol. IV (Oxford: Clarendon Press, 1956), pp. 483–84).

[26] See the essays on optimism in *Kant's gesammelte Schriften*, vol. XVII (Berlin, 1926), pp. 229–39.

[27] See *Lettres Philosophiques*, ed. R. Naves (Paris, 1956), pp. 256–57. But Voltaire's reaction was mixed: see R. G. Knapp, *The Fortunes of Pope's* Essay on Man *in 18th Century France*, Studies on Voltaire and the Eighteenth Century 82 (Geneva, 1971).

voices, Pope had caught the mood of the age: his moral philosophy was the enlightened moral philosophy of the century of enlightenment.[28]

Pope's moral philosophy was neither idiosyncratic nor original. Where did it come from? The problem of Pope's 'sources' – the question of which authors directly or indirectly, consciously or unconsciously, influenced and formed his thought – is much vexed.[29] I have nothing to say on the matter – apart from insisting that the thoughts so elegantly expressed in the *Essay on Man* were, in all essentials, antique. Pope himself, *doctus poeta*, was well aware of his venerable pedigree. With an urbane and self-conscious irony, he was clothing Stoic sentiments in Epicurean dress. For in its form, the *Essay* consciously alludes to Lucretius's Epicurean epic *On the Nature of Things*;[30] and in its content, the *Essay* is solidly Stoical. And the Stoicism which Pope rehearses is a version, mildly Christianized, of the philosophy of the Imperial Stoics – of Seneca, of Epictetus, of Marcus Aurelius.

It is in the *Meditations* of Marcus that we may find the closest ancient parallels to Pope's views. Marcus never tires of insisting that each of us is essentially a part, a $\mu\acute{\epsilon}\rho os$, of the general scheme of things – a part of Nature ($\varphi\acute{\upsilon}\sigma\iota s$), or of the universe ($\kappa\acute{o}\sigma\mu os$), or (as he once puts it) of Fate ($\epsilon\acute{\iota}\mu\alpha\rho\mu\acute{\epsilon}\nu\eta$: V xxiv). Marcus, like Pope, urges us to discover and then to remember which part we are[31] – and which parts we must play, for each of us has his lines in the cosmic drama.[32] (Marcus has the conceit, but Greek lacks the English pun.) Again like Pope, Marcus explicitly compares us to bodily organs: we stand to the universe as our hands and feet stand to our bodies.[33] Such organic parts have mutually interdependent functions and activities, and they work together ($\sigma\upsilon\nu\epsilon\rho\gamma o\tilde{\upsilon}\sigma\iota$[34]) to a common end and a common good. So with us: we are interdependent parts of an organized whole, and our mutual dependencies determine our nature and our function. Marcus, like Pope, reads his ethics from his metaphysics. The good of the part is determined by the good of the whole,[35] and both our moral duty and our psychological well-being are fixed by our particular status as parts of the stupendous whole.

Marcus's views are not presented systematically, nor – any more than Pope's – are they presented with complete rigor or consistency. But the chief matters with which I am here concerned are concisely pronounced in the following section of the *Meditations*:

[28] See, e.g., Mack, pp. 542–43.

[29] For some sane comments on this problem see Nuttall, pp. 48–52. In the surviving MS drafts, Pope refers explicitly to four ancient authors: Cicero (the *Somnium Scipionis*), Manilius, Aristotle (*Nicomachean Ethics*), and Oppian. But notes of this sort are very rare in the manuscripts, and they cannot be thought to provide a full catalogue even of expressly recognized sources. Modern philosophers may well think of Leibniz as a possible source. So did Pope's contemporaries, to whom he replied: "I never in my life read a Line of Leibnitz" (letter to Warburton, 2 Feb 1738/9, in Sherburn, p. 164).

[30] "Pope wished his poem to be read, at least to some degree, as a modern *De Rerum Natura*" (Mack, p. 525), with references to Lucretian echoes).

[31] *Meditations*, II iv, ix; IX xxii 2.

[32] *ibid.*, VI xlii 4.

[33] *ibid.*, VI xxxiii, VIII xxxiv.

[34] *ibid.*, II i 4.

[35] *ibid.*, II iii 2; VI xliv 6; liv.

First, let it be laid down that I am a part of the whole which is governed by nature; then, that I am in a certain way appropriately related to parts of the same kind.

If I remember this, then insofar as I am a part I shall not be vexed by anything allotted to me by the whole. Nothing which benefits the whole is harmful to the part. For a whole does not contain anything which is not to its benefit, and while this is common to every natural object, the nature of the universe has an additional advantage in that it cannot be compelled by any external cause to produce something harmful to itself. Thus insofar as I remember that I am a part of a whole of this sort, I shall be content with whatever happens.

And insofar as I am in a certain way appropriately related to parts of the same kind, I shall do nothing unsocial but I shall rather think of those parts and shall direct all my impulses to the common advantage and away from its opposite. Once this is done, life must flow smoothly – just as you will find a citizen's life to flow smoothly if he proceeds by way of actions which benefit his fellow-citizens and welcomes whatever his city assigns to him.[36]

We are parts of the universe. There are other parts like us. What we should do, and how we shall achieve happiness and a smooth-flowing life, are fixed by our relation to the whole and to our kindred parts.[37]

There are metaphysical notions in Marcus which are absent from Pope, and conversely. The attitudes and casts of mind of the two men are different – as different as their literary styles. But the underlying similarity of thought is evident. And it is, of course, no accidental likeness.

At the heart of Pope's moral philosophy lie two interconnected theses: there is an anthropological thesis to the effect that we are all essentially parts of the universe; and there is an axiological thesis to the effect that all value – for us – derives from our partial status. The strength of the philosophy lies in the fact that both these theses may be made to seem plausible.

As for the anthropological thesis, ask Everyman – the man in the omnibus – whether he thinks he is a part of the universe. "Well, of course," he will say, "of course I'm a part – in fact I'm a part of any number of different things. I'm part of my family. I'm part of the local bridge team. I'm part of the London Transport organization. No doubt I'm part of many other things too, which I don't at the moment care to recall. And if you suggest that I'm a part of the universe – well, why not? Maybe I wouldn't normally style myself 'Part of the Universe,' for I don't normally think of myself in such grandiloquently philosophical terms. But for all that, the description seems apt enough. Moreover, if I am a part of the universe, it

[36] ibid., X vi.

[37] For a pertinent account of Marcus's ethical thought and its relation to 'classical' Stoicism, see John Rist, "Are You a Stoic? The Case of Marcus Aurelius," ed. B. F. Meyer and E. P. Sanders, Jewish and Christian Self-Definition, vol. III (Philadelphia: Fortress Press, 1982). The best study of Marcus is now Richard Rutherford's The Meditations of Marcus Aurelius: A Study (Oxford: Clarendon Press, 1989).

seems pretty clear that I'm *essentially* a part of the universe – it could hardly be an accident that I am such a partial whole." (And, since he reads his Shakespeare, he will add that each man in his time plays many parts – and he might cite half a dozen such texts to show that the other, punning, notion of our parts is thoroughly at home in the common conception of human life.)

As for the axiological thesis, a little reflection on the goodness of familiar parts will commend it as reputable. My eyes are part of my body: their virtues and duties are plain – good eyes are simply eyes which see sharply and thus make their particular contribution to the overall economy of the body. It is the general purposes and goals of my body – that is to say, of myself – which entirely determine in what the goodness of my eyes consists, and which fix (to put it picturesquely) their interests and their duties. Again, a piston is a part of an engine; and a good piston is simply a piston which, in its own particular way, serves well the general purposes of the engine of which it is a part. The piston has no end or aspiration independent of the ends and aspirations of the engine; its interests and duties are wholly determined by those of the engine of which it forms a part.

We seem to be parts of the universe; and parts seem to have their good determined by the whole. Hence, the underlying principles of Pope's philosophy seem plausible. But seeming is not being, and plausibility is not truth. Each of the two theses requires scrutiny. I begin with the anthropological thesis.

II. MEREOLOGY

The anthropological thesis is worth setting down with some rigor, thus:

(1) Every man is essentially a part of the universe.

And if you prefer symbols to poetry – or have a catholic taste – then you may like to think of the thesis in the following terms:

$$(1^*) \quad (\forall x) \ (Hx \rightarrow Ess: (x \ll U)).$$

– where "Hx" means "x is human," "$Ess:Fx$" means "x is essentially F," "$x \ll y$" means "x is a part of y," and "U" denotes the universe.[38] Evidently, (1) entails – but is not entailed by –

(2) There is something of which every man is essentially a part.
Or:

$$(2^*) \quad (\exists y) \ (\forall x) \ (Hx \rightarrow Ess: (x \ll y)).$$

You might hold (2) without holding (1) – you might hold, say, that humans were essentially parts of the human race but not essentially parts of the Universe. (As a

[38] I take the symbols "$\ll$" and "U" from Peter Simons, *Parts – A Study in Ontology* (Oxford: Clarendon Press, 1987), p. 160. Everything I say about mereology was inspired by – and much was filched from – this immensely exciting book.

limiting case, consider the notion entertained by Aristophanes in Plato's *Symposium*, that each of us is essentially one half of a unitary pair.[39])

Again, it is evident that (2) entails – but is not entailed by –

(3) For every man, there is something of which he is essentially a part.

Or:

(3*) $(\forall x)$ $(Hx \rightarrow (\exists y)$ Ess: $(x \ll y))$.

According to (2), there is some one whole of which all humans are parts. According to (3), every human is a part of some whole – but there need be no whole of which all of us are parts.

Finally, (3) entails – but is not entailed by –

(4) For every man, it is essential that he be a part of something.

Or:

(4*) $(\forall x)$ $(Hx \rightarrow$ Ess: $(\exists y)$ $(x \ll y)$.

You might hold (4) without holding (3) or (2) or (1) – as Aristotle did. For Aristotle maintains that men are essentially parts of πόλεις, or States. He does not, of course, mean that there is some one State – Macedon, say – of which every human is essentially a part. Nor does he mean that, for each of us, there is some particular State of which he is essentially a part – Macedon for Alexander, Prussia for Hegel. Rather, he means that, for each of us, it is essential that he be a part of some State or other. I am essentially a citizen of a State. There is no State of which I am essentially a citizen. (Note, incidentally, that Aristotle claims that a citizen stands to his State as an arm or a leg stands to its body.[40] Marcus, and eventually Pope, adopt the comparison but replace the State by the universe. For them, and in a different metaphor, we are citizens of the world.)

There are different theses here, and in many contexts it is important to hold them apart. But they all have a common core; for each maintains that individual men are essentially parts of some greater whole.

Then am I in any sense essentially a part of a greater whole? Yes, replied the man in the bus. But things cannot be settled so simply. It is not that the busman is wrong. Rather, what he will or will not accede to is really quite unclear. For it is plain that the ordinary use of the word "part" is ambiguous or indeterminate or both. A simple example: it seems pretty obvious that the concept of parthood is transitive; that is to say, if x is a part of y and y is a part of z, then x is a part of z.[41] But Giorgio Belladonna's head is certainly a part of Belladonna. And Belladonna

---

[39] *Symposium*, 189c–192a.
[40] *Politics*, 1253a 19–25.
[41] See Simons, pp. 10–11, 107–8.

was certainly a part of the Squadra Azzurra. But Belladonna's head was never a part of the Squadra – it could not, after all, play bridge. Should we infer that parthood is *not* transitive? Surely we should rather suppose that the term "a part of" is ambiguous: Belladonna is not a part of the Squadra in the same sense in which Belladonna's head is a part of Belladonna.[42]

Other examples are easily adduced. And the point seems, in any case, uncontroversial. As for the man on the bus, no doubt he is right to allow that he is a part of the universe in *some* sense of the term. But it is by no means obvious that, in allowing this, he thereby admits that he stands to the universe in just the same relationship as – say – his right hand stands to his body or the piston stands to the engine of his bus. Everything turns on the *sort* of part which the anthropological thesis invokes. And the busman's amateur admission that he is some sort of a part gets us nowhere.

So let us turn to the professionals. Mereology, or the formal study of parts and wholes, is a formidable discipline; and the modern mereologist also has a view on the anthropological thesis. In fact, he will agree – for quite different reasons – with the busman. "Well, of course," he will say, "of course I'm a part of the universe. Indeed, I'm a part of innumerably many things. In most orthodox versions of mereological theory, any sum of fusion of individuals is itself an individual and a whole, of which the component individuals are parts. The universe is simply the totality of things; or, as I prefer to express it:

$$U = \sigma x' \ (\text{exists})x'.$$

And everything which exists is thereby a part of the universe:

$$(\forall x) \ (E!x \to x < U).^{43}$$

What could be simpler?"

But the mereologist, like the busman, gives us less than we want. *His* concept of parthood is not indeterminate or ambiguous. (Its sense is determined by his axioms.) But for all that it will not help us. For it is notorious that the concept of parthood about which he builds his theories – or rather, the concept about which standard mereological theories have mostly been built – has some strange consequences. A simple example: "The four wheels of a car are parts of it (each is a part of it), but there is not a fifth part consisting of the four wheels."[44] Evidently not: yet the axioms of mereology demand that the four wheels *do* constitute a fifth part. The implication of this is not, of course, that mereology is a mess or a mistake;

---

[42] Simons suggests that (1) there are distinct *generic* notions of parthood, formally analogous to one another but not falling under a single overarching concept, and also that (2) distinct restrictions upon these generic notions produce *specifically* different concepts of parthood: see pp. 104, 106, 128, and esp. 231–37.

[43] The symbol "<" designates parthood in the broad sense – the sense in which everything is a part (an 'improper part') of itself. In the text I use "part" in the normal English sense, the sense for which mereologists often use the term "proper part."

[44] Simons, p. 160.

rather, it is that orthodox mereological theory cannot determine the truth of Pope's anthropological thesis.[45]

Where shall we go, then? Plainly, we need to settle upon some relatively determinate notion of parthood, and inquire whether, in the sense fixed by that notion, we are parts of a greater whole. Moreover, it is plain that, in order to fix on an appropriate notion for Pope's anthropological thesis we shall need to keep an eye on Pope's second, axiological thesis. For the two theses are intimately connected, and the former must be grounded on a notion of parthood which will also serve the latter.

It is clear, first, that the whole of which we are supposedly parts is not a mere aggregate or agglomeration but a systematic or integral whole. The point is explicit in Pope, who talks of 'systems' in a semi-technical sense. It is also explicit in Marcus.

> Think often of the way everything in the universe is tied together and of their relation to one another. For in a way all things are interwoven with one another, and all things are for this reason friendly to one another. One thing is continuous with another because of the tonic motion and the conspiration and the unity of substance.[46]

That Pope's theses make use of a strong notion of parthood, and that this notion has something to do with the integral and systematic nature of the whole, are matters beyond doubt. The question is whether the notion can be given precise articulation – or rather, whether it can be defined with sufficient precision for us to be able to assess the truth-value of the theses to which it is to give sense.

What, then, can we make of the key concept of a system or an integral whole? The first thing to observe is that a system need not be a substance. In general, wholes need not be substances: if x is a part of y, it does not follow that y is a substance.[47] Limbs, and pistons, are parts – and parts of substances. Pope proposes that men stand to the universe as legs stand to a body. The comparison doubtless suggests that we are parts of some larger *substance* – and this suggestion will only appeal to those with extremely organic inclinations. But the suggestion is not necessarily implied by Pope's anthropological thesis, and we could in principle scout the suggestion while embracing the thesis.

For if we are parts at all, then we are surely parts not of a substance but of a *group*. We are – at best – like the musicians in an orchestra, or like the players in a team, or

---

[45] The "principal thesis" of Simons's book is that classical mereologies do not give an adequate account of the common part-whole relationship (or relationships): see p.5. He notes that "it is a central thesis of classical extensional mereologies that any two individuals possess a sum. Since individuals may be disjoint, spatio-temporally widely separated, and of quite different kinds, this assumption is very implausible" (p. 14). For an historical explanation of the prevalence of such implausible theories, see pp. 104–5.

[46] *Meditations*, VI xxxviii. See also Hume's remarks in the *Treatise* at I iv 6 [p. 257, ed. Selby-Bigge], which Simons uses for the epigraph of Part III of his book (p. 253).

[47] Compare Simons, p. 10 n. 2.

like the actors in a cast (so that the punning sort of part is again apposite). Groups are not substances. But they are continuants: they have a career and a history.[48]

Secondly, a system must have a goal or an aim or a purpose. For it must have a good, and it must have interests. If y is a system, then there must be true sentences of the form "It is good for y that P." This may seem an arbitrary stipulation. It is not: Pope's axiological thesis requires that we be able to speak of the good of the whole, so that if the anthropological thesis is to serve the axiological thesis, the wholes to which it refers must have a good. And of course some groups do have interests and goods. It is not good for the England XI that no decent fast bowlers have been produced in the last decade.[49]

Next, something about the logical structure of systems.[50] Begin with the notion of a *division* of an object. A division is simply a set of parts which together completely exhaust the object: every bit of the object is, or overlaps with, one of the items in the set. More formally:

(DD)   A set α is a division of y if and only if (1) every member of α is a part of y and (ii) every part of y is or overlaps with some member of α.

Next, a *partition*: a partition is simply a special sort of division: namely, a division in which every element is disjoint from every other element – that is, in which no element overlaps any other. Thus

(DP)   A set α is a partition of y if and only if (i) α is a division of y and (ii) every member of α is disjoint from every other member of α.

Systems, or integral wholes, are wholes which have (at least) one special sort of partition. The special sort is characterized by the fact that its members are united by a special relation (or set of relations) – they form a *family*. Families are defined in terms of binary relations. Any binary relation R has a converse. (S is converse to R just in case ySx whenever xRy.) Any binary relation R has an associated ancestral relation. (S is the ancestral of R just in case xSy whenever xRz, and z_1Rz_2 and ... and z_nRy.) Now take the relation R and its converse $\tilde{R}$. Form their disjunction, $(R \cup \tilde{R})$. Take the ancestral of this disjunction, $(R \cup \tilde{R})^*$. Call this complex relation the relation φ. Then a set forms a family with respect to a relation R if every member of the set stands in the relation φ to every other member of the set and to nothing which is not a member of the set. Thus:

---

[48] On groups see *ibid.*, pp. 145–47. Note that groups are not sets or classes in the technical sense; for their identity is not determined by their membership. The Arsenal football team and the England football team might consist of exactly the same players – but even so, they would be different teams. The England cricket XI has won precisely one of its last twenty-two matches; but no set of eleven players can claim this grisly record.

[49] Here and later I introduce sporting illustrations, the details of which will not be equally familiar to all readers. Team sports provide the best illustrations of what I want to say, and any choice of sport will leave some reader disgruntled. In fact, the sporting details never matter, and the gist will be always be plain.

[50] Here I follow (with minor modifications) the development in Simons, pp. 327–30.

(DF) A set α is family with respect to the relation R if and only if (i) for every x and every y in α, $x\varphi y$, and (ii) if x is in α and $x\varphi y$, then y is in α.

A system is a whole of which at least one partition is a family.

Or rather, the partition must form what I shall call a *substantial* family. For the formal requirements on families can be satisfied trivially. Every set α is a family with respect to the relation "... is a member of α along with ———." And every set will be a family with respect to numerous other artificial relations. A substantial family is a family with respect to a substantial relation. A relation is substantial, in this sense, if it holds between members of α in virtue not of the logical structure of α but of the substantial nature of α and its members.

Two pertinent examples may make this less bemusing. The universe, according to Marcus and his fellow Stoics, is united by συμπάθεια. Συμπάθεια is a causal notion: roughly speaking, the universe exhibits συμπάθεια inasmuch as every item in the universe is linked to every other item by some causal relation. More precisely: if "xRy" abbreviates "x is causally affected by y," then x stands in the relation of συμπάθεια to y provided that $x\varphi y$ (where φ, as before, is the ancestral of the disjunction of R with its converse). Thus on the Stoic view, there is a partition of the universe which is a causal family – a family with respect to the relation "... is causally affected by ———." The universe contains a substantial family and is therefore (*pro tanto*) a system. Or again, consider the affective notion of sympathy, or 'fellow-feeling'. On a common view, shared again by the Stoics and by Pope, the human race is – or ought to be – a sympathetic family: it is – or ought to be – a family with respect to the relation "... is regarded sympathetically by ———." Hence the human race, too, has a substantial family and is (again, *pro tanto*) a system. It is easy to think of any number of similar families and family relations.

In sum, y is a system provided that (i) it has interests or a good, and (ii) it contains a partition which is a substantial family.

The anthropological thesis has it that we are parts of such a system. But not parts of any sort: we are what I shall call 'integrating' parts. All that this means is that we are members of some partition of the system which is a substantial family. Let "$x \ll_1 y$" mean "x is an integrating part of y." Then we shall have:

(DI) $x \ll_1 y$ iff there is a substantial family of y of which x is a member.

The Popeans do not expressly say that we are *integrating* parts of a system. But this is evidently what they mean. (A system may have parts which are not integrating: if I break a tooth, I lose a part – or perhaps rather, part – of my masticatory equipment, but I do not lose an integrating part of it.)

Moreover, the anthropological thesis maintains that we are not accidentally but essentially, or naturally, parts of a system. To say that x is essentially F is to say that necessarily, if x exists, then x is F. In symbols:

Ess:Fx ↔ □(E!x → Fx).

It is helpful to express the idea of essential parthood by a somewhat more complex formula; and I shall say that x is essentially a part of y if there is an essential property of x, possession of which entails being a part of y. Or:

$$(DE) \quad Ess: x \ll_1 y \leftrightarrow (\exists F) (\Box(E!x \rightarrow Fx) \wedge (\forall z)\Box(Fz \rightarrow z \ll_1 y)).$$

The reason for producing the complex formula is that we can now present an entirely analogous account of what it is for x to be naturally a part of y: x is naturally a part of y if there is a natural property of x, possession of which entails being a part of y. Or:

$$(DN) \quad Nat: x \ll_1 y \leftrightarrow (\exists F) (Nat:Fx) \wedge (\forall z)\Box(Fz \rightarrow z \ll_1 y)).$$

There are important differences between what is essential and what is natural; but here the differences will not often matter much, and for the sake of brevity I shall sometimes use "essential" where I ought rather to use "essential or natural."

So much for the mereological groundwork. It is technical, and to some it may seem either comically or irritatingly pedantic – just the sort of thing which gives analytical philosophy a bad name. But it has a point; or rather, it has at least two points. First, it is worth showing – and only a formal definition *can* show – that the 'ordinary' notion of a system or an integral whole can be given a reasonably clear and precise sense. The concept of a whole, just like the converse concept of a part, is thoroughly vague and indeterminate; no philosophical thesis which employs it is worth anything until the concept is given some degree of precision. Secondly, it is evident that some at least of the elements in my formal definitions are to a certain extent arbitrary. That is to say, in making the ordinary concept precise, we incidentally suggest that there are more ways than one of doing so – which, of course, is only what we should expect from an indeterminate notion. (I might add that I will not go to the scaffold for the particular account of systems and integrating parts which I have just sketched. I wish to commend the practice of rigorous and formal definition, even if my own attempt to follow the practice should prove dubiously successful.)

However that may be, the question is now this: are we essentially integrating parts of a system? Is the anthropological thesis true or false?

It seems to me clear that, *pace* Marcus and Pope, I am not an integrating part of the universe. For the universe is surely not a system. No doubt I am a member of (at least) one partition of the universe; and it may be that one of these partitions is a substantial family – perhaps under the relation ". . . is causally affected by ———." (This, I take it, is an empirical question to which the answer is not evident.) But the other condition on systems is surely not satisfied by the universe. The universe has no good and no interests. The universe *does* nothing. Hence it does nothing well or badly. The universe *feels* nothing. Hence it cannot be harmed or helped. And in such circumstances it is hard to see how the universe could have a good, or how we could think there were any true propositions of the form "It is good for the universe that P."

Aristotle's suggestion, that we are parts of States, may seem more palatable than the Stoic idea. Yet Aristotle, too, is surely mistaken. We might perhaps allow that States are systems, and in particular that they have interests and a good. (This is not an uncontroversial point, but I do not wish to controvert it here.) Yet it is surely quite plain that we are not *essentially* members of States – it would be ludicrous to think that anarchism was *logically* impossible. And it seems to me false that we are *naturally* members of States – for I cannot see that anarchism is an unnatural condition for men.

Nevertheless, it might seem that Aristotle was not wide of the mark. For although we are not essentially parts of States, perhaps we are essentially – or, at any rate, naturally – parts of what we may call communities: of families, of neighborhoods, of societies, perhaps even of the human race. After all, men are naturally social in a straightforward enough sense: we possess by nature various faculties and desires which can only be exercised and satisfied in a community or society of other humans. We cannot talk to ourselves.[51]

This is platitudinous. What is disputable is whether these communities of which we are essentially or naturally integrating members are *systems*. As in the case of the universe, the crucial question is whether they have a good – whether they have interests. I do not know how to set about answering this question. I confess that it seems to me bizarre to suggest that there is such a thing as the interest of the human race. Yet it is not bizarre – or not equally bizarre – to suppose that, say, a family has interests and a good. At any rate, the supposition is commonly made, and it is implicit in much of our ordinary talk about ourselves and our aspirations and fears.

Hence I end this section lamely. It is plain that the anthropological thesis, in its strictly Popean form, is false. Yet there may be other forms of the thesis which are true. And although some of the interest of Pope's moral philosophy is dissipated once the strict thesis is rejected, nonetheless the possibility that a weaker thesis may be sustained makes it worth looking seriously at the second constituent of Pope's moral philosophy.

III. ARISTOTLE'S AXIOM

The second constituent of Pope's moral philosophy is an axiological thesis. It states that the good of any part is determined by its status as part of its whole. A particular version of this thesis is endorsed by Aristotle in the Utopian section of the *Politics*. He urges that

> one should not think that anyone of the citizens belongs to himself but that all belong to the State. For each is a part of the State; and the care of each part naturally looks to the care of the whole.[52]

---

[51] Aristotle's celebrated argument at *Pol.* 1252b28–1253a18 fails to prove that we are essentially or naturally *political* animals; for nothing in it legitimates the introduction of the crucial political notion of 'ruling and being ruled.' But the argument does indicate that, and how, we are essentially *social* animals. Here, and elsewhere in the *Politics*, Aristotle shows himself curiously insensitive to the distinction between State and society.

[52] *Politics*, 1337a 27–31.

At the end of the first Book of the *Politics*, he had already stated the thesis in perfect generality:

> Since every household is a part of the State, and individuals are parts of households, and since *the excellence of the part must look to that of the whole*, it is necessary for one to look to the State when educating children and women.[53]

The idea that we all belong to the State is found in Plato;[54] and the thought that the good of the part depends on the good of the whole is also foreshadowed in Plato's dialogues.[55]

The precise form and scope of Aristotle's claims in the *Politics* are obscure, and it is not my primary concern to provide an elucidation of the Aristotelian texts.[56] But I shall call the axiological thesis Aristotle's axiom.

Since Pope holds that our partial status determines both our interests and our duties, the axiom must have a double form. In terms of interests, the axiom maintains that the good of a part is a function of the good of the whole. There are several ways of making this vague idea precise. A rough and preliminary version might run thus:

> It is in the interest of a part that it be so-and-so if and only if it is in the interest of the whole that the part be so-and-so.

Since we are concerned with integrating parts of a system – and with items which are essentially (or naturally) parts of this sort – we may write the axiom more narrowly (and also more perspicuously) as follows:

> (1) If x is essentially (or naturally) an integrating part of some systematic whole y, then it is good for x that Fx if and only if it is good for y that Fx.

Thus if Ian Botham is essentially an integrating part of the systematic whole which is the England cricket XI, then it is good for Botham that Botham bat at number 5 if and only if it is good for the England XI that Botham bat at number 5.

But (1) as it stands is not quite enough. The connective "if and only if" is too weak: Aristotle's axiom has it that individual interests are *determined by* and *depend upon* the interests of the whole – and this asymmetrical dependence is not captured in (1). Hence we need something like the following:

> (1*) If x is essentially an integrating part of some systematic whole y, then it is good for x that Fx insofar as it is good for y that Fx.

---

[53] *ibid.*, 1260b13–17.
[54] e.g., *Laws* 923a.
[55] e.g., *Charmides* 156e; *Laws* 903b.
[56] See Jonathan Barnes, "Aristotle and Political Liberty," forthcoming in the Proceedings of the XIth Symposium Aristotelicum.

The second version of the Aristotelian axiom – the version which deals with duties – is parallel to the first. Roughly:

> A part ought to do so-and-so if and only if it is in the best interest of the whole that the part do so-and-so.

More perspicuously:

> (2) If x is essentially an integrating part of some systematic whole y, then x ought to do A if and only if it is in the best interest of y that x do A.

Thus Botham ought to bat at 5 if and only if it is in the best interest of the England XI that Botham bat at 5.

Like (1), (2) is too weak; it loses the notion of one-sided dependency between the good of the whole and the duties of the part. Hence:

> (2*) If x is essentially an integrating part of some systematic whole y, then x ought to do A insofar as it is best for y that x do A.

(I use "duty," "obligation," "ought," and so on promiscuously. The differences between these various notions – crucial in certain contexts – do not, I think, matter here.)

Now it is, I suppose, uncontroversial that membership of a whole – of a team, a cast, a band – will impose certain duties and obligations. It is also uncontroversial that my interests will to some extent be affected and modified by the interests of any group of which I am a part. At the same time, it may seem clear that theses (1*) and (2*) are far too strong – that they are simply false. For there appear to be straightforward counterexamples.

On the one hand, it is plain that the good of a part may be affected by matters quite irrelevant to the concerns of the whole. Thus it is no doubt good for Botham that he be given a knighthood. But (special conditions apart) it is quite irrelevant to the England XI and its interests that Botham be honored in this or any other way. Botham's cricketing prowess will not be affected by the honor, and it is only Botham's cricket which has any bearing on the good of the England XI.

On the other hand, the good of the England XI may, or so it seems, conflict with Botham's good. Perhaps it is good for England that England should declare when they are 495 for 6 and Botham is 97 not out. (Alas, the example is fantastical.) But this will hardly seem to be good for Botham – for him, it is better to bat on so that he may score his century and make one more entry in the record books.

Again, Botham may plainly have duties and obligations which are not determined by his membership of the England XI. He is a husband, a father, a citizen, and so on – and each of these roles carries responsibilities with it. It may seem less clear that there are counterexamples in the converse sense – cases in which England's best interests do not impose any obligation upon Botham. But various special conditions will generate such cases. Thus Botham's membership of the England XI might have a contractual basis, and the contract explicitly exclude his being required to perform certain distasteful actions – allowing himself to be run out, say. Then even if it were in the best interest of England that Botham let his partner run him out, Botham would still not be obliged to allow it to happen.

Counterexamples of these sorts are available for one main reason: there is usually more to x than its membership of y, and this fact may affect x's interests and duties in ways which either do not concern y or else conflict with the interests of y. Thus there is more to Botham than his cricketing career; and even if his membership of the England XI determines some of his interests and some of his duties – as it surely does – it is absurd to think that it must determine all his interests and all his duties.

Call a property P 'interest-generating' if an item which possesses P thereby has interests insofar as it possesses P. (And similarly for 'duty-generating'.) Then in general, there will be counterexamples to (1*) and (2*) so long as x has some property P such that (i) having P and being a part of y are independent properties, and (ii) P is an interest-generating (or a duty-generating) property. For Botham's case, there are such properties aplenty: his being a family man generates non-cricketing duties, his being a drinking man generates non-cricketing interests.

Does the Aristotelian axiom collapse in the face of these considerations? Not yet – for the putative counterexamples are inappropriate in one important respect. Botham is no doubt an integrating part of the England XI, and the England XI is a system or integral whole (I do not say an organized whole). But Botham is not *essentially* or *naturally* an integrating part of England. He does not depend for his existence and his identity on the fact that he plays for England – or even on the fact that he is a cricketer. Nor will he leave his nature unfulfilled if he turns to golf. But the Aristotelian axiom was expressly restricted to *essential* or *natural* parts. Thus Botham's case does not, as it stands, constitute a genuine counterexample either to (1*) or to (2*).

Nonetheless, the case shows where the danger lies, and at the same time indicates how we might hope to defend theses (1*) and (2*) against counterexemplary attack. In general, we could defend the theses if we could defend two further claims, namely

> (3)   If x is essentially an integrating part of a system y, then all x's essential properties are determined by x's membership of y,

and

> (4)   If P is an interest-generating or a duty-generating property of x, then P is an essential property of x.

By thesis (4), we shall only find a counterexample to (1*) and (2*) if we can find some essential property of x which is both interest-generating (or duty-generating) and also independent of x's membership of y. And by thesis (3) there can be no such property.

It might seem that thesis (3) is demonstrably false. Surely I am naturally and essentially a rational animal (if I am naturally and essentially anything at all), and surely this fact about me is independent of my membership of any system whatever? Yet this point is not beyond dispute. Indeed, Marcus supposed that the part which a man had to play in the cosmic comedy was precisely the part of a rational actor; and Aristotle similarly supposed that there was the narrowest connection between our being rational animals and our being citizens and parts of a State.

If I am an integrating part of some system, then I will be an integrating part of a particular sort and in virtue of possessing some particular properties: the piston is a part of the engine insofar as it is, precisely, a piston (and not insofar as it is a piece of steel of such-and-such a weight). If x is an integrating part of y insofar as x is F, then it seems plausible to suggest that if x is essentially a part of y, then x is essentially F. Now according to Pope's anthropological thesis, we are essentially parts of the universe insofar as we are humans – our part in the cosmic comedy is to play the man. We are, further, essentially men. And since being a man is a matter of being a rational animal, we find, after all, a tight connection between being a part of the universe and being rational.

Now of course none of this shows that thesis (3) is true; at most, it indicates how a Popean might hope to commend his own particular version of thesis (3). But let us grant (3) to the Popean, and see how far he can get with it.

Not very far at all. For thesis (4), without which (3) is idle, is surely and straightforwardly false. There are, that is to say, any number of duties and interests which I may possess or acquire in virtue of entirely accidental features of my character and my career. It is not an essential property of me that I own a cat. Yet I have an obligation to look after the cat, and I have it in virtue of the accidental fact that I own the cat. It is not an essential fact about me that I live in Oxford. Yet it is a matter of considerable interest to me whether the Oxford City Council is left-wing or right-wing – and this interest is entirely determined by the accidental fact of my being an inhabitant of Oxford. And so on and so forth. It is utterly plain that a man's duties and interests are in very many cases generated by entirely contingent facts about him. Essential properties no doubt generate duties and interests. But they are patently not the only interest-generating or duty-generating properties.

Is this the end of the road for Pope? If he concedes – as he must – that not all my interests and not all my duties can be fixed by my membership of a system, still he may, I suppose, urge that my membership imposes special duties and imports special interests.

And in one way at least this is true. For if my membership of y is essential or natural, then I cannot give it up at all – or else I cannot give it up without denying my nature. Hence any interests and duties which are fixed by membership of y will be essential interests and essential duties. They will be duties which I cannot duck, and interests which I cannot shrug off. Botham may resign from the England XI. He is then no longer bound by any of its prescriptions; and after a while he may have trained himself not to care about English cricketing fortunes, so that his interests are no longer tied up with the interests of the XI. But he cannot do this to any group of which he is essentially a part – he cannot cease to be a member of the human race, or of his own family, or (come to that) of the universe. Nor can he resign from a group of which he is naturally a part, except at an intolerable cost.

If we are essentially or naturally integrating parts of a system, and if that fact imposes duties and insinuates interests, then the duties and interests will have a permanence which other duties and interests may lack. And to this extent, our status as partial wholes may indeed affect us in a special way.

But the special status of our partial interests and duties is not particularly impressive if there is no more to it than this; for such interests and duties, inalienable though they are, may yet be few in number and trifling in content. A Popean needs something stronger. In particular, if he cannot claim that all our duties and interests are determined by our partial status, he ought at least to claim that the essential interests and duties which derive from our part in the system are interests and duties of an overriding force. More generally, he ought to hold that essential interests and duties override accidental interests and duties, in the sense that the essential always prevails over the accidental in any conflict. Gatting – to change batsmen – is an England cricketer accidentally, and a family man (let us allow) essentially. As a cricketer, he was under an obligation to play for England in the second Test. But his mother-in-law died, and as a family man he had a duty to be with his wife's family. There was a conflict of duties. The essential duty was overriding. And Gatting did not play.

In general, the Popean, having allowed that (4) cannot be sustained, might consider subscribing to the following double-barrelled thesis.

> (5)   If x is essentially φ and accidentally ψ, then
> (i) if it is in x's interest *qua* φ that Fx and in x's interest *qua* ψ that Gx, then it is more in x's interest that Fx than that Gx,
> and
> (ii) if x ought to do A *qua* φ and x ought to do B *qua* ψ, then x ought to do A rather than B.

If we are essentially integrating parts of some system, then our partial status will, it is true, no longer determine all our duties and interests, as it did in the original version of Pope's moral philosophy; but, given thesis (5), it will still determine our foremost duties and interests. For the duties and interests which it determines will not only be permanent – they will also be overriding.

Yet why should we accept the double-barreled thesis (5)? I confess that I can dream up no general arguments in its favor. And it seems to me to be false in both its barrels. Suppose that Gatting is essentially an integrating part of his family, which is itself a system. Family membership indubitably imposes various duties and obligations on him. But these duties and obligations do not appear to be invariably overriding. At any rate, it seems to me that his duties as a member of the England XI do in some cases override his familial duties. After all, some familial duties are fairly trifling, and some sporting obligations are fairly serious: Gatting should no doubt play for England rather than attend his daughter's birthday party.

As for interests, where there is a competition between, say, the good of the family and the good of the game, it is not clear that it is more in Gatting's interest to favor his family. Sometimes it may be, sometimes not.

These last considerations are vague and impressionistic and culpably subjective. But I cannot persuade myself that thesis (5) is true. Nor can I discover a weaker and defensible thesis which will yet sustain an interesting version of Aristotle's axiom.

IV. CONCLUSION

Dr. Johnson was no philosopher; and his robust common sense was often a mere unthinking dogmatism (just as his wit was often bombast and bludgeoning). Yet on Pope he gazed with a clear eye. His notorious appreciation of the *Essay on Man* contains the following delicious paragraphs.

> The essay affords an egregious instance of the predominance of genius, the dazzling splendour of imagery, and the seductive powers of eloquence. Never were penury of knowledge and vulgarity of sentiment so happily disguised. The reader feels his mind full, though he learns nothing; and when he meets it in its new array, no longer knows the talk of his mother and his nurse. When these wonder-working sounds sink into sense, and the doctrine of the essay, disrobed of its ornaments, is left to the powers of its naked excellence, what shall we discover? That we are, in comparison with our Creator, very weak and ignorant; that we do not uphold the chain of existence, and that we could not make one another with more skill than we are made. We may learn yet more; that the arts of human life were copied from the instinctive operations of other animals; that if the world be made for man, it may be said that man was made for geese. To these profound principles of natural knowledge are added some moral instructions equally new; that self-interest, well understood, will produce social concord; that men are mutual gainers by mutual benefits; that evil is sometimes balanced by good; that human advantages are sometimes unstable and fallacious, of uncertain duration, and doubtful effect; that our true honour is, not to have a great part, but to act it well; that virtue only is our own; and that happiness is always in our power.
>
> Surely a man of no very comprehensive search may venture to say that he has heard all this before; but it was never till now recommended by such a blaze of embellishment, or such sweetness of melody. The vigorous contraction of some thoughts, the luxuriant amplification of others, the incidental illustrations, and sometimes the dignity, sometimes the softness of the verses, enchain philosophy, suspend criticism, and oppress judgement by overpowering pleasure.[57]

It is crass and pedantic to comment on such a text. But philosophers are essentially pedants and naturally crass.

[57] See the Life of Pope in Samuel Johnson, *The Lives of the Most Eminent English Poets*, ed. J. H. Millar (London, 1896), vol. III, pp. 137–38.

Thus: Johnson is making two points. First, the *Essay* is not original. – Indeed it is not. Nor did Pope pretend or intend that it was. As I have said, the *Essay* is important partly because it is wholly unoriginal.

Secondly, the *Essay* is at bottom, or fundamentally, a patchwork of common knowledge and common sense. For if you take away the poetry, which charms to deceive (and, we may add, if you take away the philosophy, which impresses to betray), you will find that you are left with a sequence of commonplaces. – If I disagree with Johnson here, it is only because several of the thoughts which Johnson takes to be commonplace truths appear to me to be commonplace falsities. For Johnson's judgement is sound: Pope's moral philosophy, like most moral philosophies, is raddled prejudice painted up with meretricious theory. And many men find such things attractive.

Philosophy, Oxford University

NATURAL VIRTUES, NATURAL VICES

By Annette C. Baier

I. Nature, Artifice, Norms

David Hume has been invoked by those who want to found morality on human nature as well as by their critics. He is credited with showing us the fallacy of moving from premises about what is the case to conclusions about what ought to be the case; and yet, just a few pages after the famous *is-ought* remarks in *A Treatise of Human Nature*,[1] he embarks on his equally famous derivation of the obligations of justice from facts about the cooperative schemes accepted in human communities.[2] Is he ambivalent on the relationship between facts about human nature and human evaluations? Does he contradict himself – and, if so, which part of his whole position is most valuable?

Between the famous is-ought passage and the famous account of convention and the obligations arising from established cooperative schemes once they are morally endorsed, Hume discusses the various meanings of the term "natural." "Shou'd it be ask'd, Whether we ought to search for these principles [upon which all our notions of morals are founded] in *nature* or whether we must look for them in some other origin? I wou'd reply, that our answer to this question depends upon the definition of the word, Nature, than which there is none more ambiguous and equivocal." (T. 473–74) The natural can be opposed to the miraculous, the unusual, or the artificial. It is the last contrast that Hume wants, for his contrast between the "artificial" culturally variant, convention-dependent obligations of justice and the more invariant "natural virtues," and what he says about that contrast in this preparation for his account of the "artificial" virtues, makes it clear why he can later refer to justice as "natural" and to the general content of the rules of justice – that is, of basic human conventions of cooperation – as "Laws of Nature" (T. 484). For the "artificial" is simply what is humanly designed and projected. "We readily forget that the designs, and projects, and views of men are as necessary in their operation as heat and cold, moist and dry: But taking them to be free and entirely our own, it is usual to set them in opposition to the other principles of nature." (T. 474) So the artificial in this sense is that species of the natural whose proximate cause is human contrivance.

The "artificial" virtues depend upon our social schemes of cooperation, and so on our collective designs and projects, and these projects and projectings themselves are, for Hume, "as necessary in their operation as heat and cold." So

[1] David Hume, *A Treatise of Human Nature*, ed. L. A. Selby-Bigge and P. H. Nidditch (Oxford: Clarendon Press, 1978), pp. 469–70. Hereafter, references to this work will be supplied parenthetically in the text: e.g., T. 469–70.
[2] See *A Treatise of Human Nature*, bk. III, pt. II, especially secs. I, II, and VI.

they are "natural" in both of the other senses – there is certainly nothing miraculous about human culture and social organization, nor anything rare or unusual either in the adoption of cooperative schemes or in their moral endorsement. "If ever there was anything that cou'd be called natural in this sense [usual], the sentiments of morality certainly may; since there never was any nation in the world, nor any single person, who was utterly depriv'd of them, and who never, in any instance, shew'd the least approbation or dislike of manners." (T. 474) It is a fact about our nature that we have mores or manners, and it is a fact that we morally evaluate them. From these two facts about our nature, Hume derives his list of virtues, and (at least) the artificial virtues incorporate *ought* claims. In my discussion of how he derives his moral conclusions from his factual premises – that is, from his claims about our nature and our human condition – I shall refer both to some virtues that Hume calls "natural," and to some that he classifies as "artificial." Important as the distinction between them is for some purposes, such as seeing the limited place Hume finds for moral rules or laws, it is not so important for an understanding of his naturalism in ethics, if artifices are as natural to us as anything more spontaneous, anything less mediated by intention and convention. But since he believes that we resort to artifice when our spontaneous motivation is deemed unfortunate in its workings, the distinction becomes important for understanding the particular brand of critical or corrective naturalism that he is accepting.

The primary facts from which moral values are derived are, for Hume, the facts about the special reflective pleasure that we get from surveying certain kind of human characters. For Hume, all virtues, natural or artificial, get their status from the fact that these traits are ones we in fact welcome in human persons, once we have the relevant facts, take up a special impartial point of view, exercise our capacity for sympathy, correct its natural bias, and then finally let our reflective feelings pronounce judgment. The "is" from which Hume derives all virtue-claims is a complex one about our reflective agreement as representatives of "the party of humankind," getting satisfaction or dissatisfaction from surveying one another.

Hume accepts as an "undoubted maxim, *that no action can be virtuous, or morally good, unless there be in human nature some motive to produce it, distinct from the sense of its morality.*" (T. 479) Nor is this all. He also claims that our natural pre-moral motivation "must have a great influence" on our moral sense and moral sentiments. "'Tis according to their general force in human nature, that we praise or blame ... we always consider the *natural* or *usual* force of the passions, when we determine concerning vice and virtue; and if the passions depart very much from the common measures on either side, they are always disapprov'd as vicious. A man naturally loves his children better than his nephews, his nephews better than his cousins, his cousins better than strangers, where all else is equal. Hence arises our common measures of duty, in preferring the one to the other. Our sense of duty always follows the common and natural course of our passions." (T. 483–84) What this passage seems to say is that we can and do move from premises about what is normal in human populations to approval, and from there to conclusions about moral norms. We approve of normality. The example Hume chooses, of differential love – a preference for relatives over non-relatives, close relatives over more distant ones, and our moral approval of such preferences – encourages the thought that not only is he founding morality pretty directly on facts about our judgments and their dependence on nature, but on the sort of facts that the sociobiologists are most interested in: namely, facts about our attitudes toward those who are likely to have a similar biological inheritance to our own, to those to whom we have what Hume calls "ties of blood." So what about the supposed fallacy of moving from *is* to *ought*?

What Hume in fact says in that famous passage is that the change from *is* to *ought*, in a piece of moral reasoning, is "of the last consequence" and " 'tis necessary that it shou'd be observ'd and explain'd; and at the same time a reason shou'd be given, for what seems altogether inconceivable, how this new relation can be a deduction from others, which are entirely different from it ... This small attention wou'd subvert all the vulgar systems of morality, and let us see, that the distinction of vice and virtue is not founded merely on the relations of objects, nor is perceiv'd by reason." (T. 469–70) The references to "deduction," "relations of objects," and "reason" show that the vulgar systems of ethics to be subverted by due attention to the move from *is* to *ought* are those rationalist systems – like Samuel Clarke's or the versions of Pufendorf's natural law ethics taught in ethics classes in Scotland, i.e., deontological systems containing "that multitude of rules and precepts with which all moralists abound," (T. 457) – that typically pass without any observation or explanation from a factual claim about what God wills or ordains to normative conclusions about what we ought to do. In the rationalist versions of theological ethics that are Hume's main target, deduction is the favored way of moving from premise to conclusion, so these moralists would have to explain how one can move deductively from facts about what some alien will has ordained to conclusions about our duty.

Since Hume thinks that even facts about what any one person personally has willed (say, in a firm resolution) cannot "by a single act of our will ... render any action moral or immoral which without that act ... wou'd have been endow'd with different qualities," (T. 517) he is not likely to find alien wills, however powerful, that can magically produce *oughts* out of thin air. Observing what willing is shows us, he thinks, that it is the transition from one fact, a psychological one, to another, a fact about intentional performance. It does not generate norms, except when the performance is an edict from the occupier of some authoritative position. Then it will be the throne from which the edict comes, not just the act of will, that will give the edict its apparently normative force, and we will still face the question of what conferred authority on that seat – what made it a throne. For Hume authority is an "artifice," a human invention and a relatively late one. Only because we have other virtues and other sources of *ought*-claims besides authoritative utterances are we able to invent superiors, dignify their seats, and give then authority to declare and enforce justice. "Authority" pushes us back to the question of what it is authority about and what conferred it. For Hume, the answer to the latter is "convention and established custom."

Convention differs from mere will – it is the outcome of agreement, of *many persons' interdependent* willings to coordinate their activity, each *conditional* on the other and each *expressed*. The expression ensures that the conditions become known as according-to-fact, so that the coordination can become a fact. This still might be thought merely to move us from facts about complex conditional resolves to facts about cooperative behavior and the conditions for its continuation and its approval by moral judges. Hume calls the rules of our cooperative practices "laws of nature," and calls the demands that they put on each person "natural obligations." He does pretty carefully observe and explain how the rules of a practice or form of life arise out of the perceived interest of the players and their complex mutually referential intentions, and he never claims to rely only on deduction to get to the point where, out of facts about need, perceived interest, and agreement on a cooperative scheme, he derives obligations. But nor does he yet claim that these obligations are *moral* ones. So far, they are merely *conventional* demands on a person, backed perhaps by the threat of "bad fame" should one not comply, and the prospect of a general breakdown of the cooperative scheme should too many not comply. For these "natural" and conventional obligations to get any moral force, they must be endorsed by the moral sentiment – that is, by pleasure taken from an impartial point of view – after sympathy has been felt, or attempted, with the feelings of each person (or each representative person) that the cooperative scheme involves or concerns. Tyrannical governments, schemes of property that deny women any property rights, and property conventions that make people into property will all fail this moral test, and so will not generate any *moral* obligations.

For Hume, the duty of obedience is always "factitious."[3] Anything we obey is something we together have made into a thing of authority, a superior over us. This holds as much for moral rules as for legal rules – *we* formulate, accept, or reject them as adequate declarations of our moral sentiments. Hume is willing to use deontological terms like "duty" for the content of a few non-artificial virtues, such as parental care and benevolence to close relatives, as in the quotation above. (T. 484) But his general position is that, outside the convention-generated factitious duties of obedience to governors and the rules of justice that they are invented to help us to observe, morality consists in the cultivation of a large group of "natural virtues" which he does not himself recast as rules and precepts demanding our obedience.

Obedience is not on Hume's list of natural virtues, although it is a fair inference that he regarded something like the obedience of small children to loving parents as a childish virtue. Obedience to magistrates or to governments (and to their artificial ancestors, military commanders) are the only duties that Hume recognizes that are strictly duties of obedience. Observation of the conventions of justice becomes obedience to civil law, once we have government, but respect for those conventions is called "conformity" rather than "obedience." We conform ourselves to our own cooperative schemes, to our collective intentions, to our own inventions. They are not "superior" to us, their makers, so "obedience" is not the appropriate response to them until we have also invented rank and superiority and accepted it as morally

---

[3] See his words in the essay "Of the Origin of Government," *David Hume: Essays Moral, Political, and Literary*, ed. Eugene F. Miller (Indianapolis: Liberty Classics, 1985), p. 38.

tolerable. Hume's treatment of domination is cautious. He treats it neither as a
natural human phenomenon in the form of power exercised by any stronger one
over any weaker one (as Hobbes does), males over females, females over infant
children, nor as a useful all-purpose artifice, but as an artifice of strictly limited
scope and purpose, the artifice of *political* and *judicial* superiors.

This may introduce a note of utopianism into Hume's otherwise realistic moral
psychology, and with this optimism about the strength and limits of the urge to
dominate goes an apparent optimism also about anger, revenge, and other forms of
aggression. Hume's "artifices" are designed to redirect our acquisitive drives, not
our aggressive drives as such. He takes mercy and kindness to be natural virtues,
and so presumably traits regularly found in us, but if they are as selective in their
objects as benevolence, then their presence need not block the co-presence of
ruthlessness towards out-groups. So is Hume claiming that we do and should
approve of, or at any rate condone, ruthless inhumanity to those who are not
members of our family, folk, or nation? Is he committed to endorsing at least some
versions of a morality of double standards?

II. DOUBLE STANDARDS AND AMBIVALENCE TOWARDS THEM

That we *have* double standards is something Hume is clear enough about, since
he gives us a particularly vivid example of how they show themselves in times of
war. "When our own nation is at war with any other, we detest them under the
character of cruel, perfidious, unjust, and violent: but always esteem ourselves and
allies equitable, moderate, and merciful. If the general of our enemies be successful,
'tis with difficulty we allow him the figure and character of a man. He is a sorcerer:
He has a communication with daemons; as is reported of Oliver Cromwell, and the
Duke of Luxembourg: He is bloody-minded, and takes a pleasure in death and
destruction. But if the success be on our side, our commander has all the opposite
good qualities and is a pattern of virtue, as well as of courage and conduct. His
treachery we call policy: His cruelty is an evil inseparable from war . . ." (T. 348)
This is as unequivocal a recognition as one could wish for of in-group moral bias.
But is it an endorsement of this "method of thinking that runs thro' common life"?
(T. 348) It does not read like an endorsement. What then of the claim that "our
sense of duty always follows the natural course of our passions"? Is that, too, simply
a factual claim about our sense of duty, not an endorsement of special duties to
those close to us?

Hume's characterization of the moral point of view is as an impartial point of
view, one in which we think and feel as members of "the party of humankind." It is,
I suppose, conceivable that from such an impartial viewpoint we should approve of
patriotism, even in the form of "damnation to our enemies," as we surely can and
mostly do approve of special benevolence to close relatives. But there is a difference
between absence of benevolence and malevolence, and it is malevolence that Hume
is describing in the above description of the warlike patriot. It is perfectly open to
Hume to regard differential benevolence as a virtue, and yet regard any
malevolence as a vice. But he could only keep such a claim consistent with his claim
that vices are departures from the common measures of human passions if he

regarded hatred and malevolence as such departures. Is it at all plausible to think that he did? If he did, is his view at all plausible?

The striking thing about his treatment of natural human passions in Book Two of the *Treatise* is how little attention he gives to the "negative" passions of humility and hatred. In theory he is even-handedly analyzing pride and humility as the positive and negative poles of self-evaluation, love and hatred as the positive and negative poles of evaluation of fellow persons. But, in fact, humility and hatred get pretty short shrift. The passage quoted above, about hatred of our nation's enemies in wartime, occurs in a section entitled "Difficulties Solv'd"; in it, he allows that love and hatred are not always based on calm evaluation of the qualities of other persons, but also on the relationship in which we stand to them and on whether they present a menace or a help to our own perceived interests. If we think they have already injured us, then we will hate them. In this section he claims that we tend to love those who flatter and serve us and hate those who injure, criticize, and oppose us, regardless of their more intrinsic merits. In the following section, "Of the Love of Relations," he dwells on our automatic love of our own offspring, our delight in the company of "beings like ourselves." There is no parallel section on hatred of those unlike ourselves, nor I think is there any reason to think that Hume believed that this was a natural human phenomenon. At most he believed that our love and benevolence is stronger the closer we see our relationship and likeness to the other. He comments on the fact that love need not be species-limited. "Love in animals has not for its only object animals of the same species, but extends itself farther, and comprehends almost every sensible and thinking thing. A dog naturally loves a man above his own species, and very commonly meets with a return of affection." (T. 397) This willingness to develop affection, this conditional friendliness, is linked closely by Hume to our (and dogs'?) sociable nature. Not only is the human being dependent on things, so that "when you loosen all the holds, which he has of external objects, he immediately drops down into the deepest melancholy and despair," (T. 352) but he is dependent also on well-disposed and communicative living company: "Hence company is so naturally rejoicing, as presenting to us the liveliest of all objects, *viz.* a rational and thinking Being like ourselves, who communicates to us all the actions of his mind, makes us privy to his inmost sentiments and feelings; and lets us see, in the very instant of their production, all the emotions that are caus'd by any object." (T. 353) Again, "Every pleasure languishes when enjoy'd a-part from company.... Let all the powers and elements of nature conspire to serve and obey one man: Let the sun rise and set at his command ... he will still be miserable, till you give him one person at least, with whom he may share his happiness, and whose esteem and friendship he may enjoy." (T. 363) One person at least, or even one dog. There is nothing very exclusive about this need for company, as Hume presents it. As long as the other is friendly, living, expressive, and shares some of one's own means of expression so that mutual recognition of emotion is possible, then that one will be sufficiently "like ourselves" to be good company. Hume can consistently combine the thesis that we can welcome the company, even the friendship, of any living thing that shares our expressive body language, with the thesis that "the company of our relations and acquaintance must be peculiarly agreeable." (T. 353) Indeed, he sees the two claims as supporting each other. "Now 'tis obvious, that nature has preserv'd a great resemblance among all human creatures, and that we never remark any passion or principle in others, of which, in some degree or other, we may not find a parallel in ourselves .... This resemblance must very much contribute to make us enter into the sentiments of others, and embrace them with facility and pleasure. Accordingly we find that, where besides the general resemblance of our natures, there is any particular similarity in our manners, or character, or country, or language, it facilitates the sympathy." (T. 318) Common animal passions and common mammalian expression of them is a start; a common language, common enthusiasms, or common tastes in literature are even better.

In these particular passages where Hume is exploring our natural liking for what is like us, we do not find any racist or sexist preferences listed along with the other biases in favor of our "own kind." Both skin colors and sexes are treated by Hume as "agreeable differences," differences that need in no way interfere with sympathy and friendship unless they are (as, in fact, they often are) accompanied by differences of culture. Particularly with respect to the company of "the fair sex," Hume did his best to try to break the connection between "mixed" company and company of correspondingly mixed educational backgrounds. His early essays urge women to read history, so to ponder the courage of Boadicea, the stateswomanly virtues of Elizabeth I of England, the scholarly dedication of Lady Jane Grey, that he was later to discuss in his *History*. They could also ponder the legendary extreme measures taken by the Scythian women to free themselves from slavish tastes. Hume wrote these essays in his self-chosen role of ambassador between the "learned" and the "conversible" worlds, and his campaign was not just to make the learned more conversible, but to encourage "the Sovereigns of the Empire of Conversation" to acquire more learning and to join him in a league against "People of dull Heads and cold Hearts" ("Of Essay Writing").[4] He also gives women subtle nudges to readjust the balance between the "docility" which their culture had artificially tried to impose on them and that reactive "love of dominion" which he finds typical of married women in his society ("Of Love and Marriage").[5] His essay "Of Moral Prejudices"[6] shows one way of making that adjustment: namely. rejecting both docility and marriage but not parenthood.

Hume clearly sees that double standards, both in-group/out-group and male/female, are in no way unusual, so not in that sense unnatural to us. Are they unnatural in the other sense of "artificial" and culture-dependent? And if they are, are the artifices they depend upon morally approvable artifices? If they are the results of artifices that are neither inevitable nor morally approvable, then the more equitable alternatives to them could count as equally "natural," both in the sense of normal, expressive of normal human passions, and in the sense of preferable. Is it plausible to see both xenophobic attitudes and sexist attitudes as "unnatural," in the sense of culturally induced projects of *dysfunctional* (and avoidable) social artifices?

---

[4] *Essays*, p. 536,
[5] *Essays*, p. 558.
[6] *Essays*, p. 542ff.

According to anthropologist Christian Vogel, double standards of both these sorts are the outcome of natural selection. They therefore constitute the most "natural morality" that we have, one that he sees as conflicting head-on with the egalitarian moral standards which reflective rational persons endorse. He writes:

> We cannot remove from our genome the behavioral tendencies that have developed through natural selection, along with our predisposition to a morality of double standards. But we do have enough freedom of decision and mental power to make repeated efforts to curb these tendencies, even though we must assume that they will continue to reappear whenever we relax our efforts. As Thomas Henry Huxley (1893) wrote: "Let us understand, once for all, that the ethical progress of society depends, not on imitating the cosmic process, still less in running away from it, but in combating it!"[7]

The Huxley claim concerns "the cosmic process," but of course it is only a tiny ripple in it — namely, the developmental process producing us – that is at issue in the debate about the foundations of morality in human nature. It will seem clear to Humeans that any capacities we have that enable us to "fight" the tendencies to sexism and xenophobia that are in us must equally be "in" us, in our capacities to develop culture, to extend sympathy, to take up a moral viewpoint. And this is also what Vogel in the end is saying, that our biological inheritance is "double" and ambivalent, containing conflicting tendencies. We do have a tendency to let male bullies dominate; we do have a tendency to dehumanize our enemies in war; we do kill each other both in anger and in cold blood. Vogel quotes Sophocles: "There are many awesome things, but nothing is more awful than man."[8] Our biological inheritance is ambivalent. It gives us a "natural" tendency to double standards as well as tendency to condemn them. If we are to fight our "worse" tendencies, it will be by our "better" tendencies. As Hume wrote, "Men must, therefore, endeavour to palliate what they cannot cure."[9]

Hume, I think, is quite clear about both the "worse" and the "better" tendencies, although maybe he is overoptimistic about their relative frequency and so over-confident that we can reform the bad social artifices that reinforce our "bad nature." He gives a clear, realistic description of double standards in marriage and of the interests that they serve. When he is discussing the question of how the character of Elizabeth I of England should be judged, he refers to the difficulty of getting people to use "the true method of estimating her merits" that would require

[7] *Evolutionsbiologie und die "doppelte Moral", Jahrbuch der Akademie der Wissenschaften in Gottingen*, 1988, my free translation.
[8] Christian Vogel, *Vom Töten zum Mord: Das wirkliche Böse in der Evolutionsgeschichte* (Munich: Carl Hanser Verlag, 1989), p. 121. Where the Loeb translator has "wonders" and "wondrous" for the Greek "deina" and "deinoteron," I use "awesome things" and "awful" to preserve the negative element in the Greek which the German translation (Reklam) that Vogel quotes emphasizes by speaking here of "das Ungeheure." And it is "the terrible ambivalence of human beings" that this chorus from "Antigone" is invoked by Vogel to express.
[9] See *Essays*, p. 38.

laying aside sexist prejudices which might lead some to find her wanting in "those amiable weaknesses" that men like in women. He refers to those prejudices as "more durable, because more natural" than those stemming from political "faction and bigotry."[10] He attempts the "true method of estimating her merit," and explains (and so, to some extent, excuses – but does not endorse) the untrue but natural biased mode of judgment. The same might be said of his account of the institution of marriage in his day. It is easy enough to understand that institution. It is also not so difficult to criticize it from a moral viewpoint, and this is what Hume does in his essays "Of Polygamy and Divorces," "Of Love and Marriage," and "Of Moral Prejudices."[11]

Sexist institutions have been the norm in human societies, and so they have made sexist feelings "the usual course of our passions." But then it is equally true that religious zeal, holy wars, intermittent fear of hell, and deference to priestly authority have also been a usual display of human passions – and Hume made his own disapproval of those, and of the artifices that cultivated them, abundantly clear. Can he consistently recognize the statistical normality of religious institutions and of sexist institutions, hold that we consider the normal course of human passions when we approve or condemn, and also condemn religious and sexist institutions, the passions that they make usual in the people who are influenced by them and who accept them? Is it normal for human persons not just to tolerate immoral institutions, but to regard conformity to them as virtuous? Is this as normal as the attempt to reform them? Only if there is more moral disagreement than Hume officially allows.

III. THE "NATURAL PROGRESS OF HUMAN SENTIMENTS"

Conflict, vacillation, disagreement, and faction are facts not only about human societies but also about the passions of any one person. If our "nature" really is ambivalent, if our various passions do conflict, if some (or some versions of some) are opposed by others, then we must expect both sexism and uneasiness about sexism in one and the same persons as well as in one and the same society – both a sense of justice and a sneaking envy of the sensible knave, both patriotic zeal and cosmopolitan yearnings, both anti-religious campaigns, opposition to "monstrous doctrines" and "priestly inventions" that go against a "true" version of the public interest, and enough piety towards the faith of our fathers and mothers to make our anti-religious sentiments appear "a narrow way to thinking" to avowed atheists. (Hume was called a "Fidei Defensor" by his scornful Paris atheist friends.) There will be vacillation in thoughtful people, factions in society, and moral disagreement if our natures have conflicting tendencies and our social artifices multiple potential.

The passage I quoted earlier from Hume in which he acknowledges that not merely our behavior but our approvals and disapprovals reflect the natural or usual course of our passions (at T. 483–84) occurs when Hume is trying to persuade us that justice is an artificial virtue – that, if our partiality to ourselves and our nearest and dearest, in respect of our attitude to scarce transferable goods, is to be

---

[10] David Hume, *History of England*, end of ch. XLV (Dublin: James Williams, 1780), vol. 5, p. 445.
[11] These are to be found in *Essays*.

corrected, it will be by social artifice and culture. "Our natural uncultivated ideas of morality, instead of providing a remedy for the partiality of our affections, do rather conform themselves to that partiality and give it additional force and influence. The remedy then is not deriv'd from nature, but from artifice; or more properly speaking, nature provides a remedy in the judgment and understanding for what is irregular and incommodious in the affections." (T. 489) It is our natural understanding, along with our natural sympathy, that enables us not just to design social artifices but eventually to prefer those which are more "equitable." The victory for these less biased institutions over competitor institutions is not assured, since the motives leading persons to support racist and sexist practices may be incurable. The best we may be able to hope for is that they do not dominate our social planning. Hume, I think, supposed that equitable artifices would be more stable because they are less prone to provoke morally justified rebellion from within or resentful attack from without by those excluded from the "sweets" of the society they produce and monopolize. In his discussion in the *Enquiry Concerning the Principles of Morals*[12] of the exclusion some societies make of some people (slaves, women) from the rights that the society protects, Hume makes the ability to make resentment effectively felt the criterion of proper membership. He predicts, a bit prematurely, that sensible people, once they understand both the reasons for resentment and the power possessed by at least some of the underprivileged classes (women in particular, given their power in reproductive cooperation), will enlarge their views as they appreciate "the force of their mutual connexions. History, experience, reason, sufficiently instruct us in this natural progress of human sentiments, and in the gradual enlargement of our regards to justice."[13]

I began with the question of whether Hume's writings in ethics lend support to those, like sociobiologists, who see the discoverable facts about our nature to have great relevance for the question of what moral goals are appropriate for us, or whether, as some believe, he exposed the fallacy of moving from any factual premises to any normative conclusion. My answer has been that the former alternative is closer to the truth, but the facts on which Humean norms and moral endorsements are grounded are somewhat complicated ones, involving not just our biological and social nature and history, but our capacities for enlarged sympathy, for evaluative response to one another, and for taking steadily more "extensive views" of our situation. He is advocating that we attend carefully to the procedures by which we, and our fellow-judges, purport to move from factual premises to moral endorsements, so that we will be able to explain just what sort of move it is. The goal is to be able to endorse our own habits of moral reflection. To ignore the constraints imposed upon realistic moral goals or design of institutions by empirically discoverable facts about our nature as revealed in our history and prehistory would be to doom our moral endeavors to futility. To derive our moral goals too hastily and uncritically from our current actual practices, and from the variant of human nature that those practices nurture, would be to doom them to

[12] David Hume, *Enquiries*, ed. L. A. Selby-Bigge and P. H. Nidditch (Oxford: Clarendon Press, 1975), pp. 190–92.
[13] *ibid.*, p. 192.

34 ANNETTE C. BAIER

unreflectiveness and so to forfeiting their right to be called fully *moral* views. Hume's own recipe, and his practice, was to inform moral judgment with the available facts about human nature and human history, and about the nature and history of the society or individual about whom a judgment is being made. He would then allow wide bias-corrected sympathy, and the reflective sentiment of those who are aware of each other's reflective sentiments, to form the verdict. Uninformed by discoverable facts about human nature, moral judgment will be blind. Unwilling to do anything more than endorse the *status quo*, it will be empty. To be non-utopian, yet properly critical, moral judges must try to make sure that they have "a proper discernment" of their object, even when this discernment requires that "nice distinctions be made, just conclusions drawn, distant comparisons formed, complicated relations examined, and general facts fixed and ascertained."[14] To ensure that morality will be an active principle that "constitutes virtue our happiness" (where "we" are really all of us),[15] the final verdict must rest with the impartial but engaged "sentiment of humanity," rather than with any less extensive sentiment or sympathy.

Philosophy, University of Pittsburgh

[14] *ibid.*, p. 173.
[15] *ibid.*

LE PROMENEUR SOLITAIRE: ROUSSEAU AND THE EMERGENCE OF THE POST-SOCIAL SELF*

BY DAVID GAUTHIER

1. The portrait and the man – each is unique. "Here is the *only* portrait of a man, painted exactly from nature and completely true to it."[1] And this man, "it will be myself. . . . Myself *alone*. . . . I am different."[2] And yet this unique portrait of this unique man, "may be used as the first comparative work in the study of man, which is certainly yet to be begun."[3]

Our interest is in the study of mankind.[4] Can Rousseau be right to introduce his autobiographical writings with the claim that this study is "yet to be begun"? A century before, Hobbes could speak of reading in oneself "not this, or that particular man; but Man-kind," for beneath the opacity of actions and the differences of circumstances, Hobbes detected an identity of thoughts and passions.[5] But Rousseau represents Hobbes as misreading "a multitude of passions that are the product of society"[6] into the nature of man and creating only "dangerous dreams."[7] Rousseau himself introduces the *Discours sur l'inégalité* with

---

* For Rousseau's writings I have used the *Oeuvres Complètes*, eds. Bernard Gagnebin & Marcel Raymond (Paris: Gallimard, Bibliothèque de la Pléiade), vol. 1 (1959), vol. 3 (1964), vol. 4 (1969); these are abbreviated *OC* 1, *OC* 3 and *OC* 4 in the ensuing notes. They retain Rousseau's orthography and punctuation. The *Essai sur l'origine des langues* does not appear in the *OC*; I have used the text published by the Bibliothèque du Graphe (Paris: no date), which is a reproduction of the edition of A. Belin (1817). Particular works are referred to as follows:

> *Les Confessions de J. J. Rousseau* (1780) = *Confessions*
> *Du Contrat social* (1762) = *Contrat*
> *Dialogues: Rousseau juge de Jean Jaques* (1780) = *Premier, Deuxième, Troisième dialogue*
> *Discours sur l'Origine et les fondements de l'inégalité* (1755) = *Discours*
> *Émile ou de l'éducation* (1762) = *Émile*
> *Essai sur l'origine des Langues* = *Essai*
> *Les Rèveries du promeneur solitaire* (1780) = *Première, . . ., Dixième promenade*

The translations are my own. I am grateful to Candace Vogler for her comments on the original version of this essay.

[1] "Voici le *seul* portrait d'homme, peint exactement d'après nature et dans toute sa vérité" (*Confessions*, intro., *OC* 1, p. 3; italics mine).

[2] "ce sera moi. . . . Moi *seul*. . . . je suis autre." (*ibid.*, bk. 1, p. 5; italics mine).

[3] "peut servir de prémiére piéce de comparaison pour l'étude des hommes, qui certainement est encore à commencer" (*ibid.*, introduction, p. 3).

[4] I shall not speak here of humankind, but let 'man' and 'mankind' shift, as they will, between their sexed and unsexed resonances; at the end – mine in this paper, Rousseau's in his portrait – woman becomes too relevant to suppress the shifts.

[5] Thomas Hobbes, *Leviathan* (London: 1651), introduction, p. 2.

[6] "une multitude de passions qui sont l'ouvrage de la Société" (*Discours, première partie, OC* 3, p. 153).

[7] See Rousseau's first reference to Hobbes in the *Discours sur les sciences et les arts* (1750), where he speaks of "les dangereuses reveries des Hobbes et des Spinosas." (*OC* 3, p. 28).

the claim that, whoever you are, "here is your history, as I believe I have read it . . .
in nature."[8] What is the relation of this earlier study of mankind to the
autobiography – the *only* portrait, painted exactly from nature"? To link
Rousseau's rejection of the arguments of his predecessors, his account of the history
of mankind, and his unique self-portrayal, we must come to understand how
Rousseau's endeavor to think the conditions of man's social existence determines
his own need to live in a consciousness that is post-social. Rousseau's thought
moves from solitude to society, his self-portrait from society to solitude. And this
portrait is the "first comparative work in the study of man" as he is coming to be; it
is unique, yet exemplary. The *Discours* is our history read in nature; the *Confessions*
and *Rêveries* are our future read in Rousseau himself.

In this brief paper, we cannot trace the detail of Rousseau's journey to solitude,
but only sketch some of its stages. First, however, let us join him at the beginning of
the *Rêveries,* as he nears his destination. "So here I am *alone* on earth."[9] *Le seul
homme,* we might say, is *l'homme seul.* It was not always so. In our beginnings, every
man lived as Rousseau, "having no longer a brother, a neighbor, a friend, or any
society but myself."[10] But what was man's ordinary condition is now transformed
into the most extraordinary; what nature once gave to all is now made possible only
by "a unanimous accord."[11] "How did this change come about?"[12] We shall not
ignore this question, but it is not our prime concern. "What can legitimate it?"[13]
This is more interesting, and more difficult.

More difficult? Surely impossible. Rousseau's solitude is self-imposed. To be
sure, in his paranoia he views himself as the object of a universal hatred so deep that
he is kept in isolation, ignorance, and impotence, each detail of his life arranged by
his unknown masters. How can there be more than a pathological connection
between this lunatic, nightmare vision, which comes to pervade Rousseau's
autobiographical writings, and his political and social thought? We shall not deny
the nightmarish quality of the vision. But it shares the vocabulary of Rousseau's
endeavors to diagnose and ameliorate man's ills. Indeed, it results directly from the
success of the diagnosis and the failure of the remedies. In *Du Contrat social*
Rousseau seeks the legitimacy of our social chains. The same legitimacy extends to
his universal proscription. "But I, cut off from them and from all else, what am I
myself? That is what remains for me to find out."[14] *Les Rêveries du promeneur
solitaire* closes Rousseau's long inquiry into mankind with the man who has
emerged from society. The portrait is the anthropology of the post-social self.

2.   In his original condition, man is neither good nor evil, neither fearing ill nor
hoping for well from his fellows, a being solitary and self-sufficient.[15] His first

---

[8] "voici ton histoire telle que j'ai cru la lire . . . dans la Nature" (*Discours, OC* 3, p. 133)

[9] "Me voici donc *seul* sur la terre" (*Première promenade, OC* 1, p. 995; italics mine)

[10] "n'ayant plus de frere, de prochain, d'ami, de societé que moi-même." (*ibid.*)

[11] "un accord unanime." (*ibid.*)

[12] "Comment ce changement s'est-il fait?" (*Contrat,* bk. 1, ch. 1, *OC* 3, p. 351)

[13] "Qu'est-ce qui peut le rendre légitime?" (*ibid.*)

[14] "Mais moi, détaché d'eux et de tout, que suis-je moi-même? Voila ce qui me reste à chercher." (*Première
promenade, OC* 1, p. 995)

[15] The account of man is drawn from the *Discours sur l'inégalité.*

sentiment is "that of his existence," his first care "that of his preservation."[16] Tranquil and free, "the savage lives within himself."[17] But man's nature is not fixed like that of other animals; he has "the capacity to perfect himself."[18] The history of mankind is the history of this fatal perfectibility. In learning better to satisfy his original, simple needs and desires, man comes gradually to perceive a world beyond his own existence and to desire and need the things of that world. So long as each person's powers suffice for his needs, all is well, but once the harmony between the two is broken, he comes to be dependent on his fellows for his satisfaction, and "civilized man"[19] makes his appearance. Since his portrait is not our chief concern, we shall say of him only that he is in all respects the antithesis of his predecessor, that "always outside himself, [he] can live only in the opinion of others, and it is, so to speak, only from their judgment that he takes the sentiment of his own existence."[20]

Beasts are dangerous when wild; men dangerous when tame. In the *Confessions*, Rousseau speaks of the pleasure he took in taming animals, wanting "that they love me freely."[21] However this may be with the pigeons at Les Charmettes,[22] it is not so with men. Beneath his veneer of civility, *l'homme policé* is a slave to his *amour-propre*, the relative and competitive concern for himself that, placing his happiness and his very sense of existence in the degree of esteem he receives, makes him hostage to his equally civil fellows. He knows neither love nor liberty. The *Discours sur l'inégalité* eloquently depicts the fall of mankind under the sway of *amour-propre*; we may turn to Rousseau's essays in redemption.

One can make Émile, or one can make citizens. The former is the work of the Tutor, the latter of the Legislator. We do not begin by asking whether these are men, or gods, or Rousseau himself; we ask only what they do. Émile is made for himself, the citizens for society. Each must be given the nature proper to his calling – no easy task in a world corrupted.

The man made for himself must have powers sufficient to his needs and desires limited by his powers; only so can he be happy and free. In a society whose rule is not enough but excess, not self-sufficiency but dependence, how may the Tutor raise Émile? Rousseau's answer is clear. "Insofar as it affects him, do you not arrange all that surrounds him? . . . His works and games, his pleasures and pains – isn't everything in your hands without his knowing? No doubt he should do only what he wants, but he should want only what you want him to do; he shouldn't take

---

[16] "celui de son existence . . . celui de sa conservation." (*Discours, seconde partie, OC* 3, p. 164)

[17] "le Sauvage vit en lui-même." (*ibid.,* p. 193)

[18] "la faculté de se perfectionner." (*ibid., première partie,* p. 142)

[19] "l'homme policé" (*ibid., seconde partie,* p. 192)

[20] "toûjours hors de lui [il] ne sait vivre que dans l'opinion des autres; et c'est, pour ainsi dire, de leur seul jugement qu'il tire le sentiment de sa propre éxistence." (*ibid.,* p. 193)

[21] "qu'ils m'aimasssent en liberté." (*Confessions,* bk. 6, *OC* 1, p. 234) Note the connection between taming and liberty.

[22] The country house where Rousseau resided with Mme. de Warens, his first (and deepest) love. She will figure in our account later, as will the conjunction of love and liberty.

a step that you haven't foreseen; he shouldn't open his mouth without your knowing what he is going to say."[23] And the result? In the words of the Tutor: "It is true that I leave him the appearance of independence, but he was never so fully subject to me, since he is so because he wants to be. As long as I couldn't make myself master of his will, I remained at his side; I didn't take a step away from him. Now I sometimes leave him to himself, because I always govern him."[24]

To appreciate these remarkable passages, and to grasp their significance for the solitary walker, we must turn to the *Dialogues: Rousseau juge de Jean-Jaques*, where we find the Frenchman's description of the measures taken to constrain Jean-Jacques, "the horror of the human race,"[25] from continuing his odious crimes. "They have taken no less effective precautions in keeping him under such surveillance that he can not say a word that isn't recorded, not take a step that isn't noted, not form a plan that isn't discovered at the moment that it is conceived. They have arranged it so that, apparently free among men, he has no real society with them; he lives alone in the crowd; he knows nothing of what goes on; ... he feels himself bound in chains which he can neither show nor see the least trace. Around him they have built walls too dark for him to pierce; they have buried him alive among the living."[26]

As the Tutor knows each word that Émile utters, each step that he takes, so the anonymous and ubiquitous men of the *Dialogues* – "nos messieurs," as the Frenchman refers to them – know each word and each step of Jean-Jacques's. "In the middle of this feigned liberty he can not say a word, or take a step, or lift a finger, without their knowing and willing it."[27] As Émile does not know himself to be in the Tutor's hands, so Jean-Jacques does not know what *nos messieurs* do. To be sure, Jean-Jacques senses himself chained; Émile, presumably, is free of such presentiments. But the parallels are unmistakable. The totalitarian implications of Rousseau's remedies for our fallen condition are not a discovery of modern scholars, much less the figment of their imaginations; Rousseau knew, if only *au fond de son coeur*, the true character of the Tutor and, as we shall soon see, the Legislator.

[23] "Ne disposez-vous pas par raport à lui de tout ce qui l'environne? ... Ses travaux, ses jeux, ses plaisirs, ses peines, tout n'est-il pas dans vos mains sans qu'il le sache? Sans doute, il ne doit faire que ce qu'il veut; mais il ne doit vouloir que ce que vous voulez qu'il fasse; il ne doit pas faire un pas que vous ne l'ayez prévu, il ne doit pas ouvrir la bouche que vous ne sachiez ce qu'il va dire." (*Émile*, bk. 2, *OC* 4, pp. 362–63)

[24] "Je lui laisse, il est vrai, l'apparence de l'indépendance, mais jamais il ne me fut mieux assujeti, car il l'est parce qu'il veut l'être. Tant que je n'ai pu me rendre maitre de sa volonté, je le suis demeuré de sa personne; je ne la quittois pas d'un pas. Maintenant je le laisse quelquefois à lui-même parce que je le gouverne toujours." (*ibid.*, bk. 4, p. 661)

[25] "l'horreur du genre humain" (*Premier dialogue*, *OC* 1, p. 705) In the *Première promenade*, Rousseau employs a similar phrase in characterizing what he has become: "l'horreur de la race humaine." (*OC* 1, p. 996)

[26] "Ils ont pris des précautions non moins efficaces en le surveillant à tel point qu'il ne puisse dire un mot qui ne soit écrit, ni faire un pas qui ne soit marqué, ni former un projet qu'on ne pénètre à l'instant qu'il est conçu. Ils ont fait en sorte que, libre en apparence au milieu des hommes, il n'eut avec eux aucune société réelle, qu'il vécut seul dans la foule, qu'il ne sut rien de ce qui se fait, ... qu'il se sentit par tout chargé de chaînes dont il ne put ne montrer ni voir le moindre vestige. Ils ont élevé autour de lui des murs de tenebres impenetrables à ses regards; ils l'ont enterré vif parmi les vivans." (*Premier dialogue*, *OC* 1, p. 706)

[27] "au milieu de cette liberté feinte il ne puisse ni dire un mot, ni faire un pas, ni mouvoir un doigt qu'ils ne le sachent et ne le veuillent." (*ibid.*, p. 710)

The account in the *Dialogues* of the universal plot against Jean-Jacques is both a manifestation of Rousseau's unbridled paranoia and a portrayal of total social control of the individual on a par with Orwell's *1984*.[28] In giving such a portrayal, Rousseau is exhibiting the significance of his own social thought in a way that he doubtless did not consciously understand. When in *Émile* he enjoins the Tutor, "Prepare in advance for the rule of his liberty and the use of his powers . . . in putting him in a condition always to be master of himself and to do his will in all things,"[29] we have no reason to question his conscious sincerity. But in enjoining subjection as the means to liberty, and in recognizing that "no subjection is so perfect as that which preserves the appearance of liberty; in this way one captures the will itself,"[30] Rousseau created the conditions for his paranoia to reveal to him, as his reflection could not, that Émile is Jean-Jacques.

The Tutor's official aim is to create in Émile a person self-sufficient and, we might say, self-contained. The Legislator's aim is quite the opposite; where the Tutor strives against society for the independence of his pupil, the Legislator seeks to forge the bonds of society so tight that the dependence of the citizens is absolute. The Tutor seeks to preserve Émile in his natural condition; the Legislator seeks to destroy that condition – "to change, so to speak, human nature; to transform each individual, who in himself is a perfect and solitary whole, into part of a greater whole, from which he receives, as it were, his life and his being . . . to substitute a partial and moral existence for the physical and independent existence that we have all received from nature. It is necessary, in a word, that he deprives man of his own powers to give him ones that are alien, and that he cannot use without the aid of others."[31] The Legislator must ensure that "each citizen is nothing, and can do nothing, without *all* the others."[32] Thus the citizen differs from *l'homme policé* only (but, for Rousseau, crucially) in taking the sense of his existence from the assured recognition of his fellow-citizens, rather than from the chance recognition of strangers.

The totalitarian role of the Legislator is less concealed than that of the Tutor. But we may profit again from comparing Rousseau's account with the Frenchman's tale in the *Premier dialogue* of the measures provided by *nos messieurs* for Jean-Jacques. For, in effect, they deprive Jean-Jacques of any means to satisfy his desires on his own: "merely exhibiting the desire to find something, whatsoever

---

[28] Indeed, like Orwell, Rousseau recognizes the need to control the past; speaking, as always, of *nos messieurs*, the Frenchman says, "The further they proceed into the future, the easier it is for them to wipe out the past or to give it the twist that suits them." ["Plus ils avancent dans l'avenir, plus il leur est facile d'obliterer le passé ou de lui donner la tournure qui leur convient." (*Troisième dialogue, OC* 1, p. 944)]

[29] "Préparez de loin le régne de sa liberté et l'usage de ses forces . . . en le mettant en état d'être toujours maitre de lui-même, et de faire en toute chose sa volonté" (*Émile,* bk. 1, *OC* 4, p. 282)

[30] "Il n'y a point d'assujetissement si parfait que celui qui garde l'apparence de la liberté; on captive ainsi la volonté même." (*ibid.,* bk. 2, p. 362)

[31] "de changer, pour ainsi dire, la nature humaine; de transformer chaque individu, qui par lui-même est un tout parfait et solitaire, en partie d'un plus grand tout dont cet individu reçoive en quelque sorte sa vie et son être; . . . de substituer une existence partielle et morale à l'existence physique et indépendante que nous avons tous reçue de la nature. Il fait, en un mot, qu'il ôte à l'homme ses forces propres pour lui en donner qui lui soient étrangeres et dont il ne puisse faire usage sans le secours d'autrui." (*Contrat,* bk. 2, ch. 7, *OC* 3, pp. 381–82)

[32] "chaque Citoyen n'est rien, ne peut rien, que par *tous* les autres" (*ibid.,* p. 382; italics mine)

it be, is for him the infallible way to make it disappear."[33] But on the other hand, "and it is above all in this that there is something great, generous, and admirable in the plan of our men – that in preventing him from following his will and carrying out his evil designs, one seeks however to secure for him the sweets of life, so that everywhere he finds what he needs."[34] Indeed, "despite his opposition they give him public charity in such a way that it is impossible for him to avoid it."[35] Reduced to nothing in himself, Jean-Jacques exists through "the kindness of strangers,"[36] the powers *of nos messieurs* which he cannot escape, and to which all, save he alone, are party.

3. At this point, we should recall Rousseau's doctrine of the general will. In the *Rêveries*, Rousseau, speaking of the universal plot against him, insists that "this universal accord is too extraordinary to be entirely fortuitous. A single man who would refuse to be party to it . . . would be enough to make it miscarry. But every will . . . has strengthened the work of the men."[37] The plot is founded on a will that is general, shared by all members of society, save (it would seem) one – Rousseau himself. Instead, he is the object of that will; the plot to isolate him is the fundamental and common concern of the others. In a remarkable passage in the *Dialogues*, Rousseau states, "While he is concerned with himself, they are also concerned with him. He loves himself and they hate him; . . . he is everything for himself, he is also everything for them: for as for them, they are nothing, neither for him nor for themselves, and provided that J-J is miserable, they need no other happiness."[38] We noted that in the *Discours sur l'inégalité*, Rousseau insists that, in society, each person lives and is aware of his own existence only in the recognition of his fellows. The task of the Legislator is to assure this recognition; this has now been transformed so that each, in effect, lives through (and only through) his awareness of Jean-Jacques's misery.

But Jean-Jacques, it would seem, is a being alien to the society whose existence consists in execrating him. And one of the cardinal tenets of Rousseau's doctrine of the general will is that it must not only come from all the members of society, but apply to all. The will of society, general in relation to its members taken as a whole, is particular in relation to any other object, and even to the members taken

---

[33] "le seul desir manifesté de trouver une chose telle qu'elle soit est pour lui l'infaillible moyen de la faire disparoitre." (*Premier dialogue, OC* 1, p. 713)

[34] "et c'est là surtout ce qu'il y a de grand, de genereux, d'admirable dans le plan de nos Messieurs qu'en l'empêchant de suivre ses volontés et d'accomplir ses mauvais desseins, on cherche cependant à lui procurer les douceurs de la vie, de façon qu'il trouve par tout ce qui lui est necessaire" (*ibid.*, p. 716)

[35] "ils lui font l'aumône publiquement malgré lui de façon qu'il lui soit impossible de s'y dérober" (*ibid.*, p. 718)

[36] "Blanche [DuBois] (holding tight to his arm): Whoever you are — I have always depended on the kindness of strangers." (Tennessee Williams, *A Streetcar Named Desire*, Scene XI)

[37] "cet accord universel est trop extraordinaire pour être purement fortuit. Un seul homme qui eut refusé d'en être complice . . . suffisoit pour la faire échouer. Mais toutes les volontés . . . ont affermi l'oeuvre des hommes" (*Deuxième promenade, OC* 1, p. 1010)

[38] "Tandis qu'il [Jean-Jacques] s'occupe avec lui-même, eux [his enemies] s'occupent aussi de lui. Il s'aime et ils le haïssent; . . . il est tout pour lui-même, il est aussi tout pour eux: car quant à eux ils ne sont rien, ni pour lui, ni pour eux-mêmes, et pourvu que J. J. soit misérable, ils n'ont pas besoin d'autre bonheur." (*Deuxième dialogue, OC* 1, p. 860)

ROUSSEAU AND THE POST-SOCIAL SELF

individually. The general will is always right, insofar as it comes from all and applies to all, but as Rousseau insists, "it loses its natural rectitude whenever it is directed to any object that is individual and determinate."[39] Surely, then, it is a gross distortion of Rousseau's account to suppose that the general will of society is expressed in the universal plot against Jean-Jacques.

Here we must recall Rousseau's insistence that each individual has a private will that may differ from or oppose the general will shared by all individuals as citizens. And the person who acts on his private will, rather than conforming to the dictates of the general will, is destructive to society. Moreover, he is destructive to himself, for obedience to the general will "is the condition that, giving each citizen to the nation, ensures him against all personal dependence."[40] The Legislator, in taking from each person his own natural powers, takes from him the power to realize his private will, and in ensuring that each can act only together with his fellows, gives the citizens only the power to realize the general will. Each person is freed from living only in the opinion of others whose wills are alien to him – by being made to live only as a part of the society whose will he shares. As Rousseau notoriously says, "he is forced to be free."[41]

We have seen that Jean-Jacques is Émile; he is also the citizen, forced to be free. In the *Dialogues*, Rousseau reports Jean-Jacques as asking, "Well, sir, can't you see that the great crime – the only crime – that they fear from me, a frightful crime paralyzing them with continual terror, is my justification?"[42] Jean-Jacques's crime is that he will not admit his guilt; instead, he persists in justifying himself. For this justification, standing in opposition to society, is an affirmation of his private will against the general will, and so proof of his guilt and his enslavement. Hence he is proscribed by "a unanimous accord." He must therefore be forced to be free. He must love Big Brother.

Jean-Jacques affirms his individuality in the face of totalitarian society. The society can admit no will or judgment other than its own; Jean-Jacques defies this. His defiance is more than a denial of society's claim to express the general will – a mere claim might, after all, be mistaken. The act of affirming his own will is in itself a *demonstration* that society does not express the general will, and so has no legitimate, moral existence. If one begins, then, from the premise that society is a moral body expressing the general will, it follows that no opposed assertion of individual will can occur. Faced with the apparent fact of such an assertion, the society must seek to respond by requiring the individual to confess, thus withdrawing his assertion of individual will in favor of the general will – but, then, since this would still leave the act of assertion itself as a fact, the society must

[39] "elle perd sa rectitude naturelle lorsqu'elle tend à quelque objet individuel et déterminé" (*Contrat*, bk. 2, ch. 4, *OC* 3, p. 373)

[40] "est la condition qui donnant chaque Citoyen à la Patrie le garantit de toute dépendance personelle." (*ibid.*, bk. 1, ch. 7, p. 364)

[41] "on le forcera d'être libre" (*ibid.*)

[42] "Eh, Monsieur, pouvez-vous ne pas voir que le grand, le seul crime qu'ils redoutent de moi, crime affreux dont l'effroi les tient dans des transes continuelles, est ma justification?" (*Deuxième dialogue, OC* 1, p. 841)

respond further by making the individual a non-person, a person who never existed, so that no act asserting the individual will has ever occurred.

Jean-Jacques, however, does not confess, and most certainly not in his *Confessions*, the publication of which he saw as part of his crime of justification. What can a totalitarian society do with such a recalcitrant individual? Jean-Jacques is an enemy, affirming his individual will, but not an enemy, since no enemy is possible – the general will embraces all. Because he is an enemy – indeed, *the* enemy – execrating Jean-Jacques is an affirmation of social legitimacy which, because it acknowledges the reality of Jean-Jacques's enmity and alienation from the society, undermines that legitimacy. It purports to be the core act of the general will, since it affords not only happiness but existence to the members of society,[43] but it denies its character as such an act by taking a particular object. Jean-Jacques is therefore the object of universal but *unacknowledged* execration. In particular, he himself must never be accused, since this would openly reveal the contradiction in the general will and admit the existence – and thereby the legitimacy – of his individuality.

Rousseau's writings offer ample evidence of paranoia; nothing in our argument challenges this. Our claim is rather that the form taken by his paranoia bears an illuminating relevance to his political and social theories. One might indeed say that Rousseau's paranoia is the revenge exacted from him by his theories. Suppose that Rousseau's Legislator does his work, creating a society in which each citizen is and can be nothing without the others. But let there be one flaw in the work – Rousseau himself. Here he is, a man who, far from being molded by the socializing activity of the Legislator, is merely but fully what nature has made – "a perfect and solitary whole." He resists every attempt to deprive him of his self-sufficiency, to make him dependent on powers that can be exercised only collectively. If, as we may suspect, there is a truth about man which the Legislator has suppressed but which Rousseau's person reveals, then how shall his fellows, who know that they must not know that truth, regard him – save as the scandal of the human race? And if Rousseau is both Legislator and the man whom nature has made, then how shall he regard himself? His motto, *vitam impendere vero*,[44] sets neither him nor us an easy task.

4.   It is time to return to the question Rousseau poses in the *Première promenade*. "But I, cut off from them and from all else, what am I myself?" Rousseau may seem to begin his answer to this question even before asking it, for in the second sentence of this first walk he characterizes himself as "the most sociable and loving of men."[45] But we should be wary of an answer that precedes its question. Rousseau concludes the *Sixième promenade* with a more considered view: "I have never been truly fit for civil society, where all is constraint, obligation, duty, and . . . my independent temperament has always made me unable to bear the submission

---

[43] As we saw above, "he is also everything for them."

[44] "to consecrate one's life to truth"

[45] "Le plus sociable et le plus aimant des humains" (*Première promenade, OC* 1, p. 995)

required from whoever would live among men."[46] "He is as nature has made him,"[47] Rousseau says of Jean-Jacques – and man, as he is made by nature, is a solitary, not a sociable being.

Now one might suppose that Rousseau's insistence that he is not fit for civil society is a reaction to its corruption. Indeed, one might question our identification of the plot against Rousseau with the workings of the general will, claiming that Rousseau sees himself as the victim, not of society as such, but of the degenerate society that he depicts in the *Discours sur l'inégalité*, and seeks the remedy in the work of the Legislator and the rule of the general will which he presents in *Du Contrat social*. That this would be a misreading and misunderstanding of Rousseau is one of my principal themes; by the end of our discussion, I hope to have made it convincing. Here we should note that, in concluding that he is unfit for society, Rousseau does not appeal to its corruption, to the sway of an unbridled *amour-propre* that enslaves each to the opinions of his fellows. Rather, he appeals to obligation and duty, both essential to uncorrupted society. In *Du Contrat social* Rousseau characterizes the transformation of man from the state of nature to the civil state in moral terms: "substituting justice for instinct in his conduct . . . the voice of duty replacing impulse, and right replacing appetite."[48] This is the transformation that results when the general will replaces, or takes precedence over, the private will. And this is the transformation to which Rousseau is unable to submit.

Before considering the structure of the *Rêveries*, let us examine the argument by which Rousseau reaches his conclusion that he is unfit for society. The *Sixième Promenade* begins with Rousseau's reflections on his reason for detouring to avoid the Porte d'Enfer, on his way to botanizing near Gentilly. Near the Porte d'Enfer, a woman sets up a vending stall; her son, a cripple, begs pleasantly from passers-by. When he began walking that way, Rousseau was pleased to make the boy's acquaintance and gave him money willingly. But as time passed, "this pleasure, turning gradually into a habit, found itself . . . transformed into a type of duty which I soon felt to be a constraint."[49] And so, Rousseau now realizes, he has changed his route so that he will not encounter the lad. This leads him to a more general reflection. He realizes that he rebels against any feeling of constraint; should it harmonize with his desire, then the desire itself turns to repugnance. Although there is pleasure in freely conferring a benefit, once the recipient comes to expect it as his due the pleasure ceases; it becomes an annoyance. Rousseau's language here relates his reflection to the idea of law: "But when he who has received it [my help]. . . subjects me to a *law* that I be forever his benefactor, for having at first taken pleasure in being it, then the constraint begins."[50]

---

[46] "je n'ai jamais été vraiment propre à la societé civile où tout est gêne, obligation, devoir, et . . . mon naturel indépendant me rendit toujours incapable des assujetissemens necessaires à qui vent vivre avec les hommes." (*Sixième promenade, OC* 1, p. 1059)

[47] "Il est ce que l'a fait la nature" (*Deuxième dialogue, OC* 1, p. 799)

[48] "substituant dans sa conduite la justice à l'instinct . . . la voix du devoir succédant à l'impulsion et le droit à l'appétit" (*Contrat*, bk, 1, ch. 8, *OC* 3, p. 364)

[49] "Ce plaisir devenu par degrés habitude se trouva . . . transformé dans une espéce de devoir dont je sentis bientot la gêne" (*Sixième promenade, OC* 1, p. 1050)

[50] "Mais quand celui qui l'a receu . . . me fait *une loi* d'être à jamais son bienfaiteur pour avoir d'abord pris plaisir à l'être, dès lors la gêne commence" (*ibid.*, p. 1053; italics mine)

He continues, in a passage which sheds a surprising and profound light on his political theory, to introduce the idea of *contract*. "I know that there is a type of contract, even the most sacred of all, between the benefactor and the recipient. They form a sort of society with each other, more limited than that uniting men in general, and if the recipient tacitly commits himself to show gratitude, the benefactor equally commits himself to show the other ... the same good will that he has just exhibited, and to renew his benefits, insofar as he can, whenever they are asked of him."[51] One may refuse an initial favor without being open to reproach. But having once given, if one will not continue then "in such a refusal we have the sense of something unjust ... but it results no less from an independence dear to the heart, which it does not give up effortlessly."[52]

With this discussion, Rousseau undermines his own doctrine of the social contract. The idea that social legitimacy depends on contract appears first in the *Discours sur l'inégalité*, where Rousseau considers "the establishment of the body politic as a true contract between the people and their chosen leaders."[53] But this form of contract proves to be the device by which the rich secure their position against the naive poor, the beginning of the last act of our fall into a despotism in which each owes not merely his physical well-being, but his very sense of his own existence to the whim of a tyrant. This contract founds the society from which Rousseau seeks, through the Tutor or the Legislator, to free us.

In *Du Contrat social* Rousseau bases society not on a contract between people and rulers, but on an agreement to which each person is party in a double capacity – as an individual, alienating himself and his powers to the collective body of the state, and as a member of that body, receiving as part of the sovereign whole the lives and powers of the subjects. Rousseau supposes that in this way, "each, giving himself to all, gives himself to no one,"[54] and, sharing the general will of the sovereign body, "nevertheless obeys only himself, and remains as free as before."[55] But what one obeys is no longer appetite but duty, which Rousseau always experiences as subjection and constraint. And so he denies in his feelings what his theory requires him to affirm. The idea of a social contract turns into a chimera; for Rousseau,there can be no way of uniting with others that leaves him as free as in his independent, solitary, natural condition.

What conclusion should we draw from this? Perhaps only that Rousseau is himself unfit for the society that will remedy our ills. He sees himself, after all, as what nature has made him. He has not fallen entirely under the sway of *amour-*

---

[51] "Je sais qu'il y a une espéce de contrat et même le plus saint de tous entre le bienfaiteur et l'obligé. C'est une sorte de societé qu'ils forment l'un avec l'autre, plus étroite que celle qui unit les hommes en général, et si l'obligé s'engage tacitement à la reconnoissance, le bienfaiteur s'engage de même à conserver à l'autre ... la même bonne volonté qu'il vient de lui témoigner, et à lui renouveller les actes toutes les fois qu'il le pourra et qu'il en sera requis." (*ibid.*, p. 1054)

[52] "On sent dans ce refus je ne sais quoi d'injuste ...; mais il n'est pas moins l'effet d'une indépendance que le coeur aime, et à laquelle il ne renonce pas sans effort." (*ibid.*)

[53] "l'établissement du Corps Politique comme un vrai Contract entre et le Peuple et les Chefs qu'il se choisit" (*Discours, seconde partie, OC* 3, p. 184)

[54] "chacun se donnant à tous ne se donne à personne" (*Contrat*, bk. 1, ch. 6, *OC* 3, p. 361)

[55] "n'obéisse pourtant qu'à lui-même et reste aussi libre qu'auparavant" (*ibid.*, p. 360)

propre, and so does not need the transformative magic of the Legislator to redeem him. Perhaps we should think of him as akin to the Hottentot whose story he quotes from Kolben in a note to the *Discours*. Raised by Governor Van der Stel of the Cape as a Christian, educated in the European manner, and even employed in India by the Dutch, he nevertheless chose to return to his people's ways. Speaking generally of *les sauvages*, Rousseau insists, "nothing can overcome their invincible repugnance against adopting our customs and living as we do."[56] Perhaps Rousseau simply finds European society equally repugnant.

Were this to be our conclusion, then whatever illumination our inquiry might shed on the relation between Rousseau's life and thought would be of little relevance to our own understanding of society. But to treat Rousseau as the last savage is mistaken. His solitariness is not pre-social but post-social, the solitariness of the man who rejects society not because he has yet to acquire the needs to which it ministers, but because he has come to understand the needs which it endeavors to suppress. But I am running ahead of myself; we have yet to view the portrait of the solitary walker.

5.   How does Rousseau propose to execute this portrait? At the beginning of the *Deuxiéme promenade*, he states that his intent is to keep "a faithful record of my solitary walks and the reveries that fill them."[57] This register, written, Rousseau writes, for himself alone,[58] will give him companionship in his last days. Reading the reveries "will recall for me the sweet joy that I savor in writing them, and thus making the past live again for me, will as it were double my existence."[59] But if the register is to be relived, it is also in itself a reliving. "These ravishments, these ecstasies that I sometimes experience as I walk . . . how can I keep a faithful record of them? Wanting to recall so many sweet reveries, instead of describing them I fell once more into them."[60] In his promenades, Rousseau keeps a past ever present.

The *Rêveries* are the writings of a man no longer in dialogue with the world. Rousseau recognizes that first fear and then hope have left him, so that "complete calm has been restored [*rétabli*] in my heart."[61] *Rétabli*, Rousseau says, not *établi*; there must then have been some previous time when he enjoyed a tranquil heart. Now he is literally beyond good and evil; indeed, he says, "no longer can anyone do me either good or evil."[62] He is beyond all moral relationships; he has realized that

[56] "Rien ne peut surmonter l'invincible répugnance qu'ils ont à prendre nos moeurs et vivre à notre maniére." (*Discours, seconde partie*, note XVI, *OC* 3, p. 220)

[57] "un regître fidelle de mes promenades solitaires et des rêveries qui les remplissent" (*Deuxième promenade, OC* 1, p. 1002)

[58] So does he write for himself alone that he writes for himself alone?

[59] "me rappellera la douceur que je goute à les écrire, et faisant renaitre ainsi pour moi le tems passé doublera pour ainsi dire mon existence." (*Première promenade, OC* 1, p. 1001)

[60] "Ces ravissemens, ces extases que j'éprouvois quelquefois en me promenant . . . comment en tenir un règistre fidelle? En voulant me rappeller tant de douces rêveries, au lieu de les décrire j'y retombois." (*Deuxième promenade, OC* 1, p. 1003)

[61] "un plein calme est rétabli dans mon coeur." (*Première promenade, OC* 1, p. 997)

[62] "On ne peut plus m'y faire ni bien ni mal." (*ibid.*, p. 999)

"in relation to me, my fellows were nothing but automata who acted only by physical force."[63] He can ascribe no intention or passion to them that would make their behavior explicable.

Society gives the individual his moral existence, but for Rousseau society no longer exists. No more torn between the man nature made and the man society would form, he finds himself at rest. The moral life of man brought him only stress and conflict; Rousseau found its demands not only irksome but ultimately unintelligible. His inability to understand the behavior of his fellows in intentional terms, his dismissal of them as machines moved by external forces, is not merely a manifestation of his paranoia, but is linked to his awareness of his own unfitness for life in society. His contemporaries are moral persons, who understand themselves and their interactions in a moral vocabulary. But that vocabulary does not enable Rousseau to understand himself; thinking himself to be the natural man, he finds it alien. Of course Rousseau is not, and cannot be, the true natural man – *l'homme sauvage* who has never known society. Natural man is *before* good and evil, not, as Rousseau, *beyond* it. The self-understanding attained in the *Rêveries* must be of a man who is beyond society and the transformation it effects in men. Rousseau knows that it is impossible for mankind to undo its history and return to its original pre-social condition; is it possible that he may sometimes forget – and indeed wish to forget – that it is equally impossible for any individual man, once socialized, to return?

6. Having announced to himself (since he writes only for himself) his intent and method in the *Première promenade,* Rousseau proceeds to enlarge briefly on these matters in the *Deuxième,* and then turns, seemingly abruptly, to the retelling of an autumn walk in the countryside near Paris which led to an unfortunate accident. Walking down from Ménilmontant, Rousseau was bowled over by a Great Dane running at full speed ahead of a carriage. The fall caused him to lose consciousness. On coming to, he was aware only of the sky, of stars that were beginning to appear in the advancing night, of some foliage; it was "a moment of delight. . . . In that instant I was born into life, and it seemed to me that everything I perceived was filled with my insubstantial existence. Totally immersed in the present moment, I remembered nothing; I had no clear sense of my self, not the least idea of what had just happened to me; I did not know who I was or where I was; I felt no ill, no fear, no unrest. . . . Throughout all my being I felt an ecstatic calm."[64] Our post-social man is born.

[63] "mes contemporains n'étoient par rapport à moi que des êtres méchaniques qui n'agissoient que par impulsion" (*Huitième promenade, OC* 1, p. 1078)

[64] "un moment délicieux. . . . Je naissois dans cet instant à la vie, et il me sembloit que je remplissois de ma legere existence tous les objets que j'appercevois. Tout entier au moment présent je ne me souvenois de rien; je n'avois nulle notion distincte de mon individu, pas la moindre idée de ce qui venoit de m'arriver; je ne savois ni qui j'étois ni où j'étois; je ne sentois ni mal, ni crainte, ni inquietude. . . . Je sentois dans tout mon être un calme ravissant" (*Deuxième promenade, OC* 1, p. 1005). Candace Vogler suggests, surely correctly, that the immediacy of this experience is linked to its extra-linguistic character. It ends when Rousseau is asked where he lives; although he cannot say, he is restored to language and, through his ensuing questions, to his place in the world. Far more needs to be said about the relation of language to the post-social self than I attempt in the last paragraphs of this essay.

The next two walks are exercises in self-examination, woven around Solon's saying, "Always learning, I grow old."[65] In the *Troisième promenade*, Rousseau refuses to apply the saying to his opinions and principles, not seeking to advance his understanding but rather trusting in the reasoning by which he acquired them when his mind was at the height of its powers. He is content to reaffirm his acceptance of the *Profession de foi du Vicaire savoyard*. But he acknowledges that he has much to learn "concerning the virtues necessary to my condition"[66] and devotes the *Quatrième promenade* to his motto, *vitam impendere vero*. Despite Rousseau's earlier insistence that other persons no longer exist for him, the discussion focuses on interpersonal relationships and – until the final three paragraphs – equates truth with justice. What one owes to one's fellows is never to lie "for the damage or profit of another or oneself."[67] Although not without interest, Rousseau's account seems to be evasive. He does not ask what must surely be the obvious question: what does consecrating one's life to truth require of one? What life is open to a person so consecrated?

Finally, he draws an important distinction: "If one must be just to others, one must be true to oneself."[68] While insisting on his truthfulness in the face of considerations of interest and advantage, Rousseau recognizes his own failure, in his talk and even more in his writings, to present himself and his ideas with the truth that he owes to himself. He denies being deceitful while acknowledging being weak. But even this admission fails to address the deeper issue posed by the *Rêveries*. Could Rousseau, the man whom supposedly nature has made, present himself truthfully in and to a society that transforms man from his natural state? For Rousseau himself, truth must be equated not so much with a justice owed to others as with the solitude he must give himself.

And in the *Cinquième promenade* we come to the very heart of that solitude. Rousseau's account of his brief sojourn on the *Ile de Saint-Pierre* in the Lake of Bienne is deservedly esteemed; it conveys the beauty of his surroundings, the ecstasy of his experiences, the depth of his reveries. One paragraph will have to suffice:

> But if there is a state where the soul may find a seat firm enough to take its entire repose and gather there all its being, with no need to recall the past or to trespass on the future, where time does not matter to it, where the present lasts forever yet without any sense of its enduring or sign of time's passing, with no other sentiment, whether of privation or satisfaction, of pleasure or pain, of desire or fear, save that alone of our existence, and if this sentiment alone entirely fills the soul; then as long as this state continues, whoever finds himself in it may call himself happy, not with an imperfect, poor and relative happiness as one finds in the

[65] Rousseau quotes the saying as "Je deviens vieux en apprenant toujours." (*Troisième promenade, OC* 1, p. 1011) Perhaps one might express the thought as, "I age as I learn."
[66] "du coté des vertus necessaires à mon état." (*ibid.*, p. 1023)
[67] "pour le dommage ou le profit d'autrui ni de lui-même." (*Quatrième promenade, OC* 1, p. 1032)
[68] "S'il faut être juste pour autrui, il faut être vrai pour soi" (*ibid.*, p. 1038)

pleasures of this life, but with a happiness sufficient, perfect, and full, which leaves no emptiness in the soul that it feels the need to fill. Such is the state in which often I found myself during my solitary reveries on the *Ile de Saint-Pierre*, whether lying in my boat which I let the water carry where it will, or seated on the shores of the troubled lake, or elsewhere, on the banks of a lovely river or a brook murmuring over its gravel bed.[69]

"With no other sentiment ... save that alone of our existence." The sentiment of existence has figured prominently in our discussion; it now emerges as the central idea in Rousseau's anthropology. It is man's first sentiment, as Rousseau insists in the *Discours sur l'inégalité*; in the solitary condition of nature, each finds it within himself. We may suppose, indeed, that it is the sole innate sentiment, that all others have their origin in the experience that forces each man to recognize a world that is independent of him and sets the conditions for his conservation – which, as we noted earlier, Rousseau identifies as man's first care. But, in society, the sentiment of existence is transformed; we have referred to the conclusion of the *Discours* where Rousseau tells us that it is only from the judgment of others that "sociable man ... takes the sentiment of his own existence."[70] The role of the Legislator, in changing human nature so that each man becomes totally dependent on his fellows, is to perfect the alienation from each individual of his sentiment of existence, so that each experiences his own being only and entirely in relation to the society of which he is inseparably part. No more thoroughgoing expression of collectivism – indeed, of totalitarianism – can be conceived.

But Rousseau the man resists, so to speak, his own collectivization. The price of his resistance is, as we have seen, paranoia, but his paranoia makes possible the complete alienation from society that enables him fully to recover the single, pure sentiment of his own existence. It would not be wrong to read the *Rêveries* as exhibiting Rousseau's intent to celebrate this recovery – although, as we shall show, the attempt ultimately fails, so that such a reading would be incomplete. But the wonderful passages of the *Cinquième promenade* enable us to share the deepest expression of the sense of self that Rousseau is able to attain.

This sense of self is not suited to men in society. Rousseau insists that it would not be good for most persons if, "eager for these sweet ecstasies, they lost their taste for the active life which their ever-recurring needs prescribe as their duty."[71] One

---

[69] "Mais s'il est un état où l'ame trouve une assiete assez solide pour s'y reposer tout entiére et rassembler là tout son être, sans avoir besoin de rappeller le passé ni d'enjamber sur l'avenir; où le tems ne soit rien pour elle, où le présent dure toujours sans neanmoins marquer sa durée et sans aucune trace de succession, sans aucun autre sentiment de privation ni de jouissance, de plaisir ni de peine, de desir ni de crainte que celui seul de notre existence, et que ce sentiment seul puisse la remplir tout entiere; tant que cet état dure celui qui s'y trouve peut s'appeller heureux, non d'un bonheur imparfait, pauvre et rélatif tel que celui qu'on trouve dans les plaisirs de la vie mais d'un bonheur suffisant, parfait et plein, qui ne laisse dans l'ame aucun vuide qu'elle sente le besoin de remplir. Tel est l'état où je me suis trouvé souvent à l'Isle de St Pierre dans mes reveries solitaires, soit couché dans mon bateau que je laissois dériver au gré de l'eau, soit assis sur les rives du lac agité, soit ailleurs au bord d'une belle riviére ou d'un ruisseau murmurant sur le gravier." (*Cinquième promenade, OC* 1, pp. 1046–47)

[70] "l'homme sociable ... tire le sentiment de sa propre existence." (*Discours, seconde partie, OC* 3, p. 193)

[71] "avides de ces douces extases ils s'y dégoutassent de la vie active dont leurs besoins toujours renaissans leurs prescrivent le devoir." (*Cinquième promenade, OC* 1, p. 1047)

can be either a man or a citizen, but not both, and the citizen must not take his sense of self from within, or his pleasures from reverie. The sweetness of the sentiment of existence subverts our collectivization, and so from the totalitarian standpoint of society does not and can not exist. Rousseau must not – and does not – remain on the *Ile de Saint-Pierre*.

But Rousseau has escaped his enemies. Although they take care not to allow him to return to "such a sweet refuge,"[72] yet they do not prevent him from transporting himself there daily "on the wings of imagination,"[73] and enjoying the same pleasure as if he lived there yet. Even better – the deeper his reverie, the more vividly it paints the objects that, although the source of his pleasure, often escaped conscious notice, so, "often I am more in their midst, and even more agreeably than when I was truly among them."[74] But it will prove essential to our argument to emphasize that, important as these objects are in inducing his reverie, Rousseau's happiness comes entirely from "the sentiment of existence bare of all other affection"[75]; in experiencing this, "one is self-sufficient as God."[76] It is a sentiment without complexity, felt most fully when the soul, free of all cares, lets itself respond to such continuous, rhythmic sounds as the lapping of water. Only "fleeting and sweet ideas,"[77] enter into this effortless awareness of self and the happiness it brings.

7.   However, we must not suppose that the passivity of reverie entirely filled Rousseau's life during his sojourn on the *Ile de Saint-Pierre*. His principal work, if we may so call it, which he set himself, was to make a *Flora petrinsularis*, in which all of the island's plants would be catalogued and described. As Rousseau grew older, he came to take greater and greater pleasure in botanizing. In his few weeks on the island he was unable to do more than begin this botanical study, but he recalls that each morning he would proceed to a different part of the island to observe the various plants and to collect specimens for further study. His preoccupation with botany is the theme of the *Septième promenade*. Although it might seem to follow naturally and directly from his account of his life on the *Ile de Saint-Pierre*, another theme, equally connected with that account, is given prior attention. We have already discussed the *Sixième promenade*, in which Rousseau examines his unfitness for society; we are now in a position to realize that this conclusion is a corollary of his recognition that his truest and most complete happiness arises in the solitude of reverie.

The *Septième promenade* announces a change of emphasis in Rousseau's interests. Botany has become his principal occupation – indeed, his obsession – so that he has no time even to dream. And yet botanizing is, for Rousseau, if not quite a way of

---

[72] "un si doux azyle" (*ibid.*, p. 1049)

[73] "sur les ailes de l'imagination" (*ibid.*)

[74] "Je suis souvent plus au milieu d'eux et plus agréablement encore que quand j'y étois reellement." (*ibid.*)

[75] "Le sentiment de l'existence depouillé de toute autre affection" (*ibid.*, p. 1047)

[76] "on se suffit à soi-même comme Dieu." (*ibid.*)

[77] "de légéres et douces idées." (*ibid.*, p. 1048) Do these ideas require linguistic formulation? As the discussion of language at the end of this essay should make clear, the linguistic or extra-linguistic character of this experience is essential to determining its place in Rousseau's "post-social" existence.

dreaming, linked closely to it. As his miseries (or shall we say his belief in his miseries?) came more and more to preoccupy him, intruding even into his reveries, "an instinct ... silenced my imagination, and, directing my attention to the objects that surrounded me, brought me for the first time to examine the spectacle of nature in all its detail, which previously I had scarcely regarded save as one and in its entirety."[78] Previously the beauties of nature had provided a backdrop for reverie; now the backdrop becomes foreground. The objects – "the trees, the bushes, the plants"[79] – which he had experienced in his reveries only as fused in the unity of nature come now to be singled out for attention and examination. "Botany is the study for an idle and lazy solitary."[80]

As in the *Deuxième promenade*, a particular remembered walk conveys the core theme. Rousseau was botanizing on the Robeila, a mountain in the neighbourhood of Môtiers, a village in what was then the Principality of Neuchâtel. Making his way through the mountain fastness, he came upon "a retreat so hidden that I have never in my life seen a wilder place."[81] Surrounded by dark trees through which only glimpses of boulders and fearful precipices could be seen, hearing the cries of the wild birds of prey, Rousseau occupied himself with the several plants that he found in the enclosure. But gradually "I forgot about botany and plants ... and I set myself to dream more easily in thinking that I was in a refuge overlooked by all the world where my persecutors would not discover me ... I said to myself complacently, 'No doubt I am the first mortal to reach this place.'"[82] As this thought ran through his mind, Rousseau heard a seemingly familiar clicking noise; pushing aside the brush he saw, twenty paces off, a stocking mill. "My first reaction was a feeling of joy at finding myself again among humans when I had believed myself altogether alone."[83] But this soon gave way to "a more lasting feeling of dismay, at not being able even in the recesses of the Alps to escape from the cruel hands of men, furious to torment me."[84]

Perhaps the best commentary on this passage is found in a passage from the *Dialogues*. Rousseau is commenting on the solitude of Jean-Jacques: "I know also that absolute solitude is a sad state, contrary to nature; sentiments of affection nourish the soul, the communication of ideas activates the spirit. Our sweetest existence is relative and collective, and our true self is not entirely within us."[85]

---

[78] "un instinct . . . imposa silence à mon imagination et fixant mon attention sur les objets qui m'environnoient me fit pour la prémiére fois détailler le spectacle de la nature, que je n'avois guére contemplé jusqu'alors qu'en masse et dans son ensemble." (*Septième promenade*, OC 1, p. 1062)

[79] "Les arbres, les arbrisseaux, les plantes" (*ibid.*)

[80] "La botanique est l'étude d'un oisif et paresseux solitaire" (*ibid.*, p. 1069)

[81] "un réduit si caché que je n'ai vu de ma vie un aspect plus sauvage." (*ibid.*, p. 1070)

[82] "j'oubliai la botanique et les plantes ... et je me mis à rêver plus à mon aise en pensant que j'étois là dans un réfuge ignoré de tout l'univers où les persecuteurs ne me deterreroient pas . . . je me disois avec complaisance: sans doute je suis le prémier mortel qui ait pénétré jusqu'ici" (*ibid.*, p. 1071)

[83] "Mon prémier mouvement fut un sentiment de joye de me retrouver parmi des humains où je m'étois cru totalement seul." (*ibid.*)

[84] "un sentiment douloureux plus durable, comme ne pouvant dans les antres mêmes des alpes échaper aux cruelles mains des hommes, acharnés à me tourmenter." (*ibid.*)

[85] "je sais aussi qu'une solitude absolue est un état triste et contraire à la nature: les sentimens affectueux nourrissent l'ame, la communication des idées avive l'esprit. Notre plus douce existence est relative et collective, et notre vrai *moi* n'est pas tout entier en nous." (*Deuxième dialogue*, OC 1, p. 813)

The *Septième promenade* forces us to rethink the conclusion reached in the *Sixième*; we must relate Rousseau's unguarded, spontaneous, brief sentiment of joy to his claim that he is unfit for society. He will give us a fuller occasion for this rethinking presently.

The *Huitième promenade* draws together the ideas of its three predecessors, without the discordant note introduced by Rousseau's brief joy at finding himself among men. He begins by looking back on the apparent happiness he experienced before his discovery (as he supposes) of the universal plot against him and his realization that "my entire self was in what was alien to me"[86] without "a sentiment that could meet the test of reflection."[87] Contrasting this earlier state with his present one, in which, despite his adversity, he enjoys tranquillity, he is led to a narrative retelling of the stages of reflection that brought him from the fury and delirium which accompanied his discovery to the regaining of internal peace and "almost happiness."[88]

The key step in this process of recovery is the reconversion of *amour-propre* into *amour de soi*. In Rousseau's account in the *Discours sur l'inégalité*, the transformation of man from a solitary to a social being takes place through the conversion of *amour de soi*, the original concern each has with his own conservation, into *amour-propre*, the concern each has with being foremost. The man who has *amour de soi* at the core of his soul is the solitary individual, self-sufficient and sensing his own existence within himself. On the other hand, the man who has *amour-propre at* the core of his soul is the social being, dependent on others and sensing his existence only in their recognition of him. Rousseau's *amour-propre*, curbed first by his terrible discovery, has severed all those links with other persons that fuel its demands for recognition and priority; once again becoming *amour de soi*, it "has returned to the natural order and released me from the yoke of opinion."[89]

In the *Neuvième promenade*, Rousseau is concerned with a state of the soul very different from the complete and perfect happiness that he attained in his reveries on the *Ile de Saint-Pierre*, or the mere appearance of happiness that filled his life before he believed himself to be persecuted and cast out of society. He speaks of "contentment of spirit,"[90] and he has found it for himself not in solitude and reverie, but in observing the contentment of others: "I have often seen contented hearts, and of all that has touched me it is that which has most contented me."[91] The *promenade* relates a number of incidents from Rousseau's life, emphasizing chance relationships especially with children and youths, in which he has had the pleasure of affording visible pleasure to others.

A feeling of content that arises from observing the contentment of others can not be the work of *amour-propre*. It involves no comparison between oneself and others and in no way demands their recognition. We might indeed see it as the positive

---

[86] "j'étois tout entier à ce qui m'étoit étranger" (*Huitième promenade, OC* 1, p. 1074)

[87] "un sentiment qui pût soutenir l'epreuve de la reflexion" (*ibid.*, p. 1075)

[88] "presque la félicité." (*ibid.*, p. 1080)

[89] "est rentré dans l'ordre de la nature et m'a délivré du joug de l'opinion." (*ibid.*, p. 1079)

[90] "contentement d'esprit" (*Neuvième promenade, OC* 1, p. 1085)

[91] "j'ai souvent vu des coeurs contens, et de tous les objets qui m'ont frappé c'est celui qui m'a le plus contenté moi-même." (*ibid.*)

counterpart of *pitié*, the natural repugnance that, Rousseau supposes, we feel towards observed pain and suffering.[92] Both *pitié* and this derived content would seem to be essentially sympathetic responses; suffering and contentment are contagious, so that they are, as it were, caught by the person who observes them in his fellows. It may then seem that we may readily accommodate Rousseau's discussion of an essentially social sentiment of contentment without denying the connections between solitude, reverie, and true happiness which he develops in the *Rêveries*. But the incidents he describes are not all so readily accommodated, for several of them involve not simply his contentment in observing the contentment of others, but his contentment in bringing about their contentment.

One event in particular demands consideration. Sitting with his wife after dinner in the gardens of the *Château de la Muette*, Rousseau observed a group of some twenty little girls under the supervision of a religious sister. A man selling sweet wafers came by. Now the purchase of wafers involves a gamble; a wafer-man has a board, divided into sections each marked with a number and an arrow that one can spin which comes to rest on one of the sections. One buys a spin; one receives the number of wafers indicated by the section on which the arrow stops. The girls of course longed for the wafers; a few, who had a little money, sought the sister's permission to spin. Here was an opportunity for Rousseau to confer a benefit freely, without any fear that it might form the basis of constraining expectations. And so he interceded, telling the wafer-man to let each of the girls spin, and he would pay. Indeed, he did more: "I secretly told the wafer-man to use his usual skill in the opposite manner, so that as many good lots would fall out as possible, and I should make it worth his while."[93] Are we not in the presence of the Tutor, arranging the world of Émile?

8.   The last walk remains. And it is here that we shall be leaving Rousseau, for he does not and cannot return from it. It began so long ago. "Today, Palm Sunday, it has been exactly fifty years since my first meeting with Mme. de Warens"[94] – with the woman whom he always called *"Maman,"* even when he became her lover. We have already witnessed one nativity, on the hill from Ménilmontant, but now we are in the presence of that earlier birth when Rousseau, having fled from his master and his native Geneva, feeling himself not merely free but with the world ready to lie at his feet, was despatched by the priest of Confignon, from whom he had received hospitality, and who was eager to encourage the conversion of a young Protestant, with the words "God calls you."[95] The priest continued: "Go to Annecy, where you will find a good and charitable lady, who has been enabled by the benefactions of the king to bring other souls out of the error from which she herself has come."[96]

---

[92] See *Discours, première partie* (*OC* 3, p. 154).

[93] "je dis en secret à l'oublieur d'user de son adresse ordinaire en sens contraire en faisant tomber autant de bons lots qu'il pourroit et que je lui en tiendrois compte." (*ibid.*, p. 1091)

[94] "Aujourdui jour de paques fleuries il y a precisement cinquante ans de ma prémiére connoissance avec Mad[am]e de Warens." (*Dixième promenade, OC* 1, p. 1098)

[95] "Dieu vous appelle" (*Confessions*, bk. 2, *OC* 1, p. 47)

[96] "Allez à Annecy; vous y trouverez une bonne Dame bien charitable, que les bienfaits du Roi mettent en état de retirer d'autres ames de l'erreur dont elle est sortie elle-même." (*ibid.*) The king here referred to is Victor-Amadeus II of Sardinia, Duke of Savoy, in which Confignon and Annecy are located.

So Rousseau went. And "this first moment determined all my life for me, and brought about through an inevitable chain of events the course of the rest of my days."[97] He was sent away, but everything called him back, and he returned. "This return determined my fate, and even long before I possessed her I lived only in her and for her. There isn't a day when I don't remember with joy and tenderness this unique and short period of my life when I was fully myself, unadulterated and unopposed, and when I can truly claim to have lived. . . . during these few years, loved by a woman full of amity and sweetness, I did as I would do, I was as I would be, . . . helped by her lessons and her example, I gave my simple and fresh soul the character which best fitted it and which it has always maintained. . . . I could not suffer subjection, I was perfectly free, and better than free, because subjected only by my personal affections, I did only what I would do."[98]

Rousseau speaks of his fear that his life with *Maman* might not endure; "this fear arising from the constraint of our situation was not unfounded."[99] In the *Confessions*, he is more forthcoming. He went away – to seek a cure for his supposed illness. Again, he came back, having taken the forethought to write announcing his return to the very hour. "I had always seen my arrival marked by a sort of little party; I expected no less this time, and these attentions to which I was so receptive were well worth the trouble of being arranged."[100] But this time – nothing. "I went upstairs, I saw her at last, this dear *Maman* loved so tenderly, so ardently, so purely; . . . A young man was with her. In short, I found my place filled."[101]

And so there has not been a day when he does not remember *Maman* and the time he passed in her company. Did he remember her during his sojourn on the *Ile de Saint-Pierre*, on those afternoons when he lay in his boat filled with the pure awareness of his own existence, letting the water carry him where it would? Did he remember, in the sufficient, perfect, and full happiness of those afternoons, that earlier time when he was fully himself and lived only in her and for her? Rousseau can not ask himself these questions. The *Dixième promenade* remains unfinished. Rousseau cannot return from his last walk with *Maman*, but he can not admit that he must return without her.

9.   "But I, cut off from them and from all else, what am I myself?" Has Rousseau

---

[97] "ce premier moment decida de moi pour toute ma vie, et produisit par un enchainement inevitable le destin du reste de mes jours." (*Dixième promenade, OC* 1, p. 1098)

[98] "Ce retour fixa ma déstinée et longtems encore avant de la posseder je ne vivois plus qu'en elle et pour elle. . . . Il n'y a pas de jour où je ne me rappelle avec joye et attendrissement cet unique et court tems de ma vie où je fus moi pleinement sans mélange et sans obstacle et où je puis véritablement dire avoir vécu. . . . durant ce petit nombre d'années, aimé d'une femme pleine de complaisance et de douceur je fis ce que je voulois faire, je fus ce que je voulois être, . . . aidé de ses leçons et de son exemple, je sus donner à mon ame encore simple et neuve la forme qui lui convenoit davantage et qu'elle a gardée toujours. . . . je ne pouvois souffrir l'assujetissement, j'étois parfaitement libre, et mieux que libre, car assujeti par mes seuls attachemens, je ne faisois que ce qui je voulois faire." (*ibid.*, pp. 1098–99)

[99] "cette crainte née de la géne de notre situation n'étoit pas sans fondement." (*ibid.*, p. 1099)

[100] "J'avois vu toujours marquer mon arrivée par une espéce de petite fête: je n'en attendois pas moins cette fois, et ces empressemens qui m'étoient si sensibles valoient bien la peine d'être menagés." (*Confessions*, bk. 6, *OC* 1, p. 261)

[101] "Je monte, je la vois enfin, cette chere Maman si tendrement, si vivement, si purement aimée; . . . Un jeune homme étoit avec elle. . . . Bref je trouvai ma place prise." (*ibid.*)

then failed to answer his question? Or is the answer in the final silence? And in that final silence, may we find a part of the answer to our own quest, into the emergence of the post-social self?

Rousseau faces, both in his thought and in his person, the breakdown of the idea and the reality of natural society. In outlining this breakdown, we shall assume Rousseau's standpoint – and so his anthropological and sociological views – except where this standpoint itself becomes the explicit object of discussion. Man as nature made him is a solitary animal. But human beings have not remained in solitude; they have created society and, in turn, that society has recreated them, so that they have the appearance of social animals. However, this appearance is an illusion, and Rousseau's uniqueness lies in his awareness of the illusion. In the *Discours sur l'inégalité*, he records the passage of mankind from solitude to society. In his autobiographical writings, especially in the *Rêveries*, he records his own unique passage from society back to solitude.

Rousseau's self-portrait is the only one "painted exactly from nature" because Rousseau is the only man who is, and is aware that he is, "as nature has made him." His fellows are all more or less the work of society; they are thus living under an illusion. Indeed, the deepest form this illusion takes, as we have seen, is in the very sense of one's own existence. The primary innate sentiment of existence that characterizes natural man is lost in society, so that *l'homme policé* has only an alienated sense of himself as existing only in the opinion of others – a sense that is, so to speak, his *constitutive illusion*. Thus Rousseau's fellows can not be portrayed "exactly from nature" because they do not *exist* "exactly from [*d'après*] nature."

Rousseau understands his fellows as existing, so to speak, between nature and society. Their *amour-propre* is a corruption of their natural *amour de soi* that has not been perfected or transformed into *amour de la patrie*, the sentiment appropriate to their social existence.[102] They are the products of an imperfect socialization that denies them the self-sufficiency of *l'homme sauvage* while failing to give them the fully collective existence that, as we have seen, Rousseau takes to result from the work of the true Legislator. Instead, they are reduced to a competitive rather than a cooperative dependency on one another; they are, we might say, neither men nor citizens, but enemies. They experience their social existence as both necessary and unnatural, even though its unnaturalness is not the object of their reflective awareness. Rousseau does not suppose that men in all societies exist in this competitive dependency, but rather considers it to be characteristic of the principal European societies of his time, in contrast with the truer collectivity exemplified, as he supposes, in the ancient world, in his native city of Geneva, in Corsica, and in Poland. The malaise that he attributes to the modern world may thus be seen as the first stage in the disappearance of a supposedly natural society – the first and yet unconscious manifestation of a development akin to that which, brought to consciousness in Rousseau himself, has led him from society back to solitude.

But no development is leading mankind back to solitude! To think that men can be solitary beings – indeed, that men ever were solitary beings – is to share

---

[102] See the account of *amour de la patrie* in Rousseau's discussion of the rule of virtue in the *Discours sur l'économie politique* (1755). (*OC* 3, pp. 252–62)

Rousseau's madness. But is this true of *psychological* solitude? May Rousseau not be the harbinger of a solitude of *spirit* that is indeed part of what many other thinkers would consider a malaise of our modern world? Suppose that we agree with Rousseau, as indeed I believe that we should, that the individual is right to see the institutions and practices that make up any human society as chains whose legitimacy he may appropriately question. Now there is an answer, which we may identify with liberal individualism: the institutions and practices of society legitimately bind individuals insofar as they make possible the greater and fuller realization of those individuals' reflectively-held concerns.[103] Rousseau understands this answer; it is not absent from the argument of *Du Contrat social*. But it is patently, if implicitly, clear that he does not find this answer adequate, for two very different – and even seemingly opposed – reasons.[104]

The first arises from Rousseau's recognition of his own unfitness for society because of his inability to accept any form of internal constraint in the form of obligation or duty. This unwillingness, Rousseau insists, comes simply from the existence of the constraint, and not from the way in which it affects his interests – as we noted previously, he claims that should he come to feel an obligation to do what he otherwise desires, that desire turns into aversion. The other comes from Rousseau's recognition of the transformation society effects in human beings. To the liberal individualist, society is an instrument that men can use, provided they are able to agree on feasible terms, in order to further their several or joint aims. Rousseau may allow this, while insisting that society affects those who would use it as their instrument in ways that not merely exceed their intentions but effect a transformation in the character of their intentions so that they become quite different persons.

Whereas the first reason emphasizes the distance between the individual and a society which he finds an ever-irksome constraint, the second emphasizes the dependence of the individual on a society that determines his nature and affords him his sentiment of existence. Rousseau seems to me the first to understand, if not altogether clearly, that these seemingly opposed ways of viewing the relation between the individual and society are in fact intimately linked, and that the societies of his time are transforming human beings into individuals who are unwilling to accept social constraints. He criticizes the philosophers who spoke "unceasingly of need, avidity, oppression, desires, and pride,"[105] and so ascribed to man those characteristics that make him unfit for society, not because what they said was untrue of the men about them, but because "they spoke of savage man but described civilized man."[106] They failed to realize that those things that make men unable or unwilling to bear the constraints needed to live peaceably and sociably together are effects of social life.

---

[103] The answer admits of several variants, depending on the emphasis placed on social welfare, individual utility, or natural right. But the variants are not my topic.

[104] *Is* the answer of liberal individualism adequate? No doubt this question is of interest to the author of *Morals by Agreement*, but the present essay can only raise it.

[105] "sans cesse de besoin, d'avidité, d'oppression, de desirs, et d'orgueuil" (*Discours, OC* 3, p. 132)

[106] "Ils parloient de l'Homme Sauvage et ils peignoient l'homme Civil." (*ibid.*)

Realizing this, Rousseau is led to his deep bifurcation between the making of men and the making of citizens – the making of self-sufficient beings who can live uncorrupted in society because they do not need it and the making of totally dependent beings who could neither exist nor imagine their existence without society. The making of citizens thus proves to be, in the strictest sense, totalitarian; what might have been unexpected is that the making of men turns out to require an equally total domination of the individual will by the maker.

In his autobiographical writings, Rousseau relates his escape from domination into solitude. But the post-social man who emerges in the *Rêveries* is unable finally to rest content with the sentiment of his own existence and the self-contained, self-sufficient life that it represents. Rousseau cannot confine his memories to the *Ile de Saint-Pierre*; eventually, inevitably, he returns in thought to *Les Charmettes*, and the woman in and for whom he lived. "Our sweetest existence is relative and collective, and our true self is not entirely within us." Here the primary, innate sentiment of existence itself proves to be illusion.

10. In the *Discours sur l'inégalité* Rousseau raises, without resolving, "the difficulties concerning the origin of languages."[107] Elsewhere, in his *Essai sur l'origine des Langues*, he begins with the claim, "Speech distinguishes man among animals,"[108] but he does not take speech to be innate; it is invented, and its invention is due to our passions. In the *Discours*, he recognizes that society and language are intimately linked; he raises, but makes no attempt to answer, the question, "which was more essential – to have society in place to create languages, or to have languages invented to establish society?"[109] But we may suppose that Rousseau would have agreed that the two emerge together in the course of human development, so that man becomes a speaker in becoming social and becomes social in becoming a speaker.

The role of language is not one of Rousseau's autobiographical themes. It should have been. The journey from solitude to society requires the acquisition of language; the journey from society back to solitude does not require – indeed, does not even permit – the loss of language.[110] Post-social man remains a language-user. Now we cannot embark here on an inquiry into all of the ways in which language affects how we feel and act. Our passions may, as Rousseau claims, motivate the invention of speech; once invented, speech enters into the determination not only of which passions we experience, but even more how we experience them. Language distances; it also relates.

Man's original, innate sentiment may have been that of his existence. Rousseau treats the experience of existence as direct and pure. But neither directness nor purity marks experience when it comes to be mediated by language. And so we may ask, when the experience of existence comes to be linguistically mediated, how is it

---

[107] "les embarras de l'origine des Langues." (*ibid., première partie*, p. 146)

[108] "La parole distingue l'homme entre les animaux" (*Essai*, ch. 1, p. 501)

[109] "lequel a été le plus nécessaire, de la Société déjà liée, à l'institution des Langues, ou des Langues déjà inventées, à l'établissement de la Société?" (*Discours, première partie, OC* 3, p. 151)

[110] There are, or seem to be, extra-linguistic moments, but these are quite exceptional. See notes 64 and 77 above.

affected?[111] We might not expect that Rousseau would think to answer our question. But in the *Essai he* does, and the answer returns us to *Les Charmettes*.

The passions that give rise to speech are not the same for all men, but vary with their environment. Northern and southern languages have different bases. In the rigors of the north, "passions are born of needs, and languages, sad daughters of necessity, reflect their harsh origin."[112] Finding that "the ever-present danger of perishing did not allow them to be limited to the language of gesture ... the first word ... among them ... was ... *aidez-moi* [help me]."[113] But in the softer climes of the south, where the human race originated, different passions gave rise to language. The wells were the first places where strangers met. "There families formed their first links; there the two sexes had their first meetings; ... There, eyes accustomed to the same sights since infancy began to see sweeter ones. The heart was stirred by these new objects; ... There the first festivals occurred; feet danced with joy; the eloquence of gesture was not enough, the voice joined it in passionate tones."[114] The first words were "aimez-moi [love me]."

Language takes the innate sentiment of existence and unites it irrevocably with two ideas: help and love. It effects the deepest transformation of human nature, taking each individual "who in himself is a perfect and solitary whole" and depriving him of his self-sufficiency and completeness. The original sentiment of existence is associated with liberty; both assistance and affection constrain it. But unlike the transformation which Rousseau assigns as the task of the Legislator, language does not also deprive each individual of his separate and distinct existence or merge him into a larger social whole, but rather requires that he seek his completeness in another. Each person no longer lives in himself, but, we might say, only in his demands for assistance and for affection.

11.   We have taken as our guide to the post-social self the first man who seeks consciously to live in that condition. Understanding Rousseau in terms of his motto, *vitam impendere vero*, we have come to know his truth in a way that he does not. As a youth, he left the womb of his native Geneva, and was born to his beloved *Maman*, to whom his spirit addressed the magical words "*Aimez-moi*." Once said, the words can not be unsaid; Rousseau can no longer be "a perfect and solitary whole." He refuses to recognize, as the post-social self must, that he is not a natural man, but one formed by the artifice of society and especially of speech. But despite

[111] We may also ask how to connect the *linguistic* mediation of the experience of existence, which for Rousseau is found in the *origin* of languages, with the *social* mediation, which for Rousseau is occurring in the societies *of his time*, and is "transforming human beings into individuals who are unwilling to accept social constraints." I am thankfully spared by the limits of the present essay from addressing this question.

[112] "les passions naissent les besoins, et les langues, tristes filles de la nécessité, se sentent de leur dure origine." (*Essai*, ch. 10, p. 526)

[113] "le continuel danger de périr ne permettait pas de se borner à la langue du geste ... le premier mot ... fut. ... chez eux ... *aidez-moi*." (*ibid.*, p. 527)

[114] "Là se formèrent les premiers liens des familles, là furent les premiers rendez-vous des deux sexes. ... Là, des yeux accoutumés aux mêmes objets dès l'enfance commencèrent d'en voir de plus doux. Le coeur s'émut à ces nouveaux objets; ... il sentit le plaisir de n'être pas seul. ... Là se firent les premières fêtes: les pieds bondissaient de joie, le geste expressé ne suffisait plus, la voix l'accompagnait d'accens passionnés" (*ibid.*, ch. 9, p. 525)

his own ignorance, he shows us, as we follow him to the end of his promenades, both the real self that he has become – and in his account of the origin of languages, the fundamental factors that affect the way in which not only he, but everyone, must come to self-understanding.

Rousseau proposes to paint the portrait of the man who, rebuffed by society, has become the solitary that nature made him. But, instead, he reveals a more interesting portrait. The solitary walker whom we leave as we close the unfinished and unfinishable *Rêveries* is at once, and *au fond de son coeur*, separate and incomplete. Can he – can we – speak the words of help and of love, and yet "remain as free as before"? We have our "first comparative work," but as Rousseau would no doubt agree, the social theory "is certainly yet to be begun."

Philosophy, University of Pittsburgh

EVOLUTIONARY ETHICS AND THE SEARCH FOR PREDECESSORS: KANT, HUME, AND ALL THE WAY BACK TO ARISTOTLE?

BY MICHAEL RUSE

INTRODUCTION

Hopes of applying the findings and speculations of evolutionary theorizing to the problems of ethics have yielded a program with a (deservedly) bad reputation.[1] At the level of norms – substantival ethics – it has been a platform for some of the more grotesque socio-politico-economic suggestions of our times.[2] At the level of justification – metaethics – it has opened the way to some of the more blatant fallacies in the undergraduate textbook.[3] Recently, however, a number of people, philosophers and biologists, have sensed that a more adequate evolutionary ethics might be possible. United in the conviction that it simply has to matter that we humans are modified monkeys rather than the creation of a Good God, in His image, on the Sixth Day, they argue that recent developments in evolutionary biology, especially those dealing with the genetic basis of social behavior ("sociobiology"), open the way to a satisfactory biological understanding of morality.[4]

Despite being strongly opposed at first (like most people educated thirty years ago, I was brought up on a steady diet of G.E. Moore and the naturalistic fallacy), I have now swung round and become an enthusiast.[5] Not only do I think that evolutionary ethics is possible, but I think that this is the way that philosophical thinking about morality ought to go. But here, although I will lay out in sketchy form the case that I and others endorse, my main concern is not with exposition and defense. Apart from anything else, I have already done this elsewhere at length. My aim now is somewhat different. I am searching for predecessors.

---

[1] Michael Ruse, *Taking Darwin Seriously* (Oxford: Basil Blackwell, 1986); "Evolutionary Ethics," Peter Singer, *Companion to Ethics* (Oxford: Basil Blackwell, 1990).

[2] Although the question is still controversial, there is strong evidence linking evolutionism, via the ideas of Ernst Haeckel, with National Socialism. See Daniel Gasman, *The Scientific Origins of National Socialism: Social Darwinism, Ernst Haeckel and the Monist League* (New York: Elsevier, 1971).

[3] Most obviously, the so-called "naturalistic fallacy." See George E. Moore, *Principia Ethica* (Cambridge: Cambridge University Press, 1903). See also *Taking Darwin Seriously*, ch. 3.

[4] See Robert Richards, *Darwin and the Emergence of Evolutionary Theories of Mind and Behavior* (Chicago: University of Chicago Press, 1988); Edward O. Wilson, *On Human Nature* (Cambridge: Harvard University Press, 1978); Edward O. Wilson, *Biophilia* (Cambridge: Harvard University Press, 1984); Richard Alexander, *The Biology of Moral Systems* (New York: Aldine de Gruyter, 1987); John Mackie, "The Law of the Jungle," *Philosophy*, vol. 53 (1978), pp. 553–73; *Hume's Moral Theory* (London: Routledge and Kegan Paul, 1979); Jeffrie Murphy, *Evolution, Morality, and the Meaning of Life* (Totowa: Rowan and Littlefield, 1982); but see Philip Kitcher, *Vaulting Ambition* (Cambridge: MIT Press, 1985); Mary Midgley, *Evolution as a Religion* (London: Methuen, 1985).

[5] Michael Ruse, *Sociobiology: Sense or Nonsense?* (Dordrecht: Reidel, 1979).

Why am I engaged in such a search? Although I am on a track that most of my fellow philosophers think lies between the false and the unsavory, I am still enough of a philosopher to be deeply suspicious of any proposal that claims to be new and radical. On examination, such proposals usually turn out to be either deeply flawed or not so very original after all. And I think that, particularly in the case of ethics, this is not only as it is but as it should be. I believe it is ludicrous (and deeply insulting) to suppose *a priori* that thinkers of the depth of Kant and Hume and Aristotle (to name three of the greatest moral philosophers) had no true insights into the nature and status of human ethical thought and behavior. I expect such thinkers to be dated. I am not of the conviction that philosophy never moves forward. Indeed it does so move, usually as the result of advances in science – the one unambiguously progressive phenomenon in human culture. But I do believe that any philosophical view today which has a lien on our allegiance must show continuity with the past.

Moreover, inasmuch as one can show such continuity, so one can use the achievements of the past to illuminate the present and future. Kant, Hume, and Aristotle offer sophisticated and subtle theories of morality, pointing to ambiguities, clarifying connections, drawing implications. Inasmuch as the modern-day evolutionary ethicist can rightfully look back to the giants as predecessors (in some sense), so he or she can thereby improve and extend his or her own still-crude thoughts about the nature of morality.

This, then, is my task now. As promised, I shall first offer my evolutionary perspective on ethics. Then I shall look back through the history of moral philosophy, specifically at the three major thinkers mentioned just above, and see whether there are continuities. I am *not* trying to turn Kant or Hume or Aristotle into proto-evolutionists (although there is grist for that mill in the case of the first two). Even less am I trying to turn them into proto-evolutionary ethicists. But I do want to see if my view echoes the past – and how, therefore one might hope to enrich and develop the position that I and others hold now.

I. DARWINIAN ETHICS

Any adequate evolutionary approach to ethics has to start with the dominant biological paradigm launched by Charles Robert Darwin in his 1859 *On the Origin of Species*.[6] More organisms are born than can survive and reproduce: this leads to an ongoing 'struggle for existence'. Success in the struggle is in part due to the different (heritable) features possessed by organisms. There is thus a 'natural selection' which, given 'enough time, leads to full-blown evolution. Moreover, the kinds of features that organisms have are precisely those which help in survival and (more crucially) reproduction. They are 'adaptations'.[7]

Traditional evolutionary ethics, better known as "Social Darwinism," seizes on life's struggles, generalizes to human culture, and argues that such conflict is

---

[6] London: John Murray.

[7] I discuss these points, in depth, in my *Darwinism Defended: A Guide to the Evolution Controversies* (Reading: Addison-Wesley, 1982).

natural.[8] This is usually all cashed out as an extreme form of *laissez faire* economics, where not only do the stronger survive but this is seen as a good thing. The most famous of all representatives of this school was the nineteenth-century thinker Herbert Spencer.[9] Although it was long reviled by scholars, there is now a growing interest in his work and a realization that his thought is nowhere near as crude as popular parody would have it.[10] But there were some who fitted the traditional picture. In the words of one spokesperson for the cause, William Graham Sumner:

> Let it be understood that we cannot go outside of this alternative: liberty, inequality, survival of the fittest; not-liberty, equality, survival of the unfittest. The former carries society forward and favors all its best members; the latter carries society downwards and favors all its worst members.[11]

As you might expect, there are (like Christianity) many variants. The best-known thinker of this ilk today is the Harvard entomologist E.O. Wilson,[12] who argues that we humans exist in a symbiotic relationship with nature, and that to succeed in the struggle we must therefore cherish living things. He is active in the ecological movement.

Obviously some (metaethical) foundations must be offered for all such argumentation – Why should we care about what is natural, whether it led to extreme libertarianism or the Green movement? – and here there is general agreement (including mine) that Social Darwinism comes unstuck. To go from the way that the world works to the way that things ought to be – or to the way that we ought to behave – seems a clear and quite untenable violation of the is/ought dichotomy.[13] Whether Moore was right in thinking goodness an intuited non-natural property, he was surely right in seeing a fallacy in the equation of 'that which has evolved' with 'that which is good'.[14]

But how can one do better? The new approach to evolutionary ethics invites you to start again with the science. As Darwin realized, the struggle for existence is a struggle only in a metaphorical sense.[15] Although it can entail combat, as often as not it entails behavior which is as far from violent as it is possible to go: searching for food, courting of one's mate, care of offspring, and the like. Most particularly, as

---

[8] Richard Hofstadter, *Social Darwinism in American Thought* (New York: Braziller, 1959); Cynthia Russett, *Darwin in America: The Intellectual Response, 1865-1912* (San Francisco: Freeman, 1976); Greta Jones, *Social Darwinism and English Thought* (New York: Braziller, 1980).

[9] See especially his *Social Statics* (London: Chapman, 1851).

[10] See Richards, *Darwin and the Emergence of Evolutionary Theories of Mind and Behavior*. In this paper, I will not offer an extended treatment of Spencer's work, partly because I do not think he is in the first rank of moral philosophers, but more particularly because I have and am giving detailed discussion elsewhere. See Ruse, *Taking Darwin Seriously*, esp. chs. 2 and 3, and Ruse, *Molecules to Men: The Concept of Progress in Evolutionary Biology* (Cambridge: Harvard University Press, 1991).

[11] See William G. Sumner, *The Challenge of Facts and Other Essays* (New Haven: Yale University Press, 1914).

[12] Edward O. Wilson, *Biophilia* (Cambridge: Harvard University Press, 1984).

[13] W.D. Hudson, *Modern Moral Philosophy* (London: Macmillan, 1970).

[14] *Principia Ethica* (Cambridge: Cambridge University Press, 1903).

[15] Ruse, *Sociobiology: Sense or Nonsense?* (Dordrecht: Reidel, 1979).

Darwin also realized, the struggle can lead to cooperation between organisms (usually of the same species), simply because the costs of working with others are outweighed by the benefits of group behavior. An obvious example is the pack-hunting behavior of wolves. An individual's share of the meat from a fallen elk is far greater than that from a fallen chipmunk, even if the latter is not shared.

Cooperation for biological ends (which, in the terms of modern biology, cashes out as increasing one's genetic contribution to the composition of future generations) is known technically as 'altruism'.[16] Note that this is yet another biological metaphor – there is certainly no suggestion that such cooperation always demands deliberate subjection to the Categorical Imperative or some such thing. (This latter disinterested help – requiring Mother-Theresa-type thoughts and actions – we can refer to as unadorned, literal altruism.)

Biological altruism is widely documented through the animal (and sometimes the plant) kingdom. Moreover, much is known about its proximate mechanisms. Between relatives, biological altruism is often the result of so-called 'kin selection'.[17] Success in the struggle means increasing one's future biological representation, which in turn translates into increasing one's proportion of the units of inheritance – that is, the genes. But since relatives share copies of the same genes, when a relative reproduces, one reproduces (vicariously, as it were). Hence, evolution can promote adaptations which lead one to help the survival and reproduction of such relatives.

It is believed that this process is responsible for the widespread biological altruism to be found in the insect (especially *hymenoptera*) world. Between non-relatives, biological altruism is often the result of so-called 'reciprocal altruism'.[18] If you scratch my back, then I am much more likely to scratch yours. More generally, if you are prepared to help others, then others are more likely to help you. It is not necessary that one get instant reciprocation. Adaptations promoting such altruism can, as it were, make one willing to contribute to the general pool, so long as one can draw from the pool as needed.

What about humans? (Note that I am still talking about biological altruism and not yet about literal, moral altruism.) Darwin always firmly believed not only that we evolved but that we evolved through the mechanism of natural selection.[19] In this, he is followed absolutely and completely by modern-day Darwinians. The key to understanding humankind, including human social behaviour, is biological adaptationism. We are what we are because the successful amongst our would-be ancestors outreproduced the unsuccessful. (This is not to deny that there are those – including good biologists – who shrink from this position. In this paper, I am simply ignoring doubters and deniers. Elsewhere, I take them on with pleasure.[20])

[16] Edward O. Wilson, *Sociobiology: The New Synthesis* (Cambridge: Harvard University Press, 1975).

[17] William D. Hamilton, "The Genetical Evolution of Social Behaviour. I," *Journal of Theoretical Biology*, vol. 7 (1964), pp. 1–16; "The Genetical Evolution of Social Behaviour. II," *Journal of Theoretical Biology*, vol. 7 (1964), pp. 17–32.

[18] Robert L. Trivers, "The Evolution of Reciprocal Altruism," *Quarterly Review of Biology*, vol. 46 (1971), pp. 35–57.

[19] Charles Darwin, *Descent of Man* (London: John Murray, 1871).

[20] Ruse, *Sociobiology: Sense or Nonsense?* See also Michael Ruse, *Darwinism Defended: A Guide to the Evolution Controversies*.

Now, the thing to recognize about humans is that we are very much in need of biological altruism and – despite all the obvious qualifications – very good at it.[21] Compared to other animals, we are slow, weak, and clumsy. But we do band together, and therein lies our strength. Because we band together, we can survive and reproduce. Moreover, to forestall the immediate objections, the not-so-old stories about humans being killer apes are simply nonsense. Even if you take into account the wars of this century, our intraspecific hostility measure is below that of most other primates.[22]

How, then, does nature get us to act biologically altruistically? One possibility is that we might have been genetically determined, as are the ants. We might have been programmed by our biology to act in cooperative ways without thought, without learning, and without much chance of taking evasive action if something goes wrong. Regretfully, although mother ants who turn out millions of offspring can afford to lose a few hundred when conditions change, a human mother who (along with father) puts in masses of parental investment cannot afford to be so cavalier. Both parents and offspring must be sensitive to environmental conditions and able to respond to change. There are simply not enough offspring to waste when things go wrong. Genetic determinism is, on the whole, not for us.

Nor is the very opposite – the scenario in which we arrive in this world with brains like super-computers, ready to calculate the payoffs in any and every social transaction, willing to cooperate if it is in our interest but not otherwise. Even if it were biologically possible to produce such powerful brains, 'altruism' through this channel would suffer from crippling biological drawbacks. In life, time is money – survival and reproductive money, that is. With complex options and complex payoffs, even if we arrived at optimal solutions, the very process would take lots of time. But in life, what you usually need is a quick and dirty solution. You simply have to sacrifice perfection for efficiency. It is better to have a 90 percent effective solution to attacking tigers in 5 seconds than a 100 percent effective solution in 5 minutes.

This points to a third option, one which Darwinians today think is indeed the way that evolution has directed us. We do not come into this world with our minds or brains like unprogrammed, all-purpose computers – totally open, empty, unstructured *tabulae rasae*. Rather, we have various innate capacities or dispositions which get filled in or molded by culture as we grow up, leading us to think and act in certain biologically adaptive ways rather than others.[23] (No one, I hardly need say, is claiming that we have explicitly formulated innate ideas of the kind so effectively demolished by John Locke.[24])

Among these innate dispositions – and here it is true that we start to get speculative, but the intention is to remain firmly empirical – we find those which

---

[21] Glynn Isaac, "Aspects of Human Evolution," ed. D.S. Bendall, *Evolution from Molecules to Men* (Cambridge: Cambridge University Press, 1983), pp. 509–43.

[22] Jane Goodall, *The Chimpanzees of Gombee: Patterns of Behaviour* (Cambridge: Harvard University Press, 1987).

[23] Charles Lumsden and Edward Wilson, *Promethean Fire* (Cambridge: Harvard University Press, 1983).

[24] *An Essay Concerning Human Understanding*, ed. Peter H. Nidditch (New York: Oxford University Press, 1975).

incline us towards biological 'altruism'. But what is the content of such dispositions, as they become explicit, through ontogeny, in culture? It is simply thoughts that we *should* behave in ways which are helpful and caring towards our fellow humans. In other words, to make us biologically altruistic, nature has made us literally altruistic.'[25]

I now stress two points. First, the claim is that the literal altruism is genuine. Of course, we are all hypocrites sometimes, but we are not all like Uriah Heep – forever pretending to be helpful but really scheming otherwise. We are more efficient biological altruists if we are believers – and so it is.[26] We may have selfish genes, but we are not necessarily always selfish humans. Second, although it is speculative, the positive evidence is starting to come in. Cross-cultural studies strongly support hypotheses about a biological underpinning to human social nature. Moreover, these extend to questions of obligation – for instance, the Cambridge biologist Patrick Bateson has been considering the way in which incest *taboos* (which involve obligation) might have evolved from incest *barriers* (which do not).[27] Work such as this is increasingly backed by primate studies, especially those suggesting that apes have (what at the weakest I would term 'proto-') morality, something which one presumes our ancestors would have possessed.[28]

Yet, plausible though this evolutionary scenario may be, the philosopher will rightfully ask about its relevance to the problems of ethics. Roughly speaking, at the substantival level, while recognizing that there is much more to be teased out (some of which will come when we turn to history), I would suggest that the humans whose evolution I have just been discussing are animals whose substantival beliefs would more or less correspond with what philosophers and others would recognize as decent moral beings. They would care. They would dislike cruelty. They would think that you should give people a chance. (They would not be suckers, though; there would be strong selection against this.) They would certainly think that one ought to give out benefits and attention differentially – the young, the old, the sick, the pregnant, etc., need our help more than do others.[29]

Frankly, I do not know where the biology of human beings stands on some specific topic like, say, the controversy over abortion. But I suspect ignorance here lies less in biology and more in the difficulty of applying moral beliefs to a situation

[25] Even though I have separated biological altruism from literal altruism, without further clarification of the latter term the discussion may seem intolerably flabby. But in line with my comments at the beginning of this discussion, I see as a major aim of this paper precisely to clarify what an evolutionist might mean by moral (literal) altruism, by playing off the idea against the thoughts of the great moral philosophers. I will return to definition at the end of this paper. For the moment, however, I will stress that more is meant than just good feeling. There has to be at some level a sense of obligation.

[26] Robert L. Trivers, Foreword to R. Dawkins, *The Selfish Gene* (Oxford: Oxford University Press, 1976), pp. v–vii.

[27] "Does Evolutionary Biology Contribute to Ethics?", *Biology & Philosophy*, vol. 4 (1989), pp. 287–302.

[28] *Chimpanzee Politics* (London: Jonathan Cape, 1982). Although I stress that mine is an empirical position, I shall say no more here about the evidence, primarily because I have looked at such issues in detail elsewhere. See Ruse, *Taking Darwin Seriously; The Darwinian Paradigm* (London: Routledge, 1989); Michael Ruse and Edward O. Wilson, "Moral Philosophy as Applied Science," *Philosophy*, vol. 61 (1986), pp. 173–92.

[29] The best discussion of these points, especially about the (literal) altruist being very wary of others' cheating, is John Mackie, "The Law of the Jungle." See also, on the biological side, Robert Trivers, "The Evolution of Reciprocal Altruism," *Quarterly Review of Biology*, vol. 46 (1971), pp. 35–57.

where there is so much confusion about the facts of the case. Analogously, let me ask: does the utilitarian have an official position on abortion? What I do suspect is that, for the evolutionary ethicist, rights – especially in the sense of keeping off other people's turf (however construed) – would be important. After all, how else can you get others to give you breathing space?

But, what of foundations? Here the philosopher will fear (more likely, joyfully anticipate) trouble. Even if one agrees that one ought to be altruistic, no justification is in the fact that nature makes us altruistic for us to be effective 'altruists'. The is/ought barrier looms as large as ever. Of course, one way one might get around (or, rather, through) the barrier is by denying that there is all that sharp a division between "is" and "ought."[30] But whatever the merits of this as a general strategy, in the evolutionary case it seems a bad tack. As a general proposition "has evolved" is clearly not equivalent to "is good" or "should be taken seriously." Specifically, "We think that we ought to do x because our evolution has made us this way" does not logically entail "We ought to do x".

Moreover, the Darwinian especially wants to keep up the is/ought barrier: the whole point about moral altruism is to get us to do something we would not otherwise do. Struggle and selection obviously incline one towards selfishness – the primate who feeds him- or herself is generally fitter than the primate who feeds others. However, sometimes biological altruism is a good tactic, and so we need an extra push. This is to be found in the peculiar nature of moral altruism: obligation. Without a feeling of obligation, we are all going to start to cheat, and biological altruism will collapse. The distinctiveness of the "ought" must be maintained.

The solution is to go around rather than through. Recognizing that evolution gives no justification of (substantive) morality, the evolutionist argues that neither does anything else. Furthermore, the evolutionist argues that Darwinian evolution shows that the search for foundations is mistaken, even though there are good biological reasons why we believe in them. In other words, at the metaethical level the Darwinian urges skepticism. There is indeed a difference between "is" and "ought," but no derivation of one from the other is being attempted. Rather, claims about the world are used to explain away the apparent objective referent of morality. Substantive morality is a collective illusion of our genes. (But no less real than many other things without an objective referent, like the rules of baseball.)

Is this just special pleading – a way of escape – or is an argument being offered here? I believe it is the latter. The claim is that sometimes, when you have given a causal explanation of belief, you see that the call for reasoned justification is unneeded, even illicit. Beliefs in spiritualism are a case in point. Beliefs in morality are another. Our substantival beliefs are no more (or less) than adaptations put in place by natural selection for reproductive ends.

> The [Darwinian] may well agree . . . . that value judgments are properly
> defended in terms of other value judgments until we reach some that are
> fundamental. All of this, in a sense, is the giving of reasons. However,
> suppose we seriously raise the question of why these fundamental

---

[30] Richards, *Darwin and the Emergence of Evolutionary Theories of Mind and Behavior*.

judgments are regarded as fundamental. There may be only a causal
explanation for this! We reject simplistic utilitarianism because it entails
consequences that are morally counterintuitive, or we embrace a Rawlsian
theory of justice because it systematizes (places in 'reflective equilibrium')
our pretheoretical convictions. But what is the status of those intuitions or
convictions? Perhaps there is nothing more to be said for them than that
they involve deep preferences (or patterns of preference) built into our
biological nature. If this is so, then at a very fundamental point the
reasons/causes (and the belief we ought/really ought) distinction breaks
down, or the one transforms into the other.[31]

Yet even if you agree that morality is an adaptation, does this deny the
independent existence of morality – or the failure to build a bridge to it? Consider.
We see the speeding train because of our adaptations. Our knowledge of the train is
adaptive. Does this deny the existence of the train?[32]

However, the two cases – morality and trains – are not quite parallel. Without
the train, there is no reason to think that one would believe in its existence (odd
counter-examples excluded). With or without external morality (whatever that
might mean) one would still believe as one does, because the force of substantival
morality – as we understand it – comes from the interactions between (very real)
people. At the least, external morality is redundant, which is surely close to a
contradiction in terms. At the worst, what we believe and what morality really *is* are
two quite different things. To suppose that our beliefs and true morality coincide is
to impute a direction to evolution altogether alien to modern biological thought.[33]

There is one important point, however – and with this I can conclude the direct
exposition. Even though there may not be an objective foundation to morality, it is
part of its phenomenology that we think that there is.[34] If one says "killing is
wrong," then what one means and feels is that killing is wrong, truly and
objectively. By this means I mean that in some sense morality exists "outside us"; it
is thus neither relativistic nor subjective, in the sense of "dependent on human
feelings" or the like. This is why emotivism seems not merely implausible but
downright immoral. Murder, rape, and theft are not merely matters of emotion and
preference (or so it seems). They are matters of right and wrong!

The evolutionary ethicist is sensitive to the seeming objectivity of (substantive)
ethics, expecting and explaining it. The simple point is that unless we believe
morality to be objective, in the sense just characterized, it will not work. If everyone
recognized the illusory nature of morality (and could escape from their biology
sufficiently to take advantage of this recognition), then very soon people would
start to cheat and the whole social system would collapse. Moral altruism would go,
and with it would go biological altruism. Hence, our biology leads us to 'objectify'

[31] Murphy, *Evolution, Morality, and the Meaning of Life*.
[32] Robert Nozick, *Philosophical Explanations* (Cambridge: Harvard: University Press, 1981).
[33] Ruse, *Molecules to Men*.
[34] Mackie, *Hume's Moral Theory*.

morality.[35] Ethical skepticism may be the correct philosophy, but our genes are working flat-out to make such a conclusion counterintuitive.

I now, as promised, want to turn from the present to the past. The modern-day case for evolutionary ethics has been sketched out. The question to be pursued is how far this position mirrors ideas of the great moral thinkers in the philosophic tradition. Specifically, I want to compare the evolutionist's thinking with that of Kant, Hume, and Aristotle. Are we looking at different world systems, or are there important points of intellectual contact?

II. IMMANUEL KANT

Here and in succeeding sections, I shall lay out the central philosophical ideas so starkly as to be almost a parody. But this will leave space for comparative discussion and elaboration. In the case of Kant,[36] however, complex though his central philosophy may be, his basic moral notions are relatively straightforward. Most obviously, at the heart of his ethical theorizing we have his supreme principle of morality, that which is binding on rational beings unconditionally, the Categorical Imperative. There are various ways in which this is expressed. Most prominently, there is the universalizability version: "Act only according to that maxim by which you can at the same time will that it should become a universal law."[37] Alternatively, there is the practical version: "Act so that you treat humanity, whether in your own person or in that of another, always as an end and never as a means only."[38] From these, Kant derives his specific substantival rules about keeping promises and the like.

What of foundations? Kant is certainly not an objectivist in the sense of the intuitionist, be he Plato or G.E. Moore, believing in a morality "out there," independent of humans. Rather for him, morality is something (synthetic *a priori*) necessary which emerges from the interaction of rational (not necessarily human) beings. Consider the question of paying back debts; suppose a man decides to borrow and not repay.

> He changes the pretension of self-love into a universal law and then puts the question: How would it be if my maxim became a universal law? He immediately sees that it could never hold as a universal law of nature and be consistent with itself; rather it must necessarily contradict itself. For the universality of a law which says that anyone who believes himself to be in need could promise what he pleased with the intention of not fulfilling it would make the promise itself and the end to be accomplished by it impossible; no one would believe what was promised to him but would only laugh at any such assertion as vain pretense.[39]

---

[35] *ibid.*

[36] Immanuel Kant, *Critique of Practical Reason*, trans. L.W. Beck (Chicago: University of Chicago Press, 1949); Immanuel Kant, *Foundations of the Metaphysics of Morals*, trans. L.W. Beck (Indianapolis: Bobbs-Merrill, 1959).

[37] Kant, *Foundations*, p. 39.

[38] *ibid.*, p. 47.

[39] *ibid.*, p. 40.

When Kant argues like this, one sees the important links with social contract theory; indeed (as is well-known), today's most distinguished neo-Kantian moral philosopher, John Rawls,[40] seizes on precisely this aspect of his thought. Rawls invites us to put ourselves behind a 'veil of ignorance' and then to devise the society we would want – concluding that we would want a 'just' society, where this would be equated with 'fairness'. Likewise, when it comes to foundations, Rawls finds justification for his position not in some objective reality, but in principles of rationality.[41] He writes:

> What justifies a conception of justice is not its being true to an order antecedent to and given to us, but its congruence with our deeper understanding of ourselves and our aspirations, and our realization that, given our history and the traditions embedded in our public life, it is the most reasonable doctrine for us.[42]

Now what has all of this to do with evolutionary ethics? (Remember, I am not concerned with whether Kant was or was not an evolutionist.) In certain respects, things look rather promising. Take the substantival level. Kant and the evolutionist think that morality somehow emerges from and tracks some kind of reciprocation. Morality ultimately rests in caring about others and expecting others to care about you.[43]

Of course, this is not to say that the evolutionist will accept all of the consequences Kant draws from his imperative – but neither would anybody else. Kant's prohibition against any kind of lying owes more to his Pietistic background than to his philosophy; the same is true of his more stringent views on sexuality.

There are places here where the evolutionist can put Kant right. He argues that sodomy is treating another as a means and not an end, but his deeper objection is that it is 'unnatural'.[44] Sociobiology suggests to the contrary that, paradoxical though it may seem, such acts can have highly adaptive consequences.[45] One of the main arguments to this end centers on the already-mentioned mechanism of kin selection. If, by foregoing one's own reproduction, one thereby increases the reproduction of close relatives (being freed to help them and their children, and so forth), then natural selection might well direct one to precisely such a non-reproductive role. It is thought that homosexuality could be one way in which nature forces on people just such non-reproductive roles.

But these are, to a certain extent, details (albeit important details). Perhaps more of a strain becomes apparent when one thinks of how far imperatives are to be

[40] John Rawls, *A Theory of Justice* (Harvard: Harvard University Press, 1971).
[41] John Rawls, "Kantian Constructivism in Moral Theory," *Journal of Philosophy*, vol. 77 (1980), pp. 515–72.
[42] *ibid.*, p. 519.
[43] As Rawls, *Theory of Justice*, pp. 502–3, notes, evolutionary biology is a godsend to any Kantian or social contract theorist. Instead of having to make up stories about a fictional first parliament or a hypothetical original position, you can let the genes do the work for you.
[44] Immanuel Kant, *Critique of Pure Reason*, trans. N. Kemp Smith (London: Macmillan, 1963).
[45] Michael Ruse, *Homosexuality: A Philosophical Inquiry* (Oxford: Blackwell, 1988).

universalized – through Konigsberg? Prussia? Europe? It is hard to see how – to examine the Kantian prohibition against suicide – a case of ritual disembowelment in Japan makes much difference to me. I am hardly caught in a "contradiction" if some unknown Asian commits *hari-kari*. For this reason, the evolutionary ethicist starts to get very tense here. Given the mechanisms of biology, it seems highly improbable that there would simply be an even sentiment, applied indifferently to all and every human. One would expect stronger feelings towards close kin, weaker ones towards non-relatives in one's group, and finally a falling-away as one deals with complete strangers. If Kantianism means indifferent universalization, then biology is against it.

Note that I am talking of moral obligations here, not just feelings of affection. Of course, you love your children more than others'; the point is (says the evolutionist) that, as a parent, you have greater moral obligations, too. Note also that no one is saying that you have absolutely no obligations to the poor of the Third World – especially now that technology has made us much more of one big family. It is just that the evolutionist thinks it foolish and immoral to pretend that you ought to give all of your income to OXFAM and let your family eat at a Salvation Army soup kitchen. (This is contrary to the claim of Singer.[46])

A more serious clash between the Kantian and the Darwinian arises over the intention/consequence dichotomy. For Kant, the intention, the will, is everything. It matters not how things turn out; what counts is what you intended. The Darwinian certainly does not want to discount a good will, and I am sure, he would feel very uncomfortable about something that was totally consequentialist. However, things must get done. A saintly fool who got everything wrong would pretty soon be isolated and not long remain an object of veneration. I certainly doubt that such a socially catastrophic individual would be held as a model against the ordinary, often fallible, often sinful, but generally successful person. (Here, the Darwinian surely fits better with our intuitions. Attempted murder is very wrong, but not as much so as successful murder.)

However, in a way all of this is skirmishing, for now we come to (what I take to be) the real difference between Kantianism (including Rawls) and Darwinism. For Kant, morality rests ultimately in formal relations; as such, therefore, it is binding on any rational being whatsoever. The Categorical Imperative is as active on Andromeda as it is on Earth. But this smacks uncomfortably of directionalism to the Darwinian, inasmuch as it implies that all rational beings must think the same way. There is a flavor of teleology about any claim that the endpoint of evolution must be so constrained. As we know only too well, on this earth of ours there are many ways of getting from A to B – flying, walking, swimming, slithering, hitchhiking, swinging, etc. And as this world also shows, there are many ways of being biologically altruistic. Who would presume that all rational beings in the universe must regard each other as ends, if they are to get along? Perhaps, Cold War fashion, they might hate each other but exist in balanced harmony.

The Kantian might respond that all rational beings, even Cold Warriors, must

[46] Peter Singer, "Famine, Affluence, and Morality," *Philosophy and Public Affairs*, vol. 1, no. 3 (1972), pp. 229–43.

acknowledge and obey certain rational rules of reciprocation. This may be true, at least as we can see things. But such formal reciprocation is not itself morality. This is, of course, a point which Kant himself recognizes, when he allows that formal reciprocation might lead to better ends than everyday morality.

> Now although it is possible that a universal law of nature according to that maxim could exist, it is nevertheless impossible to will that such a principle should hold everywhere as a law of nature. For a will which resolved this would conflict with itself, since instances can often arise in which he would need the love and sympathy of others, and in which he would have robbed himself, by such a law of nature springing from his own will, of all hope of the aid he desires.[47]

The crucial factor is that the Darwinian acknowledges human nature explicitly, building it right into his morality. He recognizes that humans need love (etc.) above the purely formal rules of reciprocation. But the cost, or the result, is that morality is relative. Not, I hasten to add, necessarily on this globe – humans have a shared evolutionary past, and unless there is a shared intra-group morality then, like language or genital size, it simply will not work. But there is relativism to intergalactic morality. It is neither logically nor biologically necessary that Andromedans should need love and sympathy.[48] (In pointing to Kant's difficulty with getting morality from formal rules, one is following a line of criticism which goes back to Hegel. The point is that Kant is caught here in a way that the Darwinian is not – and the catching comes from the deepest part of Kant's philosophy.)

In the end, therefore, Kant is really not in direct line to the evolutionist. We must look elsewhere.

III. DAVID HUME

Of my view of Hume I will make no secret, for I have argued elsewhere that I regard him as a far more promising precursor.[49] His is a naturalistic approach to ethics that the Darwinian understands and appreciates. Apart from anything else, his willingness to merge the animal and the human ("no truth appears to me more evident, than that beasts are endow'd with thought and reason as well as men"[50]) strikes a note that is sweet music to the ears of today's biologist.

Hume's moral theory emerges from his analysis of human nature: specifically, his psychology of action. Reason and the emotions (the passions) are separate and distinct things, and it is only the latter which can spur one to action. Reason can certainly help one to decide about actions – how to satisfy certain desires, for instance – but ultimately it is motivationally impotent. "Reason is and ought to be

---

[47] Kant, *Foundations of the Metaphysics of Morals.*
[48] Ruse, *The Darwinian Paradiam.*
[49] Ruse, *Taking Darwin Seriously*, esp. ch. 6.
[50] David Hume, *A Treatise of Human Nature*, L.A. Selby-Bigge ed., 2d edn. Peter H. Nidditch ed. (Oxford: Oxford University Press, 1978), p. 176.

the slave of the passions."[51] Moral urges, therefore, being things which certainly do motivate us, must fall into the camp of the passions or sentiments.

But what is the basis of such urges? Hume denies that they are sparked by intuitions of (anachronistically speaking) non-natural properties. Nor do they derive ultimately from the natural, empirical world "out there." This is the message of his famous identification of the is/ought dichotomy, now rightfully known as "Hume's law." The conclusion, therefore, is that morality has to be something which comes from within, perhaps sparked by external factors but not to be derived from them.

> Take any action allow'd to be vicious: Wilful murder, for instance. Examine it in all lights, and see if you can find that matter of fact, or real existence, which you call *vice*. In which-ever way you take it, you find only certain passions, motives, volitions and thoughts. There is no other matter of fact in the case. The vice entirely escapes you, as long as you consider the object. You never can find it, till you turn your reflexion into your own breast, and find a sentiment of disapprobation, which arises in you, towards this action. Here is a matter of fact; but 'tis the object of feeling, not of reason. It lies in yourself, not in the object. So that when you pronounce any action or character to be vicious, you mean nothing, but that from the constitution of your nature you have a feeling or sentiment of blame from the contemplation of it.[52]

Quite explicitly, Hume then goes on to liken morality – specifically, things we judge good or bad – to colors (that is, secondary qualities), meaning they are things we project onto reality.

> Vice and virtue, therefore, may be compar'd to sounds, colours, heat and cold which, according to modern philosophy are not qualities in objects, but perceptions in the mind.[53]

This then leads the way to a discussion of the virtues, which he distinguishes into the artificial and the natural – the former producing "pleasure and approbation by means of an artifice or contrivance, which arises from the circumstances and necessities of mankind."[54] Among artificial virtues, we run the gamut from justice ("a constant and perpetual will of giving everyone his due"[55]) to chastity and modesty (in females). Among natural virtues, we find that they range from meekness through generosity to equity. Directly here and indirectly through to the artificial virtues, the key seems to be a sense of *sympathy* which is triggered towards our fellow humans.

[51] *ibid.*
[52] *ibid.*, p. 469.
[53] *ibid.*, p. 469.
[54] *ibid.*, p. 477.
[55] *ibid.*, p. 477.

Thus it appears *that* sympathy is a very powerful principle in human nature, *that* it has a great influence on our taste of beauty, and *that* it produces our sentiment of morals in all the artificial virtues. From thence we may presume, that it also gives rise to many of the other virtues; and that qualities acquire our approbation, because of their tendency to the good of mankind.[56]

What I have just offered is an even cruder parody of Hume than that I gave previously of Kant, but the key points of comparison with Darwinism can now be made – most particularly, that there is indeed a significant overlap between the ideas of the great British empiricist and those of today's evolutionary ethicist. (I will say nothing here about actual historical links, but as a matter of fact there is considerable evidence connecting Hume with Darwin's own thinking about morality, especially as developed in the *Descent of Man*.[57])

I do not think that the Darwinian necessarily must embrace (simply because she is a Darwinian) Hume's stark reason/emotion division. But the consequences Hume draws, most particularly that morality is centered in subjective feeling, are precisely those of the Darwinian, as are the acceptance and use of the is/ought distinction and the significance of projection. Hume likens our thinking about morality to our thinking about secondary qualities. We really do think that the sky is blue "out there," and we really do think that murder is wrong "out there."

There are also other points of contact. Take Hume's analysis of free will and determinism, a satisfactory discussion of which is presupposed by any adequate attack on the problems of morality. Hume gives the definitive discussion of the compatibilist (soft determinist) case, arguing that although we humans are causally bound, this leaves a dimension to freedom sufficiently open for any realistic understanding of morality. This is precisely the kind of argument adopted by the Darwinian.[58] Critics often accuse sociobiologists of the sin of (the already-mentioned) 'genetic determinism', meaning that they (supposedly) see humans as puppets dangling on strings from their DNA.[59] But while this may be true of ants, we have seen that it is not true of humans. Although our innate dispositions guide us, their very purpose is to leave open different ways of attack in different circumstances. In other words, even though we are clearly part of the causal chain, we have some element of choice. We have a dimension of freedom not possessed by so-called 'lower organisms' like *hymenoptera*. Hence, there is a window open for morality.

What of Hume's treatment of the virtues (and vices), and how does he handle the in-group/out-group morality differential? I take it, going the one way, that the Darwinian agrees that morality does basically come down to some kind of sympathy or fellow-feeling. I note also, going the other way, that one can find passages in Hume on the question of a sliding-scale of affection/morality which

[56] *ibid.*, pp. 577–78.
[57] See Richards, *Darwin and the Emergence of Evolutionary Theories of Mind and Behavior*.
[58] Michael Ruse, "Darwinism and Determinism," *Zygon*, vol. 22 (1986), pp. 419–42.
[59] Richard Lewontin, S. Rose, and L.J. Kamin, *Not in Our Genes* (New York: Pantheon, 1984).

sound as if they come from a modern biology textbook. Consider only the following:

> A man naturally loves his children better than his nephews, his nephews better than his cousins, his cousins better than strangers, where everything else is equal. Hence arise our common measures of duty, in preferring one to the other. Our sense of duty always follows the common and natural course of our passions.[60]

However, perhaps it is because Hume is so impressed by biological (i.e., familial) connections that, in other respects, today's evolutionist parts company with him (or, at least, would probably suggest revisions). Take the supposed artificiality of justice. No one would deny that there is a fair amount of human artifice – culture, as opposed to genes – in human social systems.[61] However, this is not to say that justice *per se* is artificial. Hume seems to think that, without specific cultural intervention, bonds of immediate family or friendship would prevent justice. To the modern biologist, however, this is to ignore or at least to overly downplay the importance of reciprocation. At least, speaking for myself, my feeling is that although Hume is right in seeing that kin relations will affect moral sentiments, he underestimates the power of reciprocation between non-relatives in human evolution. (Technically, he has seized on a kind of proto-version of kin selection, but fails to see that reciprocal altruism can also be a biological as well as a cultural mechanism.)

This is not an easy matter on which to be definitive because, like most of us, Hume does rather want to have his cake and eat it too. For all of his repeated claims that morality begins at home ("we blame a person, who either centers all his affections in his family, or is so regardless of them, as, in any opposition of interest, to give the preference to a stranger, or mere chance acquaintance"[62]), he does think that we can somehow generalize our sentiments to the rest of the human race. As long, that is, as we can "fix on some *steady* and *general* points of view."[63]

The significant factor here, perhaps is that this is a matter of reflective judgment even if not one of immediate feeling. However, my aim here is not Humean exegesis. My point, which is surely made, is that Hume is basically trying to express views very close to that of the Darwinian.

Finally, what of Hume on chastity and modesty? To modern ears he sounds, at least, quaintly old-fashioned; no doubt to some he sounds grotesquely sexist. Combine this with the bad reputation that human sociobiology has in this sphere, and the critic will grimly conclude that the coincidence is complete.

In response, I will say simply two things. First, Hume's discussion is based on

---

[60] David Hume, *A Treatise of Human Nature*, pp. 483–84.

[61] This is not to deny that some, like Charles Lumsden and Edward O. Wilson, *Genes, Mind & Culture* (Cambridge: Harvard University Press, 1981), suggest that the genes track culture much more closely than we imagine.

[62] Hume, *Treatise*, p. 489.

[63] *ibid.*, p. 581.

(and highlights) factual claims that the Darwinian accepts and likewise makes central:

> Since in the copulation of the sexes, the principle of generation goes from the man to the woman, an error may easily take place on the side of the former, tho' it be utterly impossible with regard to the latter. From this trivial and anatomical observation is deriv'd that vast difference betwixt the education and duties of the two sexes.[64]

Men and women are not the same, and this opens the way for profound differences – not the least of which are social.

Second, human *culture* is flexible, even if biologically based. In particular, various technological changes – not the least of which are cheap and efficient methods of birth control – have made significant reorderings of the relations between the sexes possible. These do not necessarily take sexuality out of the realm of the moral, or even reduce it to the level that Hume apparently finds acceptable for males. But I do not think that today's evolutionary ethicist is necessarily saddled with the views of a 25-year-old unmarried, eighteenth-century Scot.

IV. ARISTOTLE

Until recently, one might well have stopped here. It would be felt that we have gone back far enough in the history of moral philosophy. But there are two good reasons for pushing back further, to the greatest thinker of them all. First, several of today's top moral philosophers have urged upon us a neo-Aristotelian perspective.[65] They feel that, since the Reformation, we have lost our way, and we must therefore go back and find our Greek roots. If this is so, then the evolutionary ethicist had better take note. Second, specifically with respect to the philosophy expounded early in this paper, it has been claimed that its ignorance (or avoidance) of Aristotle makes it less than fully adequate. Indeed, people like me show their "profundity by feigning belief in preposterous ideas that could be seriously believed only by the insane."[66]

As commentators note, it is not easy for the modern thinker to plunge straight into Aristotle, especially the Aristotle of the *Nicomachean Ethics*.[67] Apart from anything else, he does not offer a set of prescriptions or rules for good behavior, somewhat after the fashion of Kant – or Jesus. Indeed, he is not really offering a moral handbook (in the sense of substantival norms) at all. Rather, with an intention not entirely dissimilar from Hume's, he offers a kind of moral psychology: there is an analysis of what constitutes the good life (*eudaemonia*) for man. The implicit assumption is that unless you already have some good grasp of what he is talking about, Aristotle is not for you. (For this reason, he is not in favor of ethics classes for children.)

---

[64] *ibid.*, p. 571.

[65] B. Williams, *Ethics and the Limits of Philosophy* (London: Fontana, 1985); A. MacIntyre, *After Virtue* (Notre Dame: University of Notre Dame Press, 1981).

[66] Larry Arnhart, "Darwin, Hume, Annihilism," *The Claremont Review of Books* (1988), pp. 10–12.

[67] J. Urmson, *Aristotle's Ethics* (Oxford: Blackwell, 1988).

For Aristotle, achieving the good life depends on certain crucial human dispositions or traits. These features are commonly translated as 'virtues', but are perhaps better known as 'excellences', for they certainly extend to things *we* would not normally think of as virtuous, like good health and looks ("the man who is very ugly in appearance or ill-born or solitary and childless is hardly happy"[68]). The key to true happiness depends on getting these excellences in the proper balance or harmony.

> Now if the function of man is an activity of soul in accordance with, or not without, rational principle, and if we say a so-and-so and a good so-and-so have a function which is the same in kind, e.g. a lyre-player and good lyre-player, and so without qualification in all cases, eminence in respect of excellence being added to the function (for the function of a lyre-player is to play the lyre, and that of a good lyre-player is to do so well): if this is the case, and we state the function of man to be a certain kind of life, and this to be an activity or actions of the soul implying a rational principle, and the function of a good man to be the good and noble performance of these, and if any action is well performed when it is performed in accordance with the appropriate excellence: if this is the case, human good turns out to be activity of soul in conformity with excellence, and if there are more than one excellence, in conformity with the best and most complete.[69]

As is well known, for Aristotle getting a virtue right is a question of striking a mean between unacceptable opposite extremes. To be honest, none of this sounds much like morality as we would understand it. Indeed, if anything, it sounds like, the antithesis of morality, because it all seems rather self-serving. But things start to become more familiar as we realize that a crucial aspect of Aristotle's perspective on man is that he is a social or political animal. Hence, some virtues or excellences crucially involve other human beings. It turns out that we cannot ourselves be truly happy unless we are interacting properly with our fellows, especially in such respects as bravery, liberality, and justice.

Beyond these more social features, as well as discussing excellences of character, Aristotle also offers a detailed analysis of human friendship. (Actually, important though this analysis is, given its rather separate nature, it may have been popped into the *Ethics* by his editors.) All of this leads back up to the pinnacle question of how man is to achieve his proper end of flourishing or happiness. There we learn that although the political life is one of importance, it is not the fullest end in itself, but stands beneath the life of rational contemplation. At this highest point, we become not just things behaving rationally, but part of reason itself and hence in some way identified with the supreme principle of rationality or God. In this sense, we can hope to escape our earthly bonds and become immortal.

[68] Aristotle, *Complete Works*, ed. J. Barnes (Princeton: Princeton University Press, 1984): *Nicomachean Ethics*, 1099bl.
[69] *ibid.*, 1098al, 7–17.

Strange though Aristotle may seem on first reading – especially to the modern, biologically-oriented ear – there is much within his thought that the Darwinian should find attractive. Given that Aristotle was as sensitive a biologist as he was tough-minded philosopher, even mentioning this point would be condescending were it not so self-evidently true. Most particularly, there is Aristotle's end-directed or teleological perspective on the world, especially on the world of humans. Aristotelian understanding – the fullest kind of understanding – demands that one think in terms of purposes or functions, refusing to rest satisfied with material causes. The same is true of the Darwinian, for all the valiant efforts (especially by my fellow philosophers of science) to argue otherwise.[70] The Darwinian, including the Darwinian ethicist, insists that you look at humankind from a forward perspective.[71]

Indeed, reserving for the moment some obvious queries, there is remarkable overlap between the Aristotelian and Darwinian with respect to the actual ends in terms of which organisms should be understood.

> ... for any living thing that has reached its normal development ... *the most natural act* is the production of another like itself, an animal producing an animal, a plant a plant, in order that, as far as its nature allows, it may partake in the eternal and divine. That is *the goal towards which all things strive, that for the sake of which they do whatsoever their nature renders possible* ... Since then no living thing is able to partake in what is eternal and divine by uninterrupted continuance (for nothing perishable can for ever remain one and the same), it tries to achieve that end in the only way possible to it, and success is possible in varying degrees; so it remains not indeed as the self-same individual but continues its existence in something *like* itself – not numerically one, but *one in* form.[72]

Moving next to the kinds of questions about ethics which interest us, and recognizing that in some respects the substantival/metaethical dichotomy is really quite forced in the Aristotelian context, again (notwithstanding 2500 years of intervening history) there is much to gladden and encourage the Darwinian. On the one hand, there is the absolutely central recognition of human sociality:

> It is evident that the state is a creation of nature, and that man is by nature a political animal. And he who by nature and not by mere accident is without a state, is either a bad man or above humanity.[73]

[70] Michael Ruse, *The Darwinian Paradigm.*

[71] I am not claiming that the Aristotelian and the Darwinian overlap entirely. There is a built-in teleology to the former's position quite lacking in the latter. Nevertheless, there may be a direct link between the positions *via* Cuvier. See Michael Ruse, *The Darwinian Revolution: Science Red in Tooth and Claw* (Chicago: University of Chicago Press, 1979).

[72] Aristotle, *On the Soul*, 415a, pp. 26–67, translated by Jonathan Lear, *Aristotle: The Desire to Understand* (Cambridge: Cambridge University Press, 1988), p. 100.

[73] Aristotle, *Politics* 1253a, 1–3.

Indeed, it is highly interesting how Aristotle seizes upon the importance of language, seeing that this action in some sense makes us humans even more social than the *hymenoptera*.

> Now, that man is more of a political animal than bees or any other gregarious animals is evident. Nature, as we often say, makes nothing in vain, and man is the only animal who has the gift of speech. And whereas mere voice is but an indication of pleasure or pain, and is therefore found in other animals (for their nature attains to the perception of pleasure and pain and the intimation of them to one another, and no further), the power of speech is intended to set forth the expedient and inexpedient, and therefore likewise the just and the unjust. And it is a characteristic of man that he alone has any sense of good and evil, of just and unjust, and the like, and the association of living beings who have this sense makes a family and a state.[74]

Although I am not myself very fond of notions of "highness" and "lowness" in evolution, this is precisely the position of E.O. Wilson who argues that (many popular prejudices to the contrary) humans represent the highest social forms.

> We should first note that social systems have originated repeatedly in one major group of organisms after another, achieving widely different degrees of specialization and complexity. Four groups occupy pinnacles high above the others: The colonial invertebrates, the social insects, the nonhuman mammals, and man.[75]

and

> Man has intensified [his] vertebrate traits while adding unique qualities of his own. In so doing he has achieved an extraordinary degree of cooperation with little or no sacrifice of personal survival and reproduction. Exactly how he alone has been able to cross to this fourth pinnacle, reversing the downward trend of social evolution in general, is the culminating mystery of all biology.[76]

Moreover, when one digs down into the actual ways that we are to function as a group, much that Aristotle says sounds a happy chord. Take his views on justice, which he divides into distributive and rectificatory.

> Of particular justice and that which is just in the corresponding sense, one kind is that which is manifested in distributions of honour or money or the other things that fall to be divided among those who have a share in the constitution (for in these it is possible for one man to have a share either unequal or equal to that of another), and another kind is that which plays a rectifying part in transactions.[77]

[74] *ibid.*, 1253, 7–18.
[75] Wilson, *Sociobiology*, p. 379.
[76] *ibid.*, p. 384.
[77] Aristotle, *Nicomachean Ethics*, 1130b, 30–31al.

At least, in outline this all sounds very much in tune with what has been discussed and concluded in earlier sections of this paper.

On the other hand, we have the question of foundations or justification. Here, again, there is much with which the Darwinian will sympathize. Unlike Plato, there is no Absolute Good – something which lies behind and justifies goodness and its desirability. For Aristotle action ultimately must be justified or understood in terms of their payoff for us. We do what we do, including our social doings, because we are thereby happier or fuller in some sense. Behavior, including moral behavior, is grounded at the most basic level in the ends of man. I confess I would feel uncomfortable in referring to Aristotle as a "moral skeptic" – apart from anything else, one does not find in him the sharp dichotomies (say, between "is" and "ought") that one finds in later thinkers – but his general approach to the foundations of morality is one with which the Darwinian feels comfortable.

What has been said thus far is satisfying and, from the perspective of the Darwinian, very important. One of the biggest criticisms against human sociobiology is that it is insensitive to cross-cultural differences. Supposedly, modern-day Darwinians seize on contingent aspects of their own culture and then generalize, arguing that such aspects are biologically embedded in all societies.[78] Looking at Aristotle and finding significant parallels does not prove the contrary, but it certainly shows that the cross-cultural objection is not devastating. (An especially important point, given that we in the West are a great deal closer culturally to Aristotle than we are to Stone-Age Yanomamo.)

But now let us go on to push at some of the differences. A non-exclusive, non-ordered list would certainly have to include some of the following. First, although Aristotle certainly allows (and even demands) a biological underpinning to human nature, in some respects he would give more weight to other causal factors than many modern biologists. On a nature/nurture spectrum, he would fall much closer to the nurture end of the scale than would (say) E.O. Wilson. This is especially so with respect to the excellences of character (like justice):

> Excellence, then, being of two kinds, intellectual and moral, intellectual excellence in the main owes both its birth and its growth to teaching (for which reason it requires experience and time), while moral excellence comes out as a result of habit, whence also its name is one that is formed by a slight variation from the word for 'habit'. From this it is also plain that none of the moral excellences arises in us by nature; for nothing that exists by nature can form a habit contrary to its nature.[79]

I am not sure how crucial a difference this is. Aristotle certainly recognizes some disposition or capacity for moral excellence – animals cannot be moral – so perhaps the gap with the Darwinian can be bridged. But there does seem to be a cultural bias to Aristotle which would be deplored by the Darwinian.

Second, one should be wary of thinking that even when there is overlap and

---

[78] A.L. Hughes, *Evolution and Human Kinship* (Oxford: University Press, 1988).
[79] Aristotle, *Nicomachean Ethics*, 1130b, 30–31a1.

agreement, Aristotle and the Darwinian would fill out the details in exactly the same way. Take justice. I have been suggesting that this would operate on a principle of needs, but Aristotle invokes other factors:

> awards should be according to merit; for all men agree that what is just in distribution must be according to merit in some sense, though they do not all specify the same sort of merit, but democrats identify it with the status of freeman, supporters of oligarchy with wealth (or with noble birth), and supporters of aristocracy with excellence.[80]

It is true that Aristotle is here not so much prescribing as giving a taxonomy. But this is not to conclude that he would necessarily see things our way.

Third, in discussing human relations, from a Darwinian perspective Aristotle seems not simply off-base but completely back-to-front. Take, for instance, father-son relationships. Aristotle certainly recognizes that parents will love their children before their children love them (and perhaps there will always be this inequality), not to mention that the bonds between kin will be closer than those between non-kin. But the obligations seem to go the other way.

> But there is another kind of friendship, viz. that which involves an inequality, e.g. that of father to son and in general of elder to younger, that of man to wife and in general that of ruler to subject. And these friendships differ also from each other; for it is not the same that exists between parents and children and between rulers and subjects, nor is even that of father to son the same as that of son to father, nor that of husband to wife the same as that of wife to husband. For the excellence and the function of each of these is different, and so are the reasons for which they love; the love and the friendship are therefore different also. Each party, then, neither gets the same from the other, nor ought to seek it; but when children render to parents what they ought to render to those who brought them into the world, and parents render what they should to their children, the friendship of such persons will be lasting and excellent.[81]

At the risk of sounding disrespectful towards my parents, I am not at all sure that this is the Darwinian perspective. Without implying that the relationship is entirely one-way, the biological obligations flow downwards. I have a greater obligation to my children than they have to me. (Although, of course, they have a greater obligation to their children than their children have to them.)

Fourth (and once again, I am not working in any special order), there is the notorious question of Aristotle and slavery. The human biologist is especially sensitive to matters here, since (apart from charges of sexism) he is frequently accused of being racist, right-wing, and so forth. The simple fact of the matter is that there is nothing in Darwinism suggesting that human slavery is a natural and

[80] ibid. 1158b, 12-23.
[81] ibid.

proper phenomenon. There may be slave ants. There are not necessarily slave humans. (Actually, the metaphor of slavery as applied to ants is not quite appropriate. The "slaves" are not of the same species as the "masters," whereas human slaves and masters are of the same species. One could more appropriately speak of ant domestication, instead of slavery.)

However, in fairness to Aristotle, we should not let matters just drop at this point. He argues for slavery on the grounds that some humans are incomplete or flawed, and are therefore properly (and best) fitted for slavery. Where he is a little insincere is in failing to point out that on his own philosophy, their defects might be humanly caused (that is, by the masters perpetuating the system and failing to give the slaves, or their children, full training). At one level, therefore, Aristotle's claims about the naturalness and inevitability of slavery fall down. At another level, however, he might still argue that (whatever the training) some people will be incomplete – or, at least, less capable than others. The Darwinian agrees to this. Indeed, the variability in all populations – including human populations – is one of the cornerstones of modern biology. Without in any sense arguing that the less gifted must be slaves or judged as having less than full worth in a group, both the Darwinian and the Aristotelian can agree that nature has made some people leaders and others hewers of wood and drawers of water. Nor is a recognition of this fact necessarily an unmitigated social evil.

Fifth, what about sexism? Aristotle makes feminist scholars see red almost as much as does sociobiology.[82] I suppose that all one can say is that he was a child of his time, as are we all. Certainly, there is no reason why an Aristotelian should not take a more modern-sounding stance. But Aristotle himself does not, and as I have suggested already, there is nothing inherent in modern biology suggesting that women must necessarily always assume traditional roles. So there is certainly a gap. With respect to many of the Aristotelian virtues, however, I see no reason why selection should not have promoted them as fully for women as it has done for men. Ultimately, whether or not you bring Aristotle and the Darwinian together at this point, the modern biologist does congratulate the Greek biologist on recognizing that the differences between the sexes should not be trivialized or dismissed as unimportant accidents of our culture.[83] People can be morally equal, without being biologically or socially identical.

Enough of listing points of difference. The impression I have given (or at least tried to give) is that while there are indeed many places where Darwinian and Aristotelian divide, the differences are often not as profound as one might initially think. Perhaps I underestimate the magnitude of the problems, but often they do not strike me as insuperable. Is this, then, the end of the matter? Appreciating that Aristotle was much farther from our culture than was Hume, can we nevertheless now place the Darwinian in a tradition which goes back to the Greeks?

The temptation is great, especially since there are many other things in the Aristotelian corpus one would like to claim for one's own: for instance, Aristotle's

[82] Maryanne Cline Horowitz, "Aristotle and Woman," *Journal of the History of Biology*, vol. 9, no. 2 (Fall 1976), pp. 183–213.

[83] D. Symons, *The Evolution of Human Sexuality* (Oxford: Oxford University Press, 1979).

many sensitive comments on freedom and responsibility. In the end, though, I fear that the Aristotelian and the Darwinian remain apart – not necessarily in conflict, but on differently headed tracks. Although Aristotle indeed recognizes human-kind's biological nature, for him the essence of our being is that we are rational. We are not rational merely to the end of reproduction – and our excellences are not there indirectly to serve our reproduction, even though they may just do that. Our rationality is our end, and that which gives the core meaning to human happiness – to human flourishing.

The difference is crucial. As Williams says:

> The important point is that evolutionary biology is not at all directly concerned with the well-being of the individual, but with fitness, which is the likelihood of that individual's leaving offspring.[84]

And as Lear agrees:

> Within the soul of Aristotle's virtuous man there are desires which motivate the agent to embark on a reflection which seeks to legitimate those very desires. Let us call such desires *legitimating*. A person does not stand in relation to his legitimating desires as a mere conduit for their satisfaction: in commending themselves to the person, they are not merely using him as a means to their selfish ends.[85]

What is to be done? The tough-minded biologist brushes Aristotle's world of reason aside as an epiphenomenal delusion of our genes. I hope that my discomfort with this tack is not simply unenlightened self-interest, in that as one who has chosen the vocation of professional philosophy I am aspiring to precisely that which Aristotle identifies as the highest role for humans. The tough-minded philosopher brushes Darwin aside, as too weak to say anything really pertinent about ethics. Williams again:

> The most that sociobiology might do for ethics lies in a different direction, inasmuch as it might be able to suggest that certain institutions or patterns of behavior are not realistic options for human societies. That would be an important achievement, but first sociobiology will have to be able to read the historical record of human culture much better than it does now.[86]

I trust by now that we can be a little more optimistic than that.

My own tentative suggestion towards a meeting of biology and philosophy is that we give biology all that it can do – we *have* to do that – and to recognize that as biology progresses, it may be able to do a great deal more. But we have to recognize that biology has created this different, logically separate world: the world of

---

[84] Bernard Williams, *Ethics and the Limits of Philosophy*, p. 44.
[85] Lear, *Aristotle: The Desire to Understand*, p. 189.
[86] Williams, *Ethics and the Limits of Philosophy*, p. 44.

intentions and oughts and rights and wrongs. And there may be a place for the philosophy of Aristotle here. Consider: Although the bat and ball of the player are made from molecules, you cannot deduce the world of baseball from the molecules. Likewise, you cannot deduce the world of morality of human flourishing, from the genes. (Yet, just as the molecules make and constrain baseball, so the genes do the same for morality.)

Now if we try the tack I am taking – arguing that the genes have given rise to a new world of meaning, where Aristotle might have relevance – this does not itself legitimize Aristotle and his views about harmony and the good life and rationality. Indeed, I am not even sure that today we would want to see him as legitimate. The ideal for an Athenian gentleman may not be a human universal. (The full-time musician strikes me as having a major claim on the good life.) But, my suggestion does leave us open to explore our own selves in the light of what Aristotle says. We can see if we find responsive chords in our own mental phenomenology, our own experience as moral beings. If we do, then biology is sufficiently open to allow us to incorporate them into our thinking.

As a specific example of what I have in mind (in making this last point) are some of the comments that, in line with his views about balance and harmony, Aristotle makes about self-love. He believes that only the person with a proper self-regard is functioning properly, where a major implication is that only such a person is able truly to do good to others and to operate socially. Aristotle can help us to bring this point into full focus, and help us to disregard some of the distorting effects of Christianity (not to mention Kant, who sometimes gets close to suggesting that if you want to do an action, other than from the stern call of duty, it cannot be a good one). In other words, Aristotle can (and, I would say, does) help us to enrich our moral awareness. Nothing in biology prevents this.

Whether something like this will be enough – or too much – for Aristotelian or Darwinian, I do not know. I am certainly not proposing sole ecumenical blurring of difference. Rather I hope I have shown a way for alternative approaches to interact and grow together.

V. CONCLUSION

Who dare presume to write in one paper on both the evolutionary biology of humans and the history of Western moral philosophy? I cannot pretend that I have done it particularly well, but I hope I have persuaded the reader that the effort is worthwhile. I think biology has something to tell moral philosophy. I am sure the moral philosopher has something to tell the biologist. One of my favourite metaphors is of science and philosophy as two hands reaching across a divide, trying to grasp.[87] I see a mutual job to be done, with feedback from science to philosophy and vice versa. Specifically in the case we are considering now, as our moral understanding deepens and as we become more self-reflective about this understanding, then this stimulates the biologist to explain more. Conversely, our biology stimulates our moral understanding, as I hope much in this discussion demonstrates.

In conclusion, therefore, let me use this point to recap our achievements. The Darwinian evolutionary ethicist argues that morality (literal altruism) is put in

[87] Ruse, *Taking Darwin Seriously*.

place by our genes to make us cooperators (biological altruists). There is no objective foundation to substantive ethics, for it is no more (and no less) than an adaptation of humankind to aid survival and reproduction. However, our biology leads us to "objectify" ethics, making us think that it does have a reality "out there," beyond human subjectivity. If we did not think this, we would start cheating, morality would collapse, and cooperation would be at an end.

Rightly, the critic might complain that the notion of morality on which I have relied in this discussion – what I have labelled 'literal altruism' – is a rather nebulous, ill-defined, soft concept. It seems to go beyond mere good feeling, demanding a sense of obligation – something which makes us break through our usual selfish nature – but as simply postulated says little more. Moreover, the critic might complain that the no-less-crucial notion of 'objectification' could (and should) bear a more critical examination.[88] I suggest that our trip through the ideas of the great moral philosophers helps on both of these scores.

First, Kant (and perhaps Rawls to an extent) strongly reminds us of the *social* nature of morality. It centers on people's working together and on society's failing or breaking down if these people cheat. You may or may not be able to get everything you want out of life, but how others pursue their ends rates up there with how you achieve your ends. Fairness is an important factor in human relationships. I take it that the Darwinian appreciates this clarification and indeed can handle it readily. Phylogeny stands behind Kantian "contradictions"; the natural selection of the genes is biology's answer to the hypothetical Social Contract or "original position."

One point where Kantianism does leave us without satisfactory answers is with respect to obligations to strangers, especially those from societies beyond ours.[89] The Darwinian suspects strongly that morality has to be differential, with obligations fanning out from close kin outwards and downwards. Here David Hume offers support, for he too argues that moral sentiments track blood relationships.[90] But Hume does more than merely confirm prejudice, enabling the evolutionist to seize on happy coincidences. Like the Darwinian, he approaches morality from a naturalistic perspective, trying as it were to provide a kind of moral psychology. Furthermore, although I am not convinced that Hume deals fully adequately with morality towards strangers, he does impress upon the evolutionist the need to see that morality does and must extend beyond the home. A balance must be struck.[91]

Hume also helps the evolutionist with the metaethical questions about "objectification." The critic is right: something more does need be said about this process than just a bare assertion about its existence. Hume invites us to see that the

[88] John Mackie, "Law of the Jungle," is the best discussion thus far in 'literal altruism' (a term he does not use), and Mackie, *Hume's Moral Theory* (London: Routledge and Kegan Paul, 1979), is the best discussion on "objectification" (a term he does use).

[89] Rawls admits explicitly that he speaks of a closed "well-ordered" society, leaving "questions of justice between societies," admitting that "to what extent the conception of justice for the basic structure will have to be revised in the process, cannot be foreseen in advance." John Rawls, "Kantian Constructivism in Moral Theory," *Journal of Philosophy*, vol. 77 (1980), pp. 515–72.

[90] Hume, *Treatise*, pp. 483–84.

[91] Remember: "we blame a person, who either centers all his affections in his family, or is so regardless of them, as, in any opposition of interest, to give the preference to a stranger, or mere chance acquaintance." Hume, *Treatise*, p. 489.

activity might not be confined exclusively to morality, but might be part of a more general human propensity which extends to our awareness of physical properties, such as colors and the like (and, no doubt given Hume's analysis, to causation also).[92] In fact, this stimulating suggestion has been anticipated by the sociobiologist, especially by Wilson. He argues that our thinking is structured by what he terms 'epigenetic rules', that through these we project ideas onto reality, and that these rules cover both thought about the nature of objects (including colors) and thought about relationships (including morality).[93]

Although I have not touched on this point in this paper, I suspect that Hume's sceptical views about religion might be insightful here also.[94] On the one hand, to the Humean, there is not much objective referent to religion – at least, there is a lot less than we generally think there is. Yet people do believe that claims made in the name of religion have objective validity. On the other hand – a point often skimmed over lightly by today's secular moral philosophers, but known to Hume – moral thought and religious thought are very often taken to be one and the same, or at least closely connected. Both of these factors suggest that a closer look at the way religion takes hold of people might throw light on the way we think about morality.

Again, I might note that biologists have begun to explore these and related questions. There is much interest in the possible adaptive reasons for religious belief, and indeed in the different reasons which might be given for different beliefs.[95] There is much work to be done, but a start has been made. As the reader will long have appreciated, the naturalistic inquiry into the nature of morality will draw on more than just philosophers and biologists. There will be a place for (among others) psychologists, anthropologists and – right here – students of religion.

Finally, recapping the significance of our great moral philosophers, what of Aristotle? How does he help the biological inquiry? I have already suggested that one important function he serves is to lift us beyond the concerns and assumptions of our own immediate culture. Although some, Wilson in particular, argue that there may already be biological differences between the Ancient Greeks and today's (Western) humans,[96] clearly any such differences are not going to be that great. Hence, if Aristotle's ethics were totally at odds with our biological expectations, one would have a serious counter to claims about the ultimate Darwinian base for morality. However, at a general level there is quite enough in Aristotle that the biologist can feel encouraged.

I would add – a point not stressed in the main discussion – that the fact that Aristotle's notion of the good life only partly overlaps with what (say) the Kantian would consider the good life also encourages the sociobiologist. We do today value

[92] For full discussion of this point, see Ruse, *Taking Darwin Seriously*, esp. chs. 5 and 6.

[93] See Lumsden and Wilson, *Genes, Mind, and Culture*.

[94] Most expressly as found in his *Dialogues Concerning Natural Religion*, reprinted in ed. R. Wollheim, *Hume on Religion* (London: Collins, 1963).

[95] Vernon Reynold and R.E.S. Tanner, *The Biology of Religion* (London: Longman, 1983); Edward O. Wilson, *On Human Nature* (Cambridge: Harvard University Press, 1978).

[96] Lumsden and Wilson, *Genes, Mind and Culture*.

looks and friendship and children and the like,[97] even if, in this Christianized age, we would not include them under the heading of 'virtue'. Aristotle's different taxonomy suggests that what we consider "morality" should not necessarily be put in a category absolutely separate from everything else. It is rather one of a number of things of the same logical type which go into the making of a full human being. This is very much the stance of the naturalist in morality, under which heading I locate the evolutionary ethicist. Helping to keep matters in perspective, the places where Aristotle differs from Darwin suggest that morality is not and cannot be exclusively a function of the genes. Culture, in some sense, must play a causal role. Of course, no one would deny this. The crucial question is just how great a role culture must play.[98] For the moment, I suspect that all one can say is that our encounter with Aristotle points to the need for continued cross-cultural study to locate the common elements in morality and hence the possible limits to the influence of biology. I should say that this is a matter of which biologists are fully aware. There is intense interest in questions like these, coupled with much ongoing empirical study.[99]

Whether, having said all of this, Aristotle still demands more, something which biology can never supply, is a question which I have left – and will continue to leave – essentially unanswered. Suppose one sorts out such issues as slavery and sexism, putting them down to the genes or to culture, deciding that there are or are not genuine differences between the Darwinian and the Aristotelian, and so forth. What then of the world of well-being, of reason, of human flourishing that today's philosophical scholars of Aristotle think have no connection with our animal nature? I have suggested that here there may be no contradiction with biology, but that it might be that human experience and awareness goes beyond biology – depending on it but not reducible to it.[100]

All I can do is repeat that I do not know if this will prove true. But, as a final point, let me say that I do not think that lacuna a devastating weakness in my position. It is the kind of conclusion that one expects from an approach such as mine. If one endorses a naturalistic perspective, then in philosophy as in science, one's inquiry will be open-ended – dependent always on the next empirical investigation. Thus, I can only repeat the credo of the evolutionary ethicist. As we deepen our understanding of biological altruism, and of the implications that it has for altruism in the moral realm, so then will we become more knowing of its limitations – as well as of its very considerable strengths.

Philosophy and Zoology, University of Guelph

[97] Monique Borgerhoff Mulder, "Kipsigis Bridewealth Payments," in L.L. Betzig, M. Borgerhoff Mulder, and P.W. Turke (eds.) *Human Reproductive Behavior: A Darwinian Perspective* (Cambridge: Cambridge University Press, 1988), pp. 65–82.

[98] R. Boyd and P. Richerson, *Culture and the Evolutionary Process* (Chicago: University of Chicago Press, 1985); L. Cavalli-Sforza and M. Feldman, *Cultural Transmission: A Quantitative Approach* (Princeton: Princeton University Press, 1981); Lumsden and Wilson, *Genes, Mind & Culture*.

[99] See, for instance, Laura Betzig, Monique Borgerhoff Mulder, and P.W. Turke (eds.), *Human Reproductive Behavior: A Darwinian Perspective*.

[100] Perhaps the notion of 'supervenience' would help here. In a somewhat different context, see Alexander Rosenberg, *The Structure of Biological Science* (Cambridge: Cambridge University Press, 1985).

THE BIOLOGICAL JUSTIFICATION OF ETHICS: A BEST-CASE SCENARIO

By Alexander Rosenberg

Social and behavioral scientists – that is, students of human nature – nowadays hardly ever use the term 'human nature'. This reticence reflects both a becoming modesty about the aims of their disciplines and a healthy skepticism about whether there is any one thing really worthy of the label 'human nature'.

For some feature of humankind to be identified as accounting for our 'nature', it would have to reflect some property both distinctive of our species and systematically influential enough to explain some very important aspect of our behavior. Compare: molecular structure gives the essence or the nature of water just because it explains most of its salient properties. Few students of the human sciences currently hold that there is just one or a small number of such features that can explain our actions and/or our institutions. And even among those who do, there is reluctance to label their theories as claims about 'human nature'.

Among anthropologists and sociologists, the label seems too universal and indiscriminant to be useful. The idea that there is a single underlying character that might explain similarities threatens the differences among people and cultures that these social scientists seek to uncover. Even economists, who have explicitly attempted to parlay rational choice theory into an account of all human behavior, do not claim that the maximization of transitive preferences is 'human nature'.

I think part of the reason that social scientists are reluctant to use 'human nature' is that the term has traditionally labeled a theory with normative implications as well as descriptive ones. Any one who propounds a theory of human nature seems committed to drawing conclusions from what the theory says *is* the case to what *ought* to be the case. But this is just what twentieth-century social scientists are reluctant to do. Once the lessons of David Hume and G.E. Moore were well and truly learned among social scientists, they surrendered the project (associated with the 'moral sciences' since Hobbes) of deriving 'ought' from 'is'.[1]

The few scientists who have employed the term 'human nature' do draw evaluative conclusions from their empirical theories. The best recent examples of such writers are sociobiologists like E.O. Wilson, eager to extend the writ of evolutionary biology to include both the empirical study of humans and the foundations of their moral philosophy.[2]

It is relatively easy to offer a review and philosophical critique of the excesses that are bound to creep into evolutionary biologists' attempts to transcend the

---

[1] David Hume, *A Treatise of Human Nature*, ed. L.A. Selby-Bigge (Oxford: Clarendon Press, 1888), bk. II; G.E. Moore, *Principia Ethica* (Routlege and Kegan Paul, 1907).

[2] E.O. Wilson, *On Human Nature* (Cambridge: Harvard University Press, 1978).

traditional limits of their discipline. But more useful than still another catalog of sociobiological foibles would be a sympathetic examination of the best we might hope for from the application of evolutionary biology to traditional questions about moral philosophy. Of all the intellectual fashions of the late twentieth century, it has the best claim to provide an account of human nature in the scientist's sense of 'nature', for it is undeniable that every aspect of humanity has been subjected to natural selection over blind variation literally since time immemorial. If any one thing has shaped us it is evolution, and if any piece of science is going to shed light on ethical issues, sociobiology – the application of Darwinian theory to human affairs – will. Therefore, my aim will be to identify the minimal conditions under which evolutionary biology *might* be able to tell us something about traditional issues in moral philosophy. If the rather strong assumptions evolutionary biology requires to shed light on these issues fail to obtain, then – as our best guess about human nature – biology will have no bearing on moral philosophy. This, in fact, is my strong suspicion. Nevertheless, I herewith attempt to put together the best-case scenario for the ethical significance of evolutionary biology.

I. THE POSSIBLE PROJECTS

There are several sorts of insights evolutionary biology might be supposed to offer about human nature and its relation to morality. One among them is uncontroversial and beyond the scope of moral philosophy. Like any scientific theory, evolutionary biology may well provide factual information that, together with independent normative principles, helps us make ethical decisions. It may uncover hitherto unnoticed means we can employ in meeting ethically established ends. It may even identify subsidiary goals that we need to meet in order to attain other intrinsic goals. For example, there are plain facts (about, for example, ecology, genetic diversity, and the importance to us of preserving threatened species) which biology reveals and which can be combined with moral standards into hypothetical imperatives governing human action.

More controversially, evolutionary biology may reveal constraints and limitations on human behavior that our ethical prescriptions will have to take account of. If 'ought' implies 'can', the contrapositive will be valid too: 'can't' should imply 'need not'. Like other scientific theories, evolutionary biology may help fill in the list of what we (nomologically) cannot do. However, for a theory of human nature to have ramifications for moral philosophy itself, it will have to do more than any of these things.

The most impressive accomplishment for a theory of human nature would be the derivation of particular moral principles, like the categorical imperative or the principle of utility, from biological facts about human beings. Slightly less impressive would be to derive from such facts our status as moral *agents* and *subjects*, or to establish on the strength of our biology the *intrinsic value* of human life. A derivation of agency or intrinsic value is equivalent to deriving the generic conclusion that there is some normative principle or other governing our actions. Such a derivation would be less impressive because it would leave open the question of which moral principles about agents or objects of intrinsic value were the right ones. Still less impressive but significant in its own right would be the derivation of some important component or condition or instance of morally praiseworthy conduct – like cooperation, altruism, or other-regarding behavior – as generally obligatory. To be significantly interesting the derivation need not be deductive, but it cannot be question-begging: it cannot begin from assumptions with substantial normative content. Otherwise, it will be open to the charge that these assumptions are doing all the real work, and that the biological theory makes no distinctive contribution to the derivation.

The possibility of this project, of deriving agency and/or value (or, equivalently, deriving the existence of some moral principle or other), rests on two preconditions. The first is that we can derive 'ought' from 'is': that there is some purely factual, empirical, contingent, strictly biological property of organisms, which could underwrite, explain, or justify their status as agents or loci of intrinsic value. The second is that this property is *common and peculiar* to *all Homo sapiens*, so that it will count as constituting our nature.

That the first of these two preconditions for deriving morality from human nature cannot be realized seems to me to be at least as widely held a view as any other claim in moral philosophy or metaethics. Accordingly, I will not offer new arguments to supplement the observations of Hume and Moore. I recognize, however, that the more sophisticated sociobiologists are perfectly aware of these strictures on moral justification. Among sociobiologists, those who nevertheless go on to attempt to derive some normative claims from biological findings do Moore and Hume the courtesy of noting and rejecting their arguments.[3]

But even if we grant the sociobiologist's claim that the derivation of 'ought' from 'is' has not yet been totally excluded, there remains a second precondition required by the project of deriving morality from human nature. And the failure of this condition is something on which all evolutionary biologists should be in agreement.

Humans are supposed to be moral agents. This is what distinguishes us from moral subjects, like animals, and from morally neutral objects. Now, for some biological property of human beings to ground our status as the unique set of moral agents (in our biosphere at least), that property will have to be as widely distributed among human beings as the moral property it grounds, and it will have to be peculiar to humans as well. For if it is not restricted to humans, there will be other subjects with equal claim to the standing of moral agents. The trouble is that if modern evolutionary biology teaches anything, it shows that there are no such properties common and peculiar to each member of a species. If there were, taxonomy would be a much easier subject. And since there are none, what evolutionary biology in fact shows is that there is no such thing as *the* unique human nature, any more than there is beaver nature or dodo-bird nature or E. coli nature.

Population genetics and molecular biology have shown that, up and down the entire range of living things, there are no interesting *essential* properties – no properties which will explain a range of behavior in the way that, say, molecular structure explains most of what a chemical compound does. It is not that modern

---

[3] *ibid.*, ch. 1; R. Alexander, *Darwinism and Human Affairs* (Seattle: University of Washington Press, 1979).

biology has yet to find such essential properties, which give the nature of a species. Rather, evolutionary and genetic theory *requires* that biological species have no such common and peculiar essential properties.

Gradual evolution by natural selection requires vast amounts of *variation* within and between species. This variation is provided by mutation, genetic drift, immigration, emigration, and most of all by genetic recombination in the sexual reproduction of offspring. The result is that there are no *essential* (suites of) phenotypes. Neither the typical nor average nor mean nor median values of the heritable phenotypes which face selection are their *natural, essential* values. They do not constitute the normal traits of members of a species, from which differences and divergences might count as deviations, disturbances, defects, or abnormalities. Of course there are biological properties common to every member of a species. For example, all *Homo sapiens* engage in respiration. But then so does every other organism we know about. Similarly, there are some biologically-based properties peculiar to individual humans – self-consciousness, speech, a certain level of intelligence, opposable thumbs, absence of body fur, etc. But these properties are plainly not distributed universally among humans, nor would the lack of any one of them be enough to deprive someone of membership in our moral community who was otherwise endowed with it. There is no human nature in the sense in which 'natures' are identifed in modern science.

It might well be supposed that there is some complex combination of properties – say, self-consciousness *cum* opposable thumbs *cum* a disjunction of blood-types – that is sufficient for moral agency. But the project of grounding agency in (and only in) human nature requires that this complex combination of properties be necessary for agency as well as sufficient for it, and that it be universal among *Homo sapiens*. For consider, how could a property *restricted* in its instantiation only to some members of a class provide the basis for a property *common* to all members of the class: how can we derive 'All As are Cs' from 'Some As are Bs' and 'All Bs are Cs'? Doubtless, a philosopher can solve this problem by cooking up some gruesome gerrymandered relational property. For example, one could define property C as the property of being a member of a class some of whose members have property B. Then the derivation is trivial. But, clearly, being a moral agent is not a relational property – not at any rate, if it derives solely from the nature of the individual human. And this makes the logical problem a grave one for those who seek to derive agency from human nature.

Deriving a particular moral principle, or even the generic status of moral agency, from human nature alone – at least as evolutionary biology understands it – is not a feasible project, even if we could derive 'ought' from 'is'.

A third potential project for the biological account of human nature is that of *explanation*: telling a plausible story about how a particular moral principle or 'morality' in general, or some important precondition or component of it, emerged in the evolution of *Homo sapiens*.

The qualification "plausible" cannot be emphasized too strongly here. The most we can expect of any evolutionary account of chronology is plausibility: that the narrative will be consistent with evolutionary theory and with such slim data as may be available. The reason is that the problem of explaining the emergence of morality is similar to (but even more difficult than) that faced by, say, the task of explaining the disappearance of the dinosaur. There is a saying in paleontology: "The fossil record shows at most that evolution occurred elsewhere." In the case of explaining the evolution of behavior, there are no bones, no "hard parts" left to help us choose among competing explanations. The most we can hope for is plausibility.

This raises the question of how much a merely plausible story is worth, what it is good for, and why we should want it for more than its entertainment value. The question is particularly pressing in moral philosophy and metaethics. For it is not clear that even a well-confirmed explanation for the emergence of aspects of morality from human nature has any relevance to the concerns of philosophers. It would be a genetic fallacy to infer that a particular normative conclusion was right, justified, or well grounded – or, for that matter, that it was wrong, unjustified, or groundless – from a purely causal account of its origins.

If, however, we could parlay the explanation for the emergence of aspects of morality from human nature into an argument about why it is rational to be moral, then for all its evidential weakness, the causal story would turn out to have some interest. It would address a traditional question in moral philosophy: why should I be moral? There may be some reason to think such a strategy will work. For natural selection is an optimizing force for individuals,[4] and so is self-interest. Explanations in evolutionary biology proceed by rationalizing an innovation as advantageous for an organism's survival. Egoistic justification does something quite similar. Like evolutionary explanation, it rationalizes actions as means to ends.

This, I think, is the only interesting project in moral philosophy or metaethics for a biological approach to human nature. In what follows, I sketch the outlines of such a project. I should note two things about my sketch. First, little that follows is original. Mostly, I have plucked insights from a bubbling cauldron of sociobiological and evolutionary theorizing. Second, I am by no means optimistic that this project of rationally justifying morality can succeed, even in part. My aim is to identify the strictures it will have to satisfy if it stands a chance of succeeding.

II. NATURAL SELECTION, BLIND VARIATION, FITNESS MAXIMIZATION

If the theory of natural selection is right, then the overriding fact about us is that we are all approximate fitness-maximizers. Of course, this is not a special feature of people. Indeed, it is the most widely distributed property of biological interest that there is. Every organism in every reproducing species is an approximate fitness-maximizer, for natural selection selects for fitness-maximization *uber haupt*. All the phenotypes that have been selected for in the course of evolution have this in common. And if the theory is correct, then over time, given constant environments, successive generations of organisms are better approximations to fitness-maximization than their predecessors. This is what adaptation consists in.

What exactly is fitness-maximization? This is a vexed question in the philosophy of biology. For present purposes it will suffice to adopt the following

---

[4] As is explained below, natural selection cannot operate to optimize the properties of groups, as opposed to individuals. See section II.

definitions: x is fitter than y if, over the long run, x leaves more fertile offspring than y. Thus, an organism maximizes its fitness if it leaves the largest number of fertile offspring it can over the long run. It will be convenient if we define 'offspring' in a special way: an offspring will count as one complete set of an organism's genes. Therefore, the result of asexual reproduction is one offspring, but the result of sexual reproduction is half an offspring, since each child bears only one-half the genes of each of its parents. Note that, by this means of reckoning offspring, if a childless woman's brother has one child, the woman has a quarter of an offspring. Thus five fertile nieces and nephews make for greater fitness than one child: $5/4 > 1$. This means that nature, in its relentless search for fitness-maximizing organisms, sometimes selects for fewer children and more offspring.

Nature selection has made us *approximate* fitness-maximizers, not perfect ones. There are several reasons for this. To begin with, nature selects for fitness-maximization only indirectly, by seeking adaptive phenotypes: among giraffes it selects for long necks, among cheetahs for great foot speed, among chameleons for mimicry, and among eagles for eyesight. But each of these is selected because it makes for the survival and the well-being of the organisms endowed with it. And survival, along with well-being, are in turn necessary conditions for reproductive success. Mere survival is not enough; an organism must be healthy enough to reproduce and ensure the survival of its offspring. But the point is that except where selection operates directly on the organs of reproduction, birth, feeding, and protection, every other piece of an organism's equipment is selected for direct effect on survival and well-being, and through them for indirect effects on fitness. This means that much of what nature selects may not look like it bears on reproduction and fitness.

In its culling of these properties that bear indirectly on fitness, natural selection puts a premium on quick and dirty solutions to the problem of fitness-maximization. It prefers these cheap, imperfect solutions to slow but sweet ones that may do the job better but take a long time to emerge. Nature recognizes Keynes's maxim that in the long run we are all dead, and it acts on this maxim before it's too late. Thus, all organisms are at best approximate, jury-rigged, only intermittent fitness-maximizers. As genetic recombination and the other sources of phenotypic novelty turn up variations, the best among them out-reproduce the others. But the best may not be very good on any absolute scale. It need only be good enough to survive and outlive the other variants among which it emerges.

Selection operates on what variation provides. It has no power to call forth solutions to problems of adaptation, only to pick and choose among those that recombination and mutation may offer. Here is a nice example (with thanks to Daniel Dennett). Fish need to be able to recognize predators. But fish do not have very sophisticated predator recognition capacities; they have not evolved the sort of cognitive capacities for discriminating other fish, let alone telling friend from foe. Yet in the presence of predators they invariably startle, turn, and flee. Of course they also respond this way to all fish, not just the predatory ones. Indeed, present a fish with any bilaterally symmetrical stimulus and it will emit this flight response. The reason is that selection has resulted in the emergence of a relatively simple solution to the predator detection problem: bilateral symmetry detection. This is not a very discriminating capacity, but at least it is within the cognitive powers of a fish, and it works well enough at predator detecting. Its defects are obvious – the fish wastes energy fleeing non-predators. But in its environment the cost of this imperfection is low enough, and without it fish would not have lasted long enough to give rise to those species cognitively powerful enough to do the job of predator recognition any better.

There is a related reason why natural selection leads to the evolution only of approximate fitness-maximizers. Environments change, and organisms must survive in an environment that manifests wide extremes, and they must survive when one environment is displaced by another environment. Such conditions put a premium on being a jack of many trades instead of a master of one. An environment of great uniformity lasting over epochs of geological length provides selection with the opportunity to winnow successive variations to remarkable degrees of perfection. Consider the human eye, which is the result of a series of adaptations to a solar spectrum that has remained constant for almost the whole of evolutionary history. Such fine-tuning, however, gives hostages to fortune. For when an environment changes, there is too little variation in the received phenotype for selection to operate on. A phenotype that maximizes fitness perfectly in one environment is so closely adapted to it that it may not retain enough variation to survive in any other environment.

Since we are the products of selection over changing environments, we are only approximate fitness-maximizers. Nature has produced us by selecting from what was immediately available for shaping to insure short-term survival. Doubtless, in its impatience nature has nipped in the bud potential improvements in our own species and in its predecessors. For the moment the only moral of this part of the story, for moral philosophy, is this: merely showing that altruism or other well-established patterns of morally praiseworthy action are strictly incompatible with monomaniacal, perfect, complete fitness-maximization is a poor argument for the claim that human behavior has become exempt from evolutionary selection. For we are not perfect fitness-maximizers. Natural selection has shaped us for only *approximate* fitness-maximization in the environments in which *Homo sapiens* has evolved. Approximate fitness maximization leaves a great deal of room for non-adaptive altruism and other selfless actions.

III. PARAMETERS, STRATEGIES, AND THE MAXIMIZATION OF FITNESS

Now, among approximate fitness-maximizers, what sort of social behavior should evolve? This is a problem that arises with the advent of selection for living in family groups, which of course obtained long before *Homo sapiens* emerged. Until this point fitness maximization is, in the game theorist's terms, 'parametric', not 'strategic'. Which behavior is maximizing depends only on the environment, which provides parameters fixed *independently* of which behavior the organism is going to emit. But when organisms interact, which behavior one emits may be a function of what the other is going to do. So which behavior is fitness-maximizing will depend on how other organisms behave. This means that the optimal behavior is one that reflects a *strategy*, which takes account of the prospective behavior of other organisms. When social interaction emerges, fitness-maximization becomes a strategic problem.

This does not mean that, once groups emerge, organisms begin to calculate and select strategies based on recognition of the strategies of other organisms. It means something much less implausible. It means that those behaviors will emerge as fitter which, as a matter of fact, are coordinated with one another in the way they would have been, had they been the result of reflection and deliberation. This is because there is enough time for fitness differences between the rarer but *fortuitously* coordinated behavioral phenotypes and more common uncoordinated ones to pile up and select the coordinated ones.

Coordinated behaviors are sometimes cooperative ones; they are other-regarding, involving putting oneself at the mercy (or, at least, at the advantage) of another. Thus, they constitute a significant component of morality. The emergence of coordinated behaviors makes one sort of scenario for the emergence of morality tempting. This is the *group selection* scenario, according to which nature selected societies and groups because their institutions, including their moral rules, are more adaptive for the group as a whole. On this model, selection proceeds at the level of the individual (for individual fitness-maximization) and at the level of the group (for group survival and growth). The idea that evolution might lead to the emergence of morality by selecting for groups that manifest moral rules and against groups that retain a state of nature is, on the face of it, more attractive than trying to find a story of how morality might have emerged at the level of the individual. For the fitness-maximizing individual is concerned only with maximizing its offspring; it is ready to sacrifice others to this end. The fact that there are so many immoral and amoral people around makes implausible the notion that morality emerged among *Homo sapiens* the way opposable thumbs did – as an individual response to the selection of individual organisms. But the emergence of morality as a group institution is at least compatible with the observed degree of moral imperfection among individuals. Selection at the level of the group does not require uniformity among the individuals who compose it; no championship team has ever had the best players in the league at every (or even any) position (cf. New York Mets, 1969).

So, one way to reconcile other-regarding cooperative behavior with monomaniacal evolutionary egoism is to locate selection for cooperative institutions at the level of the group and selection for individual fitness-maximization at the level of the individual. If the forces selecting for the adaptation of groups are independent of those selecting for the adaptation of individuals, then those groups within which cooperation, promise-keeping, property, fidelity, etc., emerged, for whatever reason, might do better, last longer, or have larger, healthier populations than those groups which lacked such virtuous institutions. Thus, morality is explained as an evolved holistic social constraint on individual selfishness.

This is a nice idea, but one which evolutionary biology must exclude. For no matter how much better off a society with ethical institutions might be than one without them, such a society is seriously unstable, and in the evolutionary long haul must fall victim to its own niceness. The reason is that selection at the level of the group and the level of the individual are never independent enough to allow for the long-term persistence of a moral majority and an immoral minority. In fact, they aren't independent at all. The latter will eventually swamp the former.

Consider a society of perfectly cooperative altruistic organisms, genetically programmed never to lie, cheat, steal, rape, or kill, but in which provisions for detection and elimination of organisms who do not behave in this manner are highly imperfect (as in our own society). Since everyone is perfectly cooperative, the society needs no such provision. Now suppose that a genetically programmed scoundrel emerges within this society (never mind how – it might be through mutation, recombination, immigration, etc.). By lying, cheating, stealing, raping, and otherwise free-riding whenever possible (recall the detection and enforcement mechanisms are imperfect), the scoundrel does far better than anyone else, both in terms of well-being, and in terms of eventual fitness-maximization. He leaves more offspring than anyone else. If his anti-social proclivities are hereditary, then in the long run his offspring will come to predominate in the society. Eventually, 100 percent of its membership will be composed of scoundrels and its character as a cooperative group will long since have disappeared.

Evolutionary game theorists have provided a useful jargon to describe this scenario: a group with a morally desirable other-regarding strategy is not "evolutionarily stable": left alone, it will persist, but it can be "invaded" even by a small number of egoists – who will eventually overwhelm it and convert the society into one bereft of other-regarding patterns of interaction. By contrast, a society composed wholly of fitness-maximizing egoists is an "evolutionarily stable" one: a group of such egoists cannot be successfully invaded by some other, potentially nicer pattern of behavior. Its members will all, one after another, play the nice guys for suckers and outbreed and ultimately extinguish them.

The trouble, then, with group-selectionist explanations of the emergence of morality is that a group of other-regarders might do better than a group of selfish egoists, but it is vulnerable to invasion by one such egoist, an invasion which evolutionary theory tells us must always eventually occur – since nature is always culling for improvements in individual fitness-maximization. Whether from within or without, scoundrels will eventually emerge to put an end to other-regarding groups by converting them into societies of fitness maximizers.

If morality is to emerge from the nature of organisms as approximate fitness-maximizers, it will have to happen at the level of individual selection. And it will have to be selection for optimizing behavior in the context of "strategic" interaction, where the optimum behavior of each organism depends on the behavior of other organisms. The trouble is that game theorists have increasingly come to suspect that there is no optimal strategy under these circumstances. If this is right, then there is none for evolution to choose, and no way for moral institutions to evolve from the strategic interactions of fitness maximizers.

The problem of an optimal strategy for nature to select is easily illustrated in the children's game of Rock, Paper and Scissors. In this game, kids pick one of the three choices. Rock breaks scissors and so beats it, scissors cut paper and so beat it, but paper covers rock and so beats it. Whether your choice wins depends on what the other kid picked, and no choice is better than any other. In an evolutionary situation like this, no strategy ever comes to predominate. Of course, if you know what your competitor will pick, you can always win. But what the other kid picks is going to depend on what he thinks you will pick. So, you have to know what he thinks you will pick in order to pick the best strategy, and so on backwards *ad infinitum*. There is no end to the calculation problem, and therefore no optimal strategy in the rock-paper-scissors game. Game theorists have labeled the problem of this sort of game with no finite solution – no best strategy for any player – "the problem of common knowledge." In principle, the problem of having to infinitely iterate calculations about what other players will do bedevils most strategic games.

While the problem of common knowledge cannot affect organisms which are incapable of making calculations about the strategies of others, it can affect the evolution of fitness-maximizing strategies. As nature selects the best among competing strategies for fitness-maximization, it must eventually face contexts in which the best strategy for an organism to play depends on what other strategies are available to be played by other organisms. If the game theorist can prove that, in the long run, there is no single best strategy – even with rational calculation on the part of the players – then we can expect natural selection to do no more than produce a motley of equally good or bad strategies that compete with one another, at best gaining temporary ascendancy in a random sequence. In other words, natural selection will produce nothing but noise, disorder, no real pattern in the behavior of fitness-maximizers who face strategic competiton as opposed to parametric optimization problems.

It seems safe to assume that *Homo sapiens* has not in fact suffered this fate. For the most part, our interactions do show a pattern, and an other-regarding, cooperative one at that. Morality is the rule and not the exception (and not just one among a series of cyclically succeeding patterns of behavior). It must follows, therefore, that evolution has not led us (or our evolutionary forebearers) down the cul-de-sac of the problem of common knowledge. But, if game theorists are right, almost the only way evolution could have avoided this sort of chaos is for other-regarding principles of conduct to have emerged in parametric contexts, and then to be evolutionarily stable, un-invadable when these contexts became strategic.

IV. KIN-SELECTION AND UNCERTAINTY

For a fitness-maximizing organism, interactions with offspring are close to being parametric. For, almost no matter what children and kin do to you, if you act in their interests, the result will increase your fitness. The fitness-maximizing strategy for an organism is therefore to act so as to maximize the fitness of its offspring. Thus, in selecting for fitness-maximization, nature will encourage organisms whose genetically encoded dispositions include sharing and cooperating, and even unreciprocated altruism towards kin – children, siblings, even parents. For these strategies are likely to increase one's offspring, no matter how they respond to you. This sort of kin-altruism is evolutionarily stable and un-invadable.

A short-sighted, selfish organism, who behaves as though its own survival or that of its children counted for its fitness, would end up with fewer offspring over the long haul. For sometimes it would look out for number one (or number one's kids) when sacrificing itself or a child would result in the survival of a larger number of offspring (recall, that under sexual reproduction, a child is only half an offspring). In selecting for fitness, nature will select for "inclusive fitness" and "kin selection" will emerge. Kin selection is something we can count on emerging long before *Homo sapiens* appears. It becomes an adaptive strategy as soon as the number of genetic offspring begins to exceed the number of children. (Recall, three nephews carry more of an individual's genes than one child.)

When *Homo sapiens* emerges, therefore, we are already beyond Hobbes's state of nature. Cooperation, altruism, and other-regarding behavior generally is already established inside both the nuclear and the extended family. Indeed, it is likely to already have been established a bit beyond this. Consider that individuals do not wear name tags or carry their genealogy on their sleeves for others to examine before deciding whether an interaction will be parametric or strategic. There are, of course, clear signs of kinship that even animals with limited recognition powers can use: odor, proximity to a nest or region. And there are clear signs of xenonimity – strangerness. But there is always a large area of uncertainty in between, a range of interactions in which two organisms just can't tell with any more than a certain moderate level of probability whether they are kin or not. This will be more true for males and their putative offspring than for females. Given the nature of procreation and gestation in many mammalian species – and especially in *Homo sapiens* – the male can never be as certain as the female that the young in his family are his offspring – i.e., that they share some of his genes. Unless the female is under constant and perfect surveillance during the critical period, the question of whose sperm fertilized her ovum must always be a matter of some doubt. Beyond the relation between mother and child, the degree of consanguinity between any two organisms is always a matter of probabilities, and doubts about kinship are easier to raise than to allay.

Under conditions of uncertainty about kinship, what is the optimal strategy for a fitness maximizer? Game theory tells us that the rational thing to do is to apportion the degree of one's other-regarding behavior to the strength of the evidence of consanguinity. In the long run, as natural selection operates, it must favor this strategy as well. Even in cases where the available positive evidence of consanguinity (subtle similarities of smell, coat color, shape of beak, pitch of mating call, etc.) is difficult to detect, one can expect nature to select for cooperation and other-regarding behavior between kin, provided only that it has enough time to fine-tune the detection mechanisms. Considering the job it has done in optimizing the eye for vision within the time constraint of four million years, it may seem reasonable to suppose it can fine-tune kin-selection strategies as well. And if everyone turns out probably to be closely enough related to everyone else, then natural selection might be expected by itself to produce other-regarding behavior up to levels of frequency that match the probability of universal consanguinity. Here we have the emergence of morality, or at least a crucial aspect of it, without having to solve the problems common knowledge makes for strategic games.

However, the amount of other-regarding behavior that might in fact be fitness-maximizing just because of the fact that we are all each other's seventh cousin hardly seems sufficient to explain the emergence and persistence of moral conduct. The problem with this neat explanation is that we have no independent idea of whether the payoffs (in more offspring) for being other-regarding are really great enough when the probability of being related falls to the level that obtains between you and me. And there doesn't seem to be any easy way to find out. In short, our explanation isn't robust enough. It rests on a certain variable taking on a very limited range of values, one within which we have no reason to think it falls. We need a better explanation for the emergence and persistence of other-regarding behavior than kin selection and the uncertainty of relatedness can give us. It's all right to start with kin selection, but we need an explanation that carries other-regarding conduct into the realm of strategic interactions among fitness maximizers *unlikely* to be kin.

To do this, we need to help ourselves to another brace of healthy assumptions about morality and game theory. First, let us accept without argument that the institutions of morality are public goods: they cannot be provided to one consumer without being provided to all others, so that any one consumer has an incentive to understate the value of the good to him and so decline to pay its full value provided he is confident that others will pay enough to provide it. Certainly, the institution of generalized cooperation is like this. No one can count on it unless everyone can, and we all have an incentive to understate its value to us whenever we are asked to pay our fair share to maintain it. Moreover, fitness-maximizers have an incentive to cheat, to decline to cooperate, if they can get away with it undetected or unpunished. But if everyone knows this, and everyone knows that everyone knows this, etc., then the institution of cooperation will break down because of our common knowledge. The public good is lost, and every one is worse off. The prisoner's dilemma graphically illustrates this problem of the provision of public goods. Individual rational agents have an incentive to be free-riders, to decline to cooperate. The result is a non-optimal equilibrium in which no cooperation is visible. The natural selection version of this collapse from the fortuitous provision of public goods to a non-optimal equilibrium takes time, as individual defectors emerge through recombination or mutation and out-reproduce cooperators.

The second assumption we need is that most of our morally relevant interactions are moves in an indefinitely long sequence of prisoner's dilemma games. This seems a not unreasonable assumption: honoring moral obligations is not a one-shot, all-or-nothing affair. It is a matter of repeated interactions largely among the same individuals. Interactions with strangers are by definition less frequent than with people we have interacted with and will interact with in the future. Now, one important fruit of the joint research of game theorists and evolutionary biologists has been the conclusion that, even among strangers, being a free-rider (always declining to cooperate, always taking advantage) is not the fitness-maximizing strategy in an iterated prisoner's dilemma. Rather, the best strategy is what is known as "tit-for-tat": that is, for optimal results one should cooperate on the initial occasion for interaction, and on each subsequent occasion do what the other player did on the last round. This strategy will maximize fitness even when everyone knows that everyone else is employing this strategy. For even on the assumption that there is complete common knowledge of what strategies will be chosen, tit-for-tat remains the best strategy. Once in place, it assures cooperation even among unrelated fitness-maximizers. It circumvents the common-knowledge problem.

V. ETHICS – QUICK AND DIRTY

There is one rather serious obstacle to natural selection's helping itself to this strategy: the problem of getting it into place. For tit-for-tat cannot invade and overwhelm the strategy of narrow selfishness that is required by strict fitness-maximization. In a group of organisms that never cooperate, anyone playing tit-for-tat will be taken advantage of at least once by every other player. This advantage is enough to prevent tit-for-tat players eventually swamping selfishness. In fact, it may be enough of an advantage for tit-for-tat to be driven to extinction by the strategy of selfishness every time it appears as a strategy for interaction.

This is where nature's preference for the quick and dirty, *approximate* solution to the problem of selecting for fitness-maximization comes in. Our approximate fitness-maximizers' optimum strategy involves other-regarding behavior with kin, and selfishness with others. How will fitness be maximized in the borderline area where kinship and its absence are difficult or impossible to determine? When the only choice for an organism is to cooperate or decline to do so, how does it behave? By flipping a coin weighted to reflect the evidence for kinship, and doing as the coin indicates? A few pages back I derided this suggestion, though we cannot put it past nature to have evolved a device within us that has this effect. On the other hand, nature will prefer quick and dirty solutions to mathematically elegant ones, provided they are cheap to build, early to emerge, and do the job under a variety of circumstances, etc. If tit-for-tat is almost as good a strategy for fitness-maximization in cases of uncertainty as employing the probability calculus and far easier for nature to implement, then on initial encounters under uncertainty about kinship, individuals playing this strategy will cooperate. But this means they will cooperate therafter as well. Thus, interactions at the borderline come to have the character of interactions within the family; parties to any and every interactive situation will generally cooperate.

Now suppose that among organisms genetically programmed to be other-regarding within the family and to play tit-for-tat at the borderlines, one or more individuals emerge with a new variation: their genome is programmed to encourage tit-for-tat always and everywhere, or at least whenever interacting with strangers. Interaction with selfish strangers will be costly to such organisms and should lead to their extinction. But suppose such interaction is rare. Furthermore, suppose (as seems reasonable) that the strategy of always playing tit-for-tat is otherwise an adaptive one, with advantages over other more complex strategies, especially for organisms lacking complex cognitive and calculational powers. For the cost of maintaining and using a storage system for kin and non-kin may be greater than the cost of being taken for a sucker in just the first round of an indefinitely iterated interaction. This will likely be true when the chances of meeting a stranger are extremely low, as they will be in the earlier stages of the evolution of mammalian species living in family groups. It is, in general, easy to imagine scenarios that make tit-for-tat the best overall strategy under most circumstances in a given environment. But this means that natural selection for approximate fitness maximization among individuals has led to the emergence of cooperative, other-regarding strategies. It has solved the problem of providing public goods to individual organisms geared always and only to look out for themselves and their kin. If ethical institutions are, after all, public goods, then we have explained how they might emerge among approximate fitness-maximizers.

Of course, this entire story applies to us only to the extent that we are approximate fitness-maximizers. This is not hard to show. In fact, if anything, it's too easy to show. For the story does not include any indication of how good an approximation to perfect fitness-maximization is required for the emergence of other-regarding strategies. Even if it did, we have no idea of whether *Homo sapiens* is in fact a good enough fitness-maximizer for this scenario actually to obtain. For these reasons, the claim that we are in fact approximate fitness maximizers will have vanishingly small empirical content. But then empirical content was never the strong point of any evolutionary theory, and is of little interest in moral philosophy anyway.

That we are fitness-maximizers to some degree of approximation goes without saying. After all, the only alternative to being an approximate fitness-maximizer is being extinct. And how did nature shape us for fitness-maximization? What phenotypical properties of *Homo sapiens* did it shape in this direction? Well, the quickest and dirtiest way of making us approach fitness-maximization is to make us *approximate utility-maximizers,* to shape us into systems organized to maximize our well-being, by linking well-being to the avoidance of discomfort, pain, and distress, and the attainment of comfort, pleasure, and feelings of security. The reason is obvious: an organism's reproductive potential is, *ceteris paribus,* a function of its well-being. So, in order to select for fitness-maximization, nature will select for organisms that by-and-large maximize their well-being. The by-and-large clause reflects the fact that there are certain departures from utility-maximization that nature will select for too. For example, it will select for organisms that sacrifice their own well-being to offspring, especially after they have passed the age of optimal procreation. Or, equivalently, nature will select for preference structures that make kin-altruism pleasing to the individual. This is a quick and dirty solution to the problem of programming kin-selection, one which corresponds to the philosopher's claim that altruism is just the reflection of a perverse preference structure.

If the quick and dirty solution to the problems of designing an approximate fitness-maximizer is to design an approximate utility-maximizer, then our merely plausible explanation for the emergence of morality or of one important component of it may have another role to play. It may turn out to be a part of a (weak) *justification* of morality, or at least of one important component of it.

One traditional question of interest to moral philosophers is that of how to convince the rational egoist to be moral, how to show the egoist that being moral is in his interest. Nowadays this problem is often set forth as that of showing how morality could be part of a strategy that maximizes individual utility. In its own way, natural selection provides reason to suppose that morality is part of a utility-maximizing strategy, and our story provides a plausible scenario for how this might have happened.

It is clear that nature began selecting for utility-maximizers long before it began selecting for other-regarding cooperators. For one thing, maximizing well-being is a strategy to be found across the phylogenetic spectrum; it doubtless characterized our ancestors long before the rearing of offspring in nuclear or extended families and the emergence of social groups made other-regarding cooperation possible and necessary. Having laid down very early in evolution approximate utility-maximization as a quick and dirty strategy for approximating fitness-maximization, nature is unlikely ever to "rip it out" and start over. This means that when it lays down other strategies, they will at least have to be compatible with utility maximizing. It is much more likely that the new strategy will be new ways to maximize utility under new circumstances. But if cooperation and other-regarding behavior generally is nature's way of most efficiently maximizing utility, then it should be good enough for us. That is, in our own calculations and reflection on how to maximize our utilities, we should expect to come eventually to the same conclusion which it has taken nature several geological epochs to arrive at. Both rational agents and nature operate in accordance with principles of instrumental rationality; they both seek the most efficient means to their ends. Since nature's end (approximate fitness-maximization) is served by our ends (approximate utility-maximization), our means and nature's will often coincide.

VI. CONCLUSION

It's a nice story, and it seems to have a moral for moral philosophy. I think it is absolutely the best biology can do by way of shedding light on anything worth calling 'human nature' and drawing out its implications for matters of interest to moral philosophers. But before taking any comfort in it at all, we need to recall and weigh the hostages to fortune it leaves – the many special assumptions about us and about the nature of moral conduct that it requires just to get off the ground: to begin with, the idea that just because one is cooperative or other-regarding, one has attained the status of a moral agent or some important precondition to it. Then there are the claims about humankind as approximate fitness-maximizers. Even if you accept this view of 'human nature', as I do, you are committed to a level of fitness-maximization that you cannot specify beyond saying it is high enough to allow for the scenario I have tried to unfold. Then you have to find a way to draw the force or circumvent the difficulty of the problem of strategic games, in which there seem to be no stable equilibria in the behavior of fitness-maximizers, let alone equilibria that underwrite any part of morality. (And you can't call upon group selection to help solve this problem.) Then you have to buy into the theory of kin-selection and its application to conditions of uncertainty. This is one of the smaller gnats to strain on, given the independent evolutionary evidence for kin selection. But the trouble is that it will not suffice when interactions begin to transcend the family. At this point, we need to assimilate morality further to strategies of choice to be analyzed by the tools of economics and game theory. Finally, we need to be able to fudge our account enough to say that morality emerges because we are not perfect fitness-maximizers, since the best nature can do is make us approximate utility-maximizers.

But perhaps the most difficult consequence of this story to swallow is this: if nature had been able to do any better, morality might never have emerged at all.

Philosophy, University of California, Riverside

THE VARIETIES OF SELF-INTEREST*

By Richard A. Epstein

I. Variety and Constancy in Self-Interest

In this paper, I want to explore the relationship between the various forms of individual self-interest and the appropriate structures of government. I shall begin with the former, and by degrees extend the analysis to the latter. I do so in order to mount a defense of principles of limited government, private property, and individual liberty. The ordinary analysis of self-interest treats it as though it were not only a given but also a constant of human nature, and thus makes few allowances for differences between persons. Yet common experience tells us that personality and behavior are as unique as fingerprints. The positive inquiry, therefore, is how we find what is constant about self-interest in a world of natural human diversity. The normative inquiry must take into account both the constant and variable features of human nature in order to determine what forms of social arrangements hold the greatest prospect of long-term social advantage. The gulf between 'is' and 'ought' must be overcome here, as it must be in all normative discourse. Yet we cannot make sensible judgments of what ought to be the case in the domain of rules unless we first have some idea of what is the case in the domain of behavior.

The initial inquiry asks why self-interest (to be suitably qualified to take into account inclusive fitness)[1] is regarded as a constant of human behavior. The explanation derives more from the biological and less from the social. The powerful pressures of natural selection weed out any organisms for whom (genetic) self-interest is not the paramount consideration. The organisms that are self-regarding keep all of what they produce and are able to obtain some fraction of the output of other organisms whose altruism is genuine and powerful. In time, genuine altruists lose "market share" to the committed egoists. The process is in a sense inexorable, so that altruists in the long run face extinction. The battle over resources is a function of scarcity, not of the particulars of any physical or social arrangements.[2]

* An earlier version of this paper was given at the Midwest Faculty Seminars at the University of Chicago in April, 1989. I should like to thank Timothy Fuller for his valuable comments on an earlier draft of this paper and Ellyn Acker for her usual diligent research assistance.

[1] Inclusive fitness holds that all organisms act to maximize not only their individual fitness, but the fitness of their entire genetic line as well. Thus parents will normally take into account the welfare of their children to reflect the 50 percent of the genetic endowment that they have in common. The level of overlap with grandchildren is 25 percent, and the level between siblings is 50 percent (half of the genes each offspring receives from one parent will be held by the other offspring). See generally W.D. Hamilton, "The Genetical Evolution of Social Behavior," *Journal of Theoretical Biology*, vol. 7 (1964), p. 1. Given inclusive fitness, organisms then act to maximize not their individual welfare, but their overall genetic endowment over time.

[2] I have examined this theme in a related paper, "The Utilitarian Foundations of Natural Law," *Harvard Journal of Law and Public Policy* (1989), p. 713.

It therefore works as a constant across different climates, continents, and social arrangements, so much so that it is quite impossible to understand human beings by rejecting the self-interest postulate in favor of some (undefined) behavioral alternative. Without self-interest, what is it that people maximize?

Self-interest is an attitude, disposition, or approach that persons bring toward their initial endowments. It states that they will use these endowments so as to maximize their private returns, subject to whatever external constraints – natural, social, or legal – under which they labor. It is the universal function which transforms natural endowments (the arguments of the function) into individual satisfactions (its dependent variable). These initial endowments differ across individuals in almost every conceivable dimension: height, weight, hearing, seeing, intelligence, temperament, and the like. The diversity in individual traits is also a constant because it improves the expected yield from offspring in the next generation. If all offspring were identical, then their life prospects would tend to converge. Wholly apart from the risk of a bad genetic draw, that convergence would place every person in direct competition with every other person, as each would rank the desirability of external resources in the same order. Even in good times their level of success would be limited by that competition, for with genetic convergence conflict cannot be avoided by a strategy of nonconfrontation (by A seeking out resources that he values more than B, and vice versa.) In bad times their want of diversity could lead them to all perish together. Diversity thus increases output in good times and the odds of survival in bad times. It should be a dominant biological strategy. And it is.

Diversity also increases the payoffs from survival. So long as the payoff from having one offspring in state A of the world is higher than having the nth offspring in state B, then there are gains to diversity along a wide variety of dimensions, but none in the relaxation of the self-interest constant. Evolution therefore tends to favor the diversity in common traits that we see, much as competent financial analysts typically favor diversifying an investment portfolio. The hard questions concern the level of diversification that is optimal along different dimensions, not the gains from diversity as such.

To explain what given individuals will *do* in certain circumstances requires an understanding of the interaction between the self-interest constant and the diverse individual endowments, as these play themselves out in diferent environments. Tall people and short people will both act out of self-interest (inclusive fitness is quite irrelevant in this context) in deciding whether to gather an apple from a high branch, even if both value it equally. But the cost for the tall man of taking possession of the apple could be extending his arm up over his head, while the short man may have to climb some rickety structure. The differences in cost are dependent on differences in natural attributes, which in turn lead to differences in predicted behavior. Far from falsifying the self-interest hypothesis, these differences in behavior and outcome show its power. Presumptively it would be falsified if the short person were, *ceteris paribus*, more likely to take the risk than the tall man. But if the low cost alternatives are observed, then we can use a single norm of self-interest to explain divergent forms of conduct.

Once the process of differentiation starts, it snowballs unaided. A second decision will depend both on initial and acquired endowments, and so on down the line. In each case the divergences between persons can increase, since the variation in their total endowments increases as they respond to prior choices and the succeeding consequences. The particulars of some individual's condition, taken into account in ordinary life, become critical to concrete assessments of what given individuals have done and will do. Their behavior paths should be expected to diverge substantially over time.

II. Gains from Trade

This process of differentiation in skills and tastes has important implications for the theory of social control. The basic theory of self-interest is strong enough to explain disparate behaviors and choices. But the exact pattern of individual encounters and personal decisions involves the very features of individual life that outsiders find hardest to observe and understand. As outsiders, we do know that different natural endowments generate different preferences, costs, and behaviors across individuals. But it is only a modest task to identify the source of these differences and to explain why they remain robust over time and circumstance. It is a far more ambitious task to determine how these differences work in any particular case, for we lack the tools of measurement needed for these refined calculations.

The problem here is especially acute because most of the important questions involve differences not in the direction of preferences and behaviors, but only in the level of intensity. The differences between persons are often not in "sign," but only in "slope." While there are surely some situations in which I value positively what you value negatively, there are doubtless a great many more where the relevant inquiry is *how much* more or less I like (or dislike) a certain good or prospect than you do. Stated otherwise, the common biological and cultural heritage of most persons means that there is a high likelihood that goods that are positively valued by one person will be also positively valued by another. That positive correlation is likely to become stronger as the individuals have more in common in both their background and their environment. Thus there are a few individuals who prefer pain to pleasure, starvation to satiation, or cold to warmth (or, indeed, extreme heat to warmth). Yet, by the same token, different persons have different thresholds for pain, different tastes in food, and different tolerances for heat and for cold.

These differences among human beings create opportunities for gains through trade which would not arise if all persons had identical preferences and skills. Even if two persons attach positive value to the same good, one person will attach a higher value to (any given unit of) that good than the other. In a world without exchange, the value of the good is measured solely by its use to the person who currently possesses it. In a world with costless exchange, its value is measured by the desire of the person who desires it most. In a world of costly exchange, the critical question is whether the joint gains from trade exceed the costs of bringing that trade about. If a given good is valued at X by A and $2X$ by B, then a sale from A to B at $1.5X$ will leave both sides better off than they were before, so long as transaction costs are less than $0.5X$ for each. The same result could be achieved without voluntary exchange only if some central authority knew the relative values that each party attached to the good and then costlessly forced the transfer of possession.

Our collective knowledge is only sufficient to show the *existence* of potential gains from trade. It is not strong enough to allow us to *identify* which trades should be made, or at what price. The persistence of self-interest and the variations and graduations in preferences offer one of the strongest justifications for the use of decentralized systems of property allocation – that is, markets – instead of centralized social planning and control. Night watchmen need only know the rules of trespass, just as umpires need only know the rules of the game. They need not learn the preference maps of the various players in order to discharge their public functions. Nor need they adopt the same complex strategies that are appropriate for players within the game for whom compliance with the rules is the minimum condition, not the ultimate objective. There is a clear and workable distinction between legal boundaries and personal or business decisions. The use of collective force is better deployed at setting the rules of the road than in determining the composition of the traffic.[3]

III. INTERDEPENDENT UTILITIES AND INCLUSIVE FITNESS

Thus far I have talked only about the simplest model of self-interest, that which mirrors individual self-interest in transactions with strangers. In that context, the assumptions of the model are good enough because there are few if any interdependent utilities between the two (or more) parties to the trade. The biological situation is, of course, far more complex. Individual self-interest does not account for parenting and reproduction. A selfish individual has no concern for what happened before he arrived on this earth, and – more importantly – none for what will happen after he departs it. Wholly egoistic preferences are incompatible with the life cycle of all species, including human beings, and with the

---

[3] See F.A. Hayek, *The Road To Serfdom* 74 (1944); the more ambitious program is set out in *National Broadcasting Co. v United States*, 319 U.S. 190 (1943) (per Frankfurter J.). The source of the conflict is this: Hayek uses the example of the highway to explain how it is possible to develop an institution of common property without having to know the reasons and purposes for which people want to use the road. Lane assignments, speed limits, and other traffic rules can be set well without that knowledge. Frankfurter rejected this model of rules in determining the Federal Communication Commission's (FCC) administrative allocation of broadcast licenses. A Hayekian mode of analysis would only ask whether the license trespassed (that is, interfered) with broadcasters using nearby frequencies. But Frankfurter held that the FCC could not only determine these relatively simple matters, but do far more:

> But the [Federal Communications] Act does not restrict the Commission merely to supervision of the traffic. It puts upon the Commission the burden of determining the composition of that traffic. The facilities of radio are not large enough to accommodate all who wish to use them. Methods must be divided for choosing from among the many who wish to apply. And since Congress could not do this, it committed the task to the Commission. [p. 215]

Frankfurter's analysis completely overlooks the possibility that, with property rights established, the frequencies could be allotted by bid. See generally, for a devastating criticism of Frankfurter's approach, R.H. Coase, "The Federal Communications Commission," *Journal of Law and Economics*, vol. 2 (1959), p. 1. On the conflict between Hayek and Frankfurter, my sympathies lie with Hayek. See R.A. Epstein, "Beyond the Rule of Law: Civic Virtue and Constitutional Structure," *George Washington Law Review*, vol. 56 (1987), p. 149.

evolution of the species. Genes may maximize their welfare in an unconscious, but selfish manner. However, persons cannot.

One major source of variation in self-interest lies in the way in which the standard of self-interest is modified to take into account the biological imperatives of reproduction. In this context the subject of sex differences looms to the fore. It is an issue emphasized by feminist writers who emphasize that women as a group speak in a "different voice" from men.[4] I think that the proposition has a good deal of truth to it, but that its origins lie as much in the biological imperatives of reproduction as in the social conditioning and conventions that all young persons receive from their parents. On the standard analysis, mothers have greater influence on children because they have lower opportunity costs for providing nourishment and assistance, especially in the earlier years.

In order to address this subject, I think therefore that it is useful to suppress for the moment the differences between separate individuals and to focus instead on the systematic differences that apply across the two sexes – the phenomenon of "sexual dimorphism" that exists as much with humans as with many other species. It is as important to have some appreciation of the differences *between* the sexes as well as the differences *within* each sex. It is pointless (or, worse, dangerous) to assume that any intelligent assessment can be made of various forms of social organization if one part of the overall picture is studiously ignored.

The power of the sociobiological theory of sexual dimorphism rests upon its ability to explain systematic differences in sex without relaxing the rigorous self-interest assumption on which behavioral analysis depends. The argument here, as I understand it, proceeds in several stages. The first stage of the argument asks a simple question: why do organisms have two parents, instead of one or three? The answer requires a comparison of the gains from further diversity with the costs of obtaining those gains. The move from one sex to two sexes creates the possibility of enormous diversification in the next generation, with the consequent benefits alluded to above. Instead of simple organisms producing clones of themselves, two individuals can combine in 2^n ways, with n – the number of different genes – very large indeed. The possibilities are almost infinite. Three parents increase the possible gains to 3^n. But while the numerical difference between the two figures is very large, the practical payoff (given the law of diminishing returns) does not lie in a large n. The chance of producing two identical offspring with two parents is trivial, save in the case of identical twins – which, in any event, could happen with three sexes. The added diversity from the third sex is therefore likely to be very small.

The picture is very different when we look at the changes on the cost side. Here the first question is simple union. How is mating to take place? The transaction costs (again!) of getting three organisms together are far greater. Allocating responsibilities for caring for the next generation after mating is also more complicated. The point here is not just that there is a 50 percent increase in the number of parents involved. Rather, it is that the movement from two to three parties opens up the possibility not only of bargains (e.g., courtship) between two

---

[4] See, e.g., Carol Gilligan, *In a Different Voice: Psychological Theory and Women's Development* (Cambridge: Harvard University Press, 1982) as part of a vast literature on the subject.

persons, but coalitions and sequential exchanges, which are vastly more complex to analyze (or, for that matter, organize). The many-body problem in physics becomes vastly more difficult when there are three bodies, not two. The movement from two to three has similarly enormous consequences in game theory precisely because of the added possibilities for strategic bargaining.

It follows, then, that we have taken into account all the relevant possibilities. One parent has low diversity, which yields benefits even smaller than its low cost. Two parents, has moderately higher costs but far greater diversity (not to mention some modest insurance if something should happen to one parent). Three parents yields small increases in diversity, but imposes large increases in costs. Any larger number of parents is inferior to three, so long as three is inferior to two. There is no doubt a sense that this analysis engages in a form of reverse engineering, and postulates that what is the case has to be the case as well. But the unique peak in output with two sexes seems evident on the strength of a theory which looks at bargaining games and transaction costs in a wide range of social situations. We should not stint on our instincts. We can be confident that two sexes is all that there will ever be, here or anywhere else in (why be modest?) the universe.

The next step in the argument asks why the sexes are different. Here, the initial question is mating. Again, there are three possibilities. We could have two (like) males, two (like) females, or one of each. The defining characteristic of males are large numbers of small sperm, and that of females is small numbers of large eggs. Again, the simple dynamics of procreation explain the differences in outcomes in these three worlds. Two males may find union easy to obtain, perhaps too easy. The combined offspring are too numerous, so neither parent can provide them with nutrition and protection. The system will work only if the offspring can make it on their own, where the attrition rate is necessarily enormous. In principle that (R-selectionist)[5] strategy can work; indeed, it does work with many forms of life. Fish, which lay huge numbers of eggs, adopt basically this strategy. But its utility is sharply limited when the offspring are not self-sufficient at birth, as is the case with mammals and marsupials – where lots of parental protection, nutrition, and instruction are required for the offspring to reach reproductive maturity.

The other (K-selectionist) strategy, female to female (or few, but large ova), could in principle allow parents to assist their offspring after birth. Nonetheless, there are other obstacles that prevent this from becoming a dominant strategy. The cycle of reproduction is only as robust as its weakest link; with the female-to-female strategy, it is just not clear how the two will come to meet or which of the two mothers will house the offspring. The mixed strategy universally adopted in primates – many male sperm chasing after a single female egg – is viable, but it requires a sharp differentiation in social roles, which in turn allows for gains from trade. The female parent has the greater investment in the egg, and can ill afford to lose it on some long journey. The sperm are relatively cheap and easily expendable. It therefore follows that the female will carry the fertilized egg with her, leaving the male relatively free to go elsewhere.

[5] See David P. Barash, *Sociobiology and Behavior*, pp. 181–82 (1977).

Given the asymmetry of sexual reproduction, males and females have different natural endowments and accordingly will adopt different reproductive strategies, even though they both act out of the same underlying self-interest. The female will tend to be selective in the males whom she accepts, given the small number of offspring that she can carry to term. The males will tend to be aggressive in courting different females because they are more likely to get a higher rate of return with a second successful mating than by devoting the same resources to protecting their own offspring from the first. Of course the law of diminishing returns applies here as well, but it does not necessarily follow that the first ounce of energy spent on protecting offspring helps the male more than the last ounce of energy spent in trying to mate with new females. It may happen (as with polygamous marriages) but it need not. For these purposes, the critical point is that the *marginal* rates of substitution differ systematically for males and females. So long as reproduction is the central objective in evolution, we should expect that any trait that is relevant to reproduction will be central to all aspects of the behavior of both sexes. The implication of asymmetrical sex roles is that males should be less risk-averse (or more risk-preferring) than females when each act out of their own self-interest.[6] If one male dominates, then he can totally exclude his rivals from reproduction and keep the gains for himself. If one female dominates, she cannot carry the offspring of all the males: she has less to gain by the exclusion and therefore should invest far fewer resources to obtain it. A population with one vigorous male and a hundred females can flourish (although the death or incapacitation of the male leaves no backup), but a population with one female and a hundred males is at the edge of extinction; even if she reproduces, the total population is limited to her offspring, itself a tiny fraction of the original population.

It follows therefore that asymmetrical behavior – especially on matters of intensity – should be the norm, not the exception. Whenever the payoffs to some activities differ systematically, the rates of substitution will vary across activities. Even if men and women were equally adept at activity A, we should not expect them to engage in it at equal levels. The differences in risk preferences and behavior on matters of reproduction and child-rearing change the relative opportunity costs in everything that men and women do.

There is a question, of course, as to how much these differences survive in human beings, given the manifest importance of cultural influences on human behavior. But the presence of culture does not negate the influence of biology: it

---

[6] There is here a limiting condition that applies in some cases. Thus, with some kinds of birds there is very little sexual dimorphism between the male and female, while in others the differences are enormous. The cases of convergence between the sexes are those in which the efforts of the male are necessary to ensure the survival of the newborn chicks after birth, which itself is dependent upon the difficulty of acquiring food. The cases in which the female is able to acquire sufficient food for the offspring by herself are those in which the sexual dimorphisms are the greatest. Note that the sexual symmetry in birds is possible in part because once the egg is laid, the male is able to help with warming and feeding as much as the female. There seems to be no situation in the case of birds in which females will adopt higher risk strategies than males. In mammals that condition is never reached, given pregnancy and nursing. See generally, Bruce Beehler, "The Birds of Paradise," *Scientific American* (December, 1989), pp. 116–23.

only makes its role somewhat more difficult to analyze, and may in practice *reinforce*, not undermine, these basic natural differences. The point, again, rests in the marginal returns to various forms of labor. If men are relatively better at activity A and women at activity B, then the principle of comparative advantage says that each should specialize investments in areas of strength and divide the gains through trade. If cultures are therefore in competition with one another, then those which hit upon rules that imitate and facilitate nature should be able to outperform those which do not. At least in a nonself-conscious era, where persons do not wish to redefine sex roles or restructure society through collective means, culture is not a random factor – nor need its dictates and norms cut against biological predilections. Rather, cultural evolution will tend toward low-cost solutions that maximize the gains from trade by taking into account differential endowments within and between the sexes.

Consider, for example, patterns of courtship. The male primate typically seeks out the female who plays hard (but not too hard) to get. Her motivation is clear. She has only a limited quantity of eggs and must therefore be selective to be sure that she has chosen the right mate. Yielding to the first proposal could be very costly, for the optimal search (the same for mates as it is for low-priced autos) usually requires more than a single observation. Indeed, the greater variation in the early responses, the more substantial the gains from a continued search, because the greater variance raises the prospects of a highly favorable match. Within courtship, therefore, the female has a strong incentive to check to see if she has drawn a male from the top portion of the sample. But males need only have weaker incentives to see that they have selected a female from the top of the distribution, as well as fewer scruples because they can father numerous offspring in a single cycle. We should expect, therefore, to see males pursue females. We should expect females to be selective in their choice of mates by showing an initial reluctance that can only be overcome by some showing of general fitness. Yet females need not be as aggressive, as they incur enormous risks to advance relatively little in the queue.

In this account, it is assumed that both males and females act out of their own self-interest, the one biological constant they both share. All that differs are the strategies that are used to maximize that self-interest. The differential behavior observed in this area largely depends on costs of foregoing any particular mating opportunity, for these are high for the female and low for the male. The female is more selective because she has more to lose. It is not the case that one sex is "active" and the other "passive." Females have extensive influence over their choice of mates. The cultural response has been both to recognize natural inclinations and to respect them, within limits. Thus with courtship, and the sexual interactions that follow, the standard pattern is for the man to take the initiative (because he has less to lose from starting the interaction) and the women to have the right to respond in either the affirmative or negative (to preserve her options since she has more to lose from attachment in the particular case). This arrangement allows matters to proceed at a slower rate than if women took the initiative – to which men would, all too promptly, respond. The basic pattern of behavior that one sees seems to work to the long-term interests of both sides. Symmetrical rules for courtship

would hardly be optimal, given the differences that are found in initial
endowments. We should not be wildly optimistic about any set of rules governing
marriage to work without a hitch, given the divergent interests of the two spouses.
Marriage contracts are necessarily a form of barter: the male must like what the
female has to offer and vice versa.[7] Ordinary contracts of sale have the strong
functional justification allowing transactional specialization: I am a seller (for
whom a dollar is a dollar), and you are the choosy buyer. Next time I will be the
choosy buyer, and someone else the indifferent seller. With marriage, however,
both parties are choosy at the same time. The difficulty of the contracting process
should therefore lead us to expect a high failure rate, no matter what the
contractual rules are.

Asymmetry in social interactions, then, is a sign of sensible rules, not foolish
ones. There is less by way of exploitation and more by way of mutual
accommodation in this commonly observed pattern of behavior, and we should
expect strong resistance from *both* men and women who are just "uncomfortable"
with modifying the traditional rules for the dating game, even if they don't know
quite why. Birth control has led to a change in the costs of sexual relations, and
society (at least our society) has responded to this change by weakening the double
standard on sexual behavior. But the evolutionary legacy lags behind the rapid shift
in technology. Even today we should expect the behavioral patterns between males
and females to diverge, notwithstanding the technological and social changes. To
the extent that biological dispositions constrain personal choice, we should not
expect the actions of men and women to respond only to the most recent shifts in
the technology of birth control devices. Their behaviors will respond as well to the
built-in attitudes and dispositions of their biological inheritance, and these in-born
attributes change in accord with far slower evolutionary clock. Changes in
technology will narrow the gaps in the behavior of men and women. But given the
durable differences in biological predispositions, important (if reduced) differences
in behavior will remain.

The problem of sex differences is, of course, not limited to courtship, but affects
the roles that men and women play relative both to each other and to their
offspring. Here it has often been said that the differences between men and women
are differences between individuals whose orientation is "atomistic" and those who
have a stronger sense of community ties.[8] Perceptions of these asymmetrical
positions do not fall within the bailiwick of any single political persuasion. But the
point is surely overdrawn if it is assumed that males care only for themselves, while
women care equally for other persons. The interdependence of utility functions is
common to both sexes, even though it plays out in different ways for each.
Fathering has positive payoffs, even if they are lower than those from mothering.
So too where there are no common genes between two individuals, the degree of
"separateness" is the same for women as it is for men. There is no genetic altruism
between two unrelated females, just as there is none between two unrelated males.

[7] See Lloyd Cohen, "Marriage, Divorce, and Quasi Rents; or, 'I Gave Him The Best Years of My Life'," *Journal of Legal Studies*, vol. 16 (1987), p. 267.
[8] See Robin West, "Jurisprudence and Gender," *University of Chicago Law Review*, vol. 55 (1988), p. 1.

Nonetheless, the different natural endowments may make it more likely that, in transactions with strangers, women will be more likely to seek gains from cooperation than from aggression. Even within the world of bargains, we should expect to see differences in the strategies by which men and women bargain and interact. For biological reasons alone, men are more likely to take risks in their business dealings than women.[9] The attitudes taken in sexual relations can hardly be segregated from the rest of people's lives. Thus, the effort to become a dominant male does not begin at the point of sexual conflict. It begins far earlier, when young males nurse, hunt, play, and engage in combat. Evolution is a blunt instrument that does the best it can with what it has. Even if it were optimal in some abstract world to partition the attitudes that people bring toward sexual relations from those which they have towards business relations, it is doubtful that any evolutionary system could refine emotional behavior to respond fully to these subtle demands. In case after case, we see biological systems that overrespond to certain kinds of stimuli precisely because the costs of reducing those errors are greater than the costs of the errors themselves.[10] The reproductive ends shape other parts of the human experience, and it is a legacy that cannot be willed away by wishing it were otherwise. Evolution made us what we are, not necessarily what we want to be.

IV. FROM TASTES TO MARKETS

Moreover, these differences in taste for risk and behavior have important consequences for patterns of investment, both in terms of financial and human capital. The simplest form of corporate structure gives each investor common stock for the original investment. The use of common stock across the board has this advantage: it makes it easy to divide the gains and losses of the firm's business, as each shareholder participates *pro rata* to the extent of the original investment. The conflicts of interest between the shareholders are reduced, as are the administrative costs of running the entire enterprise.

Nonetheless, many firms do not organize themselves along these simple lines: specialization is too lucrative. Firms with common stock often incur debt. Other firms engage in the proliferation of different classes of stocks: preferred and common, with and without voting rights. Other firms issue warrants, which allow the purchase of shares at some minimum price, usually set above its current market value – a still riskier form of investment. One driving force behind these

[9] See, e.g., John Markoff, "Computing in America: It's a Masculine Mystique," *New York Times*, February 13, 1989, p. 7. "Men tend to be more adventurous and riskier," according to Sydney Springer, a female programmer at Sun Microsystems. It might also be added that they doubtless make more mistakes as well. The key to assessing risk therefore lies in the payoffs, which are apt to be enormous on the high side. The issue is also picked up in Margaret Hennig & Anne Jardim, *The Managerial Woman* (1976), pp. 47–50, 107ff, which notes that women are less comfortable with risk than men, because they tend to treat it only as negative and never as positive. Their explanations for the phenomenon have nothing to do with the biological determinants but stress socialization as an independent variable, which they then analyze in Freudian terms.

[10] The point is emphasized in this volume by Alexander Rosenberg, "Human Nature and Ethics: What Can Biology Tell Us?" His example is that fish, who are unable to distinguish between predators and other fish, flee at the sight of any fish. The costs of this practice include the unnecessary expenditure of energy. But these costs are relatively low. A fish that remains when it should flee is committing a fatal error. Given the inability to develop perfect discrimination between friend and foe, the corner solution – always flee – dominates any intermediate response, notwithstanding its admitted error cost.

complicated capital structures is to exploit the differences for taste in risk among investors and differences in degrees of control which they have over the operation of the firm. The demand for these costly and complicated capital structures would be sharply reduced if all individuals had identical tastes for risk. Yet it is precisely because there are major differences in the willingness to bear risks across persons (and across sexes) that these structures are found in combination with the cheaper but less sensitive forms of investment. The two, moreover, are likely to remain in equilibrium, for there is no universal reason to believe that the benefits of simplicity will outweigh those of complexity (or vice versa) for all organizations at all times. Let each type be offered at its lowest possible price and the observed outcome is likely to be in the social interest – that is, maximal satisfaction of the preferences of all market participants.

The same pattern of risk division may be found in the structure of employment relationships. A powerful parallel arises between debt and equity in capital markets, and employee and employer in human capital transactions. In capital markets, the owner of the equity is the "residual claimant" who faces the brunt of price moves in the underlying assets. Similarly, the employee of a business receives a fixed salary, while the employer is the residual claimant of the flow of income generated by the firm. If all individuals had an equal taste for risk, then there would be less reason for people to organize firms with employees and greater reason to have simple partnerships – the direct analogy to the firm whose entire capital structure consists of one class of equity stock. But given different tastes for risk, it is now possible *ex ante* to make transactions with mutual gain by having some individuals assume the position of workers and the others of employers. As risk and control go hand in hand, it follows that those who bear the greatest risk will have the greatest say over the decisions of the business.

These basic propositions have direct implications for the likely distribution of sex roles within the firm. If there is a systematic difference in risk taking between men and women, then we should again expect on average to see the asymmetries – debt/equity, employer/employee – emerge in various kinds of labor and capital markets, again without having to appeal to any notion of employee (or sex) exploitation. There should on average be more entrepreneurial men than entrepreneurial women, as the higher rate of return goes with the greater level of risk. The separation of the market into different levels of risk works well for all the participants in it, so long as the additional costs of policing the asymmetrical relations are lower than the gains derivable from specialization.

An important caveat is again in order here. It is quite clear that the rates of change associated with women in the workplace over the past generation (or, indeed, over the past century) cannot be explained by evolutionary or biological theories: the rates of change have been far too rapid, and the magnitude far too great. Instead, many of the key variables appear to be technological. Today women (and their families) are able to reduce the cost of providing care for their young and, more generally, of maintaining a household economy. At the simplest level, baby formula is a low-cost substitute for nursing, and there are a thousand household aids available that reduce the costs of doing what was traditionally regarded as women's work. As the cost of not performing certain traditional household functions goes down, then we should expect more women to abandon or reshape their traditional roles, even if there are no biological changes at all. Stated otherwise, the choice of sex roles for both men and women moves along several margins at the same time, so that there can be important social shifts that have no biological origins. Nonetheless, since biological influences do matter, there can be no ready inference from a radical shift in male's and female's roles to the quite different proposition that sex roles will turn out to be irrelevant in modern times. The differences in biology, as they relate to the taste for risk or any other factor, are not rendered irrelevant or unimportant by changes in technology or social attitudes.

The totality of evidence then suggests that differentiation of sex roles will remain important for the foreseeable future.[11] There is, of course, no reason to use this information to *mandate* that men work as employers and women as employees. Any such rule will surely be wrong in many cases and is gratuitously coercive even when (or if) the arguments made here are correct. But by the same token, these biological observations have a valuable defensive use: that is, to deflect criticism and lawsuits which use evidence of differential employment patterns as evidence of wrongful discrimination by employers. The biological arguments explain why certain patterns sometimes emerge in the workplace wholly without employer discrimination: e.g., the greater willingness of men to sell on a commission–only basis than women, given the differential taste for risk.[12]

Differential tastes for risk are, of course, not the only factor that drives specialization in labor markets; however, it cannot be ignored. A rule that mandated an equal number or fraction of men or women in particular trades or

[11] See, e.g., Victor R. Fuchs, *Women's Quest for Economic Equality* (Cambridge: Harvard University Press, 1988), ch. 3, noting that the differences in job patterns are significantly greater between sexes than they are between races. Fuchs rejects "prejudice and exploitation" as an explanation for those differences, and notes the role that biology might play (including differences in "upper body strength," etc.).

[12] See, e.g., *EEOC v. Sears, Roebuck & Co.*, 839 F.2d 302 (7th Cir. 1988) where Judge Wood, in an excellent opinion, rejected the EEOC's effort to prove that Sears had discriminated in its hiring of its commissioned sales force by showing that a somewhat greater percentage of men had taken these jobs than women. The key witness for Sears for the proposition that some difference in "interest" between men and women might explain why women gravitate toward noncommissioned sales was Professor Rosalind Rosenberg who has in turn been savaged (no lesser word will do) by other feminists. See, e.g., Joan C. Williams, "Deconstructing Gender," *Michigan Law Review*, vol. 87 (1989), p. 797. Rosenberg has been defended by Thomas Haskell & Sanford Levinson, "Academic Freedom and Expert Witnessing: Historians and the *Sears* Case," *Texas Law Review*, vol. 66, p. 1629, to which see the reply of Alice Kessler-Harris, *"Academic Freedom and Expert Witnessing:* A Response to Haskell and Levinson," *Texas Law Review*, vol. 67 (1988), p. 429, and the rejoinder thereto, Thomas Haskell & Sanford Levinson, "On Academic Freedom and Hypothetical Pools: A Reply to Alice Kessler-Harris," *Texas Law Review*, vol. 67 (1989), p. 1591. The major objection to Kessler-Harris's work is her analysis of sex differences either as nonexistent or as all-or-nothing phenomena. Thus Kessler-Harris writes of Rosenberg's argument: "her argument contended that family and work orientations of women would make them unlikely candidates for commission sales jobs. This position ignored the history and perspectives of the working poor. Women are a diverse group, but research about wage earners demonstrates that women, like men, work primarily for income" [p. 436]. But the relevant question is not whether women are "unlikely candidates for commission sales jobs." Rather, it is the differential inquiry: whether they are *less likely* candidates, in part because of preferences about risk. That both men and women work "primarily for income" is again beside the point. The question is: is the preferred level of risk for an income stream identical for men and women? Everything turns on marginal analysis. Small differences in employee taste will lead to disparate patterns of employment without any employer discrimination.

professions is far more intrusive than even the present antidiscrimination law, and it cannot be achieved without some substantial social cost: the demand for equality places an effective break on the gains from trade which specialization itself promises. Social structures that ignore private preferences have an enduring capacity to end up frustrating them.

V. To the Social Level

The theory of natural individual differences, then, has important implications for what we should expect and desire to see emerge in the patterns of both individual behavior and social organizations. It also gives us an important clue as to the kinds of measures that we should use in order to assess competing forms of social order. In this context, we can isolate two distinct approaches toward determining the proper role of government in the social order. One line argues that there are certain "public" or "social" values which the society should strive to achieve because they are regarded as good in themselves by some abstract and impersonal criterion. Theories of this form might be classified as 'utilitarian' (more so among philosophers than lawyers and economists)[13] if they rest upon the belief that the function of social rules is to maximize some disembodied form of "utility" that transcends the tastes and preferences of ordinary individuals.[14] Alternatively, these theories could be "communitarian" or "authoritarian" if utility is repudiated and some other goal – be it community self-realization or heaven on earth – is adopted as the organizing principle for evaluating social rules and individual conduct. Within the framework of any of these moral theories, someone could assert that a particular "end state" (to use Robert Nozick's terms), such as equal division of wealth, or an equal percentage of men and women in certain trades and professions, is a good on which the society should devote at least some of its resources. The identification of the desired collective end state is to justify the public use of force.

The difficulties that lie in the path of these various collective schemes are considerable because of what they leave out. At every point in the process people must be forced to assume roles and attitudes that they would not adopt if left to their own devices. The social goals (imposed by some) are at systematic tension with the preferences (both internal and revealed) of the individuals within the system. The external social goal places a powerful constraint upon the voluntary exchanges that could otherwise take place. Without, for example, an equal income constraint, it is possible to form corporations with complex capital and employment relations. But since these initial business practices will (as the probabilities play themselves out) yield to some dispersion in income (depending

[13] See, for the difference in approach, R.A. Epstein, "The Utilitarian Foundations of Natural Law," *Harvard Journal of Law & Public Policy*, vol. 12 (1989), p. 713, and the criticism thereof in Eric Mack, "A Costly Road to Natural Law," p. 753, and my reply, "Postscript: Subjective Utilitarianism," p. 769.

[14] The utilitarian theories do not always lie in the "objective camp." See below for a discussion of utilitarian theories that rest upon a more subjective view of what value is and that stresses how difficult value may be to compare across persons. See generally Jules Coleman, "Efficiency, Utility and Wealth Maximization," *Hofstra Law Review*, vol. 8 (1980), p. 509, for a discussion of the connections among the various strands of social theory.

on whether risk succeeds or fails), these arrangements themselves could not be tolerated under the basic social norm. There must be a mandated redistribution *ex post* which unravels the (differential) private gains from specialized contracting, which is in a *de facto* sense banned.

To give a simple example, if persons had to bargain under a constraint of equal outcomes, then a world in which each of two persons has 10 is preferable to one in which one has 11 and the other has 15. One could not even reach the state where each one has 11 if the required redistribution takes more than four units to achieve. And it will typically be quite impossible in practice to have production of 26 total units if an equal 13/13 split of the proceeds is required. If equality of outcome is required when initial conditions are unequal, then all transactions in which the size of the potential gains are smaller than the initial wealth differences are necessarily eliminated from consideration. When equality *ex post* is not achievable, then the greater inequalities *ex ante* remain fixed and unchangeable. Thus if one person has 5 in the initial position and the second has 10, any insistence on *ex post* equality will prevent the parties from bargaining to a position where the first person obtains 9 and the second 11.

The constraint of *ex post* equality can exert an important influence in day-to-day affairs. Let me give here one recent legal example that illustrates the logic of the situation. The case concerns the mandatory provision of health insurance to workers. Under the Pregnancy Discrimination Act of 1978, any employer who chooses to provide health insurance must provide coverage for pregnancy as for any other disability. However, there is no obligation to provide any coverage at all. Under the prior legal regime, pregnancy could have been excluded from coverage. When this was done, the resulting disability insurance worked a clear redistribution in favor of women (even without pregnancy) insofar as equal premiums were collected from members of both sexes, but a larger fraction of benefits was paid out to the women. By banning the pregnancy exclusion, the legislation in effect provided that women had to receive two sets of benefits in order for either men or women to receive one. In some instances it may well pay an employer to provide that additional insurance for all workers notwithstanding the external constraint: there may be too few women likely to become pregnant for the costs to matter much. But in other situations, it surely will not. Note now the collective preference functions that emerge. Without insurance men and women have differential risks, so that (say) the value of the job package to men was 10 and to women 8. With the insurance, the new position was 12 to 11, a clear social improvement to both sides. Once pregnancy coverage is required, then the benefit structure for all employees moves (say) to 12 to 15, but at a cost that employers find prohibitive. Better therefore to have the formal equality of no insurance (10 to 8) than the formal equality of insurance without pregnancy benefits (12 to 11) – or so the statute requires because of some collective vision of the good.

The risks of these collective social visions (whether based upon consensus or an intuitive apprehension of the just social organization) have real costs, not the least of which are the dangers of authoritarian excess. The question is how then to formulate a social test of what counts as the "common good" without an appeal to these collective notions. The clue to the exercise is found in the set of examples given above; it rests on the critical assumption that each person can consistently order his or her own preferences, even if they cannot with equal skill compare preferences across separate persons. Here I do not mean to argue that we can never make any interpersonal comparisons of utility, for it is clear that in our ordinary involvements with family, religion, and charity we routinely and confidently make just these sorts of comparisons. But it is one thing for each of us to use our individual judgments to guide our individual conduct when motivated by love, piety, or benevolence – the classical cases of "imperfect obligation." It is quite another thing to use these judgments to *coerce* others in a political setting when none of these factors are operative. Here the easy cases (we should help those in great pain) yield to harder cases, as with the pregnancy insurance example where the social dislocations can become larger.

Nonetheless, if we are rightly skeptical about our ability to rest coercion on these interpersonal comparisons of preferences, then the task that remains is to show how individual conceptions of self-interest can yield social comparisons of just states of the world. A simple rule which says "Adopt that state of the world which leaves things best for me" recognizes the subjective elements of good. But egoism is not a social principle, because it cannot resolve the conflicts between two persons who have inconsistent but intense desires.

It is therefore necessary to develop social measures of welfare from individual subjective states of desire. I think that the escape from egoism lies in the use of the various economic measures of social welfare that were pioneered in the first part of this century, and which recently have moved to greater prominence. In the simplest form, if one distribution of goods A leaves everyone better off by his or her own lights than a second distribution B, then there is no reason to prefer state of the world B to A. It is possible by this person-by-person measurement to make a social judgment: that is to take into account the well-being of every person in the relevant social set. Yet at the same time it is not necessary to make any collective determination of the good, determinations that are difficult to make, given the known differences in natural endowments and subjective preferences held by all persons. Indeed, the test here is in a sense too strong, for if one person is better off in state A, and one is worse off, then here too we can prefer state A to state B without having to abandon the subjectivity of value in the pursuit of an "objective" social measure of welfare. It was just arguments of this sort that I advanced above: that social measures of efficiency based upon the so-called "Pareto" standards are wholly inconsistent with any external constraint of (say) an equal division of the spoils, or indeed with any other standard of "justice" that operates without regard to the sum of individual human preferences.

The difficult question is how these various Pareto-like tests play themselves out in different types of social settings. In this regard, we can see the value that is associated with both well-defined sets of individual property rights and systems of voluntary exchange. The theory about each voluntary contract is that between the parties it generates an outcome which leaves both sides better than they were before, as measured by their own subjective lights: the pregnancy insurance case illustrates this proposition of how regulation can defeat optimal insurance contracting.[15] As a first approximation, therefore, the enforcement of these contracts looks as though it advances the common good, given that no one is thereby left worse off.

The difficulty with this argument (which is not even hinted at in the above cases) concerns the persistence of "externalities" to the relationship. Will the transaction between A and B have adverse effects upon the welfare of strangers to the transaction? If so, then we have a harder row to hoe because the strong Pareto test for social welfare flounders as we move our evaluative eye from contracting parties to strangers. Yet here there are a number of responses that mute – but do not entirely eliminate – the force of the objection. The original agreement between A and B should increase their joint stock of wealth, which in the aggregate should increase the opportunities for trade that are available to any third party. Therefore it looks as if most trade has external benefits, not external costs. But in any given transaction the benefits and costs are not evenly distributed across all strangers. C and D, who routinely deal with A and B respectively, may be pleased if each is made better off by a trade between them, but they will not be so inclined if A and B are now less willing to deal with them by virtue of the agreement between themselves. It is of no consolation to C and D, being egoists, that E and F have now received enhanced opportunities by virtue of the trade between A and B. At best, the trade between A and B asks us to compare their joint gains (and perhaps those of E and F) with the losses of C and D, and it is precisely that calculation which we cannot easily make without making strong assumptions about the relative strength of subjective preferences, the very difficulty that a Pareto standard of social welfare was trying to avoid.

The reason why social theory is so difficult, I believe, that there is no clean escape from this objection: all voluntary transactions generate negative externalities, especially if some individuals resent the gains which others are able to obtain. Nevertheless, there are still some helpful signposts along the way that should lead us to be suspicious of using this argument as the thin edge of the wedge toward greater social control. First, it is a mistake to ask whether this or that particular contract has any negative externalities which frustrate the operation of the Pareto standard. Rather, the right question is: what is the likelihood that these negative externalities will persist if voluntary exchanges are routine for broad classes of transactions, even if some third-parties do object? Here, the concern with interpersonal comparisons of utilities means that we have to tote up each person's gains and losses from each transaction separately, subject only to the all-or-nothing constraint of allowing all routine transfers and property and services or none. Once this assumption is made, the likelihood that any one person would find himself the loser from an extensive network of transactions which generate large gains between the parties and large positive externalities seems to be most unlikely. Indeed, if people were forced to bet whether they would gain or lose under a system of free trade, relative to that which gives *everyone* a blocking position over any trade by any

---

one else, I think that the answer is clear: no one is prepared to sacrifice his own independence for the right to frustrate all other transactions.

If there is any doubt on this score, then the matter can be taken one step further. Place folks behind the veil of ignorance, so that they do not know whom they will be when the veil is lifted. At this point, people have to bet between being the typical person or the odd man out – if he can be found at all. Move the initial point of judgment back far enough, and the pressure to opt into a system that has large positive gains is therefore overwhelming, even from the point of view of the classical Pareto criterion.[16] It is hard to find anyone who turns out to be a systematic loser. By the same token, a comprehensive restriction on voluntary exchanges produces losses for the immediate parties, and losses for the strangers who wish to trade with them. The cycle therefore expands itself in reverse as losses mount when the right to prohibit bargains by others becomes a universal rule. The evidence in practice confirms the basic theoretical point. There are few people who want general prohibition on all voluntary contracts. But as has been clear from the time of Adam Smith, they are eager to endorse *selective* prohibitions that work to their immediate advantage while keeping the normal system of markets and free exchange alive in other domains, especially those in which they operate. Those persons who benefit under rent control or zoning want specific restraints on voluntary transactions, not a system of universal price controls – which, when tried, was quickly abandoned in the 1970s.

VI. To the Social Contract

How should these arguments be put into place to determine some larger social contract under which all persons with distinctive subjective preferences could agree to live? The contracts are of necessity hypothetical because the bargaining difficulties (time, space, language, strategic behavior) are quite impossible to overcome as numbers become large. Hence, we have to ask whether there is a set of rules which offers the best chance of satisfying the rather stringent Pareto criterion, given the differences found in social preferences. I confess that I don't think that this task can be done with quite the rigor that I have demanded. The risk of the single perverse holdout has never been fully overcome, and I suspect that it never will be. If individuals were as self-interested and egoistic as the standard models assume, then the society that we observe would require the use of some coercion in order to be viable. But with coercion comes the risk of abuse, and the key to political success, I think, is to keep the scope of coercive government action as narrow as possible.

Part of the explanation for the limited scope of government rests in the varieties of self-interest. Government decisions are collective decisions which bind even those who disagree. There is no question that collective decisions are part of everyone's life, given family, business, and pleasure. But the critical point rests upon *who* is part of the collectivity that makes the decision. Within political society, membership is coincident with geography and the accidents of birth. Everyone is in

---

[16] See, for further elaboration, R.A. Epstein, "The Utilitarian Foundations of Natural Law," pp. 713, 745–49, esp. n. 60.

the game. On critical matters, therefore, there is apt to be a wide difference on the points of the greatest importance to the people who are governed. What other outcome could be expected, given the differences in individual tastes and the difficulties of measurement and quantification? It therefore follows that collective decisions undertaken at the government level have to reconcile divergent tastes of individuals who otherwise have no independent sentiments and affections to bind them together. While politicians like to speak of our nation as one large "family," there is in truth a vast difference between the impersonal ties that link people together in political life, especially at the state or national level, and the affective ties that link individuals to their family and narrow circle of friends, which is usually smaller than the "community" of which they are a part. At this point we therefore need consider only the substantial variation in preferences that exist with respect to any collective decision. The broader the dispersion, the greater the residual dissatisfaction regardless of the decision made. The best that can be done is to choose that decision which satisfies the median voter. But where preferences are widely spread out, then even this choice will result in very large losses.[17] Matters can be much improved, however, if membership in decisional organizations is done on a voluntary basis, for then two groups can each decide to go their separate way. The total amount of variance is reduced substantially, and with it the pressures on collective decisionmaking.

The use of separate groups is possible for any number of important functions. But it cannot be used to decide how we shall govern, for here there is some need for a monopoly of force within the territory. Nonetheless, the theory points quickly to limiting the use of government to police the separate spheres in which individual preferences dominate: and private property and individual liberty are surely an important part of any such overall strategy. So long as there is widespread agreement on this function, then we should have tolerable public agreement on the core functions of political union without having to battle the high level of disagreement about a wide range of other issues. The modern tendency to make every important decision collective, or political, therefore cuts in exactly the wrong direction. As the issues become more explosive, political consensus will weaken and with it the capacity of government to operate well.

I think, therefore, that there is an intimate connection between the structure of the preferences of self-interested persons and the structure of government. Where differences are regarded as natural and powerful, then limited government becomes the preferred political approach. It is no longer wise to use force to change the way people think about each other. It is only appropriate to see that they do not

---

[17] Thus assume a social loss function that measures each person's dissatisfaction by $(p_i - x)^2$ where p_i is the individual preference and x the collective choice. The squared function is used to represent what seems to be the case, that the further one moves from the median the more vigorous the dissent. Without the squared function, there would be a great deal more freedom in choosing the optimal social choice. With the squared function, the objective should be to get close to the *mean*, which ordinary voting (dominated on single issues by the *median*) does not do particularly well when distributions are heavily skewed. The point is seen in the simplest of examples: A has a preference for -2 and B for $+2$. If the social loss function were linear, any place along the line between -2 and $+2$ would be as good as any other. But once the squared function is introduced, the only place to minimize the loss is at 0, which is right between them. Thus at either extreme the total loss is 16, at either $+1$ or -1 it is 10 ($3^2 + 1^2$), and at 0 it is 8 ($2^2 + 2^2$).

use force to get their own way, and occasionally to overcome bargaining problems that cannot be solved by voluntary agreement (e.g., the formation of the state itself). In contrast, so long as these individual preferences are regarded as malleable or arbitrary, then it will be possible to find a social "problem" whenever some people have the wrong tastes or desires. On this view of the world, it will never be possible to confine political power within any narrow grounds. Surely huge portions of the feminist program for restructuring society rest upon the conviction that certain natural differences are illegitimate and should have no role to play in the world of commerce and public affairs. If individual choices are a function of social conditioning and not natural inclination, then plausibly government has a far grander mission. The source of social distress becomes nothing more than the asymmetrical and arbitrary transactions entered into by persons with different endowments and tastes. Private property or personal liberty will always generate a set of outcomes that do not conform to some overall unified conception of the proper distribution of social power and economic preferment. To justify coercion to rectify these imbalances opens us up to the risk of the authoritarian police state. The cure is far worse than the supposed disease.

VII. Conclusion

The purpose of this paper is to indicate the connection between what we know about human biology and the structure of social institutions. At the outset the raw data that we have consists of individual preferences, which are shaped and influenced by a wide range of social and biological forces. All too often, the modern tendency is to assume that the social parts of the equation wholly dominate the biological ones. Thus, personality and human institutions are said to be "social constructs" that reflect the institutions of dominant social classes. Biology is then viewed largely as a common template onto which these preferences are embedded, but not as a source of the differences in preferences as they emerge in any complex modern setting. The implication is that strong social control from the center is often needed to insure that individual personality is saved from the baleful influences that have led, among other things, to differences in sexual preferences and behavior.

I have taken quite the opposite view here, and have urged that the influences of biology are far more persistent and pervasive, and that it would be as dangerous to ignore the biological determinants of human behavior as it would be to ignore the social determinants of that behavior. So long as both sets of inputs are powerful, then it becomes far more difficult to condemn as illegitimate various patterns of different social and sexual roles that are common in the United States and elsewhere. I therefore have far less of a reformist impulse. I do not think that these biological arguments, even if correct, justify the use of force against those who disagree with me. But by the same token I think that these biological arguments offer powerful reasons to resist those who think that any difference in sex roles is so morally unacceptable that it gives them a general warrant to remake individual behaviors and social institutions from the center.

Law, University of Chicago

THE ORIGINS OF MORALITY: AN ESSAY IN PHILOSOPHICAL ANTHROPOLOGY

By Andrew Oldenquist

I. Introduction

By what steps, historically, did morality emerge? Our remote ancestors evolved into social animals. Sociality requires, among other things, restraints on disruptive sexual, hostile, aggressive, vengeful, and acquisitive behavior. Since we are innately social and not social by convention, we can assume the biological evolution of the emotional equipment – numerous predispositions to want, fear, feel anxious or secure – required for social living, just as we can assume cultural evolution of various means to control antisocial behavior and reinforce the prosocial kind. Small clans consisting, say, of several extended families whose members cooperated in hunting, gathering, defense, and child-rearing could not exist without a combination of innate and social restraints on individual behavior.

I shall argue for a naturalistic theory of morality, by which I do not mean the definitional claims G.E. Moore sought to refute,[1] but a broader and more complex theory that maintains that a sufficient understanding of human nature, history, and culture can fully explain morality; that nothing is left hanging. A theory that coherently brings together the needed biological, psychological, and cultural facts I shall call a philosophical anthropology; it is a theory that:

1) takes the good for humans – both an ultimate good (if there is any) and other important goods – to depend on human nature;

2) argues that a rudimentary but improving scientific and philosophical theory of human nature now exists, and thus denies that people are "essenceless";

3) takes this theory to be evolutionary and historical, making the question "How did morality originate?" pivotal for ethical theory, but leaves open the empirical question of the relative importance of biological and cultural evolution; and

4) takes the origin of the moral ideas to be explainable in terms of human nature and history.

Scientific facts and hypotheses will have roughly the role in this explanation that virtues, means and ends, the parts of the soul, habit, and practical reason had for Aristotle. Aristotle was the first philosophical anthropologist, and accomplished wonders given the non-evolutionary, rudimentary science of his time. As Aristotle would have put it, trying to understand morality without understanding human nature is like trying to know the good for a thing without knowing what kind of thing it is. And trying to understand human nature without understanding human

---

[1] For example, Jeremy Bentham's claim that "good" means "pleasant," a similar claim that Moore attributed to John Stuart Mill, and the claim of some moralists that "right" means "commanded by God."

evolution is, as Boyd and Richerson put it, quoting Darwin, "like puzzling at astronomy without mechanics."[2]

When I say that a naturalistic theory explains morality and leaves nothing hanging, I do not mean that scientific premises yield moral conclusions. Hume's Law forbidding the deduction of "ought" from "is" will stand. Rather, a philosophical anthropology should explain the origin of the moral ideas, explain why we have the basic moral beliefs we do, and say something about their relative importance to most people; finally (and fundamentally for ethical theory), it should explain why they are *moral* beliefs and not just aversions or desires.

Moral reasoning will remain untouched. The same logical constraints and moral psychological claims hold for both this theory and theories that affirm objective or unique moral facts: the objective defectiveness of moral beliefs based on factual ignorance, bad inference, or confusion; the superiority of empathy and knowledge by acquaintance over description in reaching moral agreement; and the existence of basic principles and values that large numbers of people find acceptable without argument.

First I defend a general schema for causally explaining the existence of a moral belief, given certain empirical and logical conditions. Then I suggest causal explanations of several actual species-wide moral beliefs in terms of the schema, together with hypotheses from human ethology and evolutionary biology. Next I take up, tentatively, the idea that explaining the genesis of virtues and moral rules, and their relation to human nature, implies a case for the reasonableness of at least some of them. Finally, I consider some problems regarding determinism and reductionism.

The crucial step in a naturalistic account, as I construe it, is an argument that lets one infer, from the facts of ancient social living, that a society has a morality. This is accomplished if one can describe the problems, attitudes, behavior, feelings, and talk of an ancient society in such a way that people today, reflecting on these descriptions, conclude that, yes, they had moral beliefs. This is not to say we have evidence that, say, a particular Cro-Magnon clan in southern France 30,000 years ago had feelings and behavior that revealed that they had a morality, rather than mere aversions and desires. We cannot know that. I mean that late hominids or early humans at some time reached a stage at which they manifested these feelings and behavior, and that this is in principle a dateable (though gradual) occurrence.

I do not conclude that they had true moral beliefs, false ones, or that moral beliefs have truth-values at all, but simply that they had moral beliefs. If one thinks moral beliefs (whether Cro-Magnon or contemporary) are about moral facts,[3] that will require an additional theory – one in moral epistemology or moral ontology. We can establish that a hypothetical society has (or doesn't have) a morality

---

[2] Robert Boyd and Peter J. Richerson, *Culture and the Evolutionary Process* (Chicago: University of Chicago Press, 1985), p. 1.

[3] Philosophers who defend an objective status for morality, currently called "moral realism," are defensive about what they mean by "moral facts" or "moral properties," and spend more time saying what they do not mean than what they do. Philosophers' claims about moral facts range from hard ontological claims about moral properties to a mere indication that they take folk morality at face value, by which I mean they endorse lay claims that torture is wrong and (if asked by philosophers) that it is true that torture is wrong.

without having to answer these latter questions; that is, the criteria for a group having a morality can be satisfied whether or not there are moral facts and moral properties, and whether or not non-descriptivism is true. It will also remain open, as far as logic is concerned, whether a utilitarian, a Kantian, a divine command, or any other normative theory is correct. But this openness is just logical. The theory will fit well with a form of rule-utilitarianism and a meta-ethical theory that is non-descriptivist and close to the theories of Hume[4] and Stevenson.[5]

II. Bridge Theories

I want to offer a theory of how an aversion, hate, or fear turns into a moral belief under the right conditions.[6] I propose that an aversion or desire is a moral belief when enough of the following characteristics are present:

1. One can intentionally communicate it to others, presumably though language, in the form of a judgment.

2. The judgment is supported by reasons, unless it is a basic or ultimate one, and the reasons one supports it with have a general appeal within one's community.

3. It is an all-things-considered judgment.

4. One is willing to universalize it, within a domain that bounds one's moral community.

5. The judgment can recommend action contrary to self-interest and still tend to motivate the agent.

6. The object of the judgment is the good or ill of humans, human institutions, and the higher animals.

7. One is disposed to use moral language – to call the object of the judgment bad, evil, and so on.

8. Expressions of the judgment are often ritualized, made in ceremonial circumstances, thereby indicating that the community and not just an individual is speaking.

The theory that an aversion or dislike is a moral belief (and its verbal expression a moral judgment) when these logical and empirical characteristics apply is what I will call a bridge theory. A bridge theory allows us to bridge the gulf between aversion and moral disapproval, and show under what conditions the former turns into the latter. It does this without referring to moral facts, moral properties, or anything else mysterious. It is essential that characteristics 1–8 individually not contain or imply any moral expressions. If one hates an action and enough of characteristics 1–8 apply, one thinks the action is morally wrong. We conclude something like "Jones believes that what S did is immoral," which tells us that Jones (and Jones's society) has a morality, but leaves Hume's Law intact. There is a general bridge theory, which I have just stated, and specific bridge theories for other moral concepts. The theory of retributive justice as "sanitized revenge," for

---

[4] In the *Treatise*, bk. III, pt. I, sec. I, where I interpret his remarks to imply a proto-emotivism.

[5] As developed by him in *Ethics and Language* (New Haven: Yale University Press, 1944).

[6] I shall emphasize aversions rather than desires, because most moral rules are prohibitory and function to protect people from what they very much fear. Nonetheless, the bridge theory also lets us infer moral beliefs about positive duties of compassion, loyalty, and so on.

example, explains a judgment of retributive justice as a desire for revenge that is impartial, publicly promulgated, made in a cool hour by neutral officials, ritualized, and so on.[7]

The conditions listed are not intended to be necessary and sufficient conditions for having a moral belief; it is not a traditional philosophical analysis. It instead explains "moral belief" as a cluster concept – sometimes the presence or absence of a condition will make the difference between aversion and moral belief, and sometimes not. It depends on the particular circumstances and on how forcefully or weakly the other conditions apply. One result is that there will be borderline cases of moral beliefs, not so much in the sense that individuals will not know whether they hate an action or think it wrong (although that can happen), but rather that people will disagree about whether something is a matter of morality.

It might be thought a trivial matter to derive the fact that someone has a moral belief from an attitude together with a number of empirical and logical conditions – on the ground that the only important thing is whether the moral belief is true. But this derivation is, I believe, more important to a philosophical understanding of morality if it actually tells us when a person, and hence the person's society, has a morality; after all, it remains problematic, after a few thousand years of inquiry, whether anyone can prove that moral beliefs are true or even whether they have truth values.

Other people may find the derivation unacceptable since, even if it doesn't violate Hume's Law, it is clearly a kind of reductionism. It is indeed that, and what is being "reduced" are moral beliefs and judgments. That is, moral beliefs and judgments are being identified with psychological states and bodily actions together with facts about the person's biology and culture. Surely, one may say, what morality is about, badness and rightness, cannot themselves be reduced to culture and biology. But this depends on one's theory of what morality is about. A bridge theory is an embarrassment to moral realism since it identifies moral beliefs with attitudes and certain conditions, leaving no role for the moral facts or moral properties moral beliefs are said to be about. Moral facts would not be refuted, but simply left out of the overall explanation of morality. On the other hand, if a nondescriptivist theory is true – for example, one similar to those of Hume, Stevenson, or Richard Hare[8] – nothing is left behind and morality itself is indeed reduced to culture and biology.

Our ancient ancestors had aversions, hates, and fears; then, later, they had what we call morality. Therefore, there was a describable change: we had ancestors that lacked a morality, they had descendants who did have a morality, and the question of what accounted for the change is of the greatest philosophical importance. The conditions listed in the bridge theory schema are part of an attempt to describe the change, though hardly to date it or locate it geographically. By a premoral period of society I mean generically premoral, not immoral or egoistic: their hypothesized attitudes do not satisfy our criteria for being moral concepts and beliefs.

---

[7] I give an explanation of a bridge theory for retributive justice, together with an argument for the social necessity of retribution, in "An Explanation of Retribution," *Journal of Philosophy* (September 1988).

[8] In Hare's *Freedom and Reason* (New York: Oxford University Press, 1963).

It is tempting to suppose that hominid or early human premoral society would be like the early stages in the cognitive-developmental theories of Jean Piaget and Lawrence Kohlberg. Kohlberg, whose six stages of moral development represent familiar philosophical positions ranging from an egoistic Stage One to a Rawlsian/neo-Kantian Stage Six,[9] says young children inevitably start in Stage One and advance without regressing, with the exceptions of morally backward adults who can be stuck at One, and college students who, Kohlberg says, regress. The idea that moral ontogeny recapitulates moral phylogeny, the former (in the form of Kohlberg's stages) therefore offering clues to the latter, unfortunately is not plausible – partly because of controversy over how to describe the stages and over which is higher. Aristotle, for example, would appear to be a Two-plus on Kohlberg's scale.

But the idea remains beguiling – the idea of the egoism of the young child paralleling presocial ancestors that lived long before there was morality, rather like the fetus with gills, and the herd morality of the older child paralleling early humans. The ethological evidence together with my model suggests a different scenario than the Kohlbergian one. It is that late hominids were thoroughly social – and strongly group-egoist and conventional – before they had any morality. And then as conceptualization, language, and third-party involvement in conflicts developed, dispositions that were just aversions began to satisfy the criteria for being moral beliefs, perhaps at roughly the same time for all of Kohlberg's stages.

It is plausible that in proto-moral early human society there were precursors of beliefs in rights, equality, the primacy of the self, and limits on the authority of the collective over the individual. Yet, innately social, precariously surviving, technologically stagnant clans can be expected to have a strongly group-egoist and collectivist social morality. We have strong evidence that contemporary traditional societies are highly socially conservative in the sense of being conformist, group-subservient, and intolerant of deviations from established ways.[10] It is easy to understand why they are so, and to extrapolate back to prehistoric societies.

[9] Laurence Kohlberg's stages are described in many of his writings. A late version of them is in *The Unstudied Curriculum* (Washington: Association for Supervision and Curriculum Development, 1970):
The Pre-Conventional Level
Stage 1. The punishment and obedience orientation. Morality is avoidance of punishment and unquestioning deference to power.
Stage 2. The instrumental relativist orientation. Right action is what gets you what you want, sometimes by trading favors.
The Conventional Level
Stage 3. The "good boy – nice girl" orientation. Morality is earning approval by conforming and being "nice."
Stage 4. The "law and order" orientation. Morality is doing one's duty in the sense of respecting authority and the social order.
The Post-Conventional or Principled Level
Stage 5. The social-contract orientation. Morality is based on law, rights, and social utility.
Stage 6. The universal ethical principle orientation. Morality is a matter of self-chosen universal principles of justice.
[10] See, for example, numerous passages in Franz Boas's *The Mind of Primitive Man* (New York: The Macmillan Co., 1938), Ruth Benedict's *Patterns of Culture* (Boston: Houghton Mifflin Co., 1959), I. M. Lewis, *Social Anthropology in Perspective* (New York: Penguin Books, 1976), and Edward Shils, *Tradition* (Chicago: University of Chicago Press, 1981).

Autonomy, individualism, and social experimentation are luxuries that could only begin to gain social approval with an increase in physical security.

One can suggest a relatively recent, historical, moral development, after humans began to gain some degree of mastery over food supply, predators, and shelter, in the sense of a cultural evolution of what is considered immoral; for example, an outward extension of who counts as an outsider and hence can be killed at will, a decrease in casual cruelty to humans and animals, and a rejection of slavery. These are all recent, historical changes, and hence long postdate the origin of codes of morality. If you lived almost anywhere 70,000 years ago and were precocious about individual rights, the equality of women, the rights of children, and the moral equality of outsiders, you would have a lonely and difficult time of it.

In addition to proto-moral taboos, and even proto-taboos existing before intra-clan communication deserved to be called language, there are some quasi-normative ideas, such as alienation, that we can easily suppose applied in prehistoric clans even if they had no words for it. This is because alienation less obviously requires reasoning and conceptualization than does morality, at least according to each of the three main understandings of it – the Marxist, which defines alienation in terms of objective economic relations of production,[11] the social-psychological, deriving prominently from the work of Melvin Seeman and which defines it in terms of feelings of powerlessness, normlessness, meaningless-ness, isolation, and self-estrangement,[12] and the communitarian, whose preemin-ent exponent was Emile Durkheim,[13] and also finds expression in the work of biologically oriented German philosophical anthropologists such as Arnold Gehlen.[14] On each of these theories, alienation would have been (and now is) a rare phenomenon in traditional societies. I believe that for ancient peoples it was a negative value, whether or not they themselves could say so or even think so.[15]

The significance of alienation is that it is one of those shadow-land normative notions – shame and courage being others – for which we need only a rudimentary bridge theory in order to attribute them as norms to late hominid or early human society. There is no daunting moral word, such as "moral," that we feel must pop into place: we can find alienation, as we can courage, when we postulate certain feelings, behavior, causes, and favorable or unfavorable reactions of others. Our ancient ancestors "knew" courage and alienation, much as we know them, as surely as they "knew" love, compassion, jealousy, hate, and revenge, even if they lacked a full-fledged language. These attributes and attitudes are steps or stages in the evolution of a morality as we know it.

[11] Marx explains alienation in the *Economic and Philosophical Manuscripts of 1844* (first published in 1932).

[12] Melvin Seeman, "On the Meaning of Alienation," *American Sociological Review,* 1959.

[13] Discussed and defended at length by Durkheim in *Suicide,* first published in Paris in 1897.

[14] See especially Gehlen's *Der Mensch, Seine Natur und Seine Stellung in der Welt* (Wiesbaden: AULA Verlag, 1986).

[15] Most modern analyses of alienation view alienated people as victims either of the social/economic system or of something else that is not their responsibility. Common moral opinion, however, is that people ought to have a sense of possession and regard for their family, community, or organization, and that alienated people are proper objects of criticism. In modern industrial societies, however, the matter is complicated because of the general sense that there is also something wrong with the social structure if it produces significant numbers of alienated people.

More than one theory is possible, of course. Perhaps the properties of goodness and badness existed from the time of the Big Bang, waiting for our ancestors to become smart enough to apprehend them, at which time people acquired a morality. Or, somewhat more diffidently, one might suggest (as have Peter Singer and Elliott Sober[16]) that we evolved big brains and morality arose as a rational by-product of our intelligence, much as did trigonometry. Such theories will not explain the affective side of morality, the things Hume spoke of – that morals move us and that matters of fact do not, that morals are more properly felt than thought of.[17] Yet Singer and Sober also seem to be correct when they say that the acquisition of morality is a natural (indeed, necessary) development of social beings as they acquired intelligence; Darwin himself makes the same point, as we shall see shortly. How analogous the case is to trigonometry is another matter. Part of what the bridge theory does is show how morality arises in social beings with intelligence, such features as universalizability, having reasons, and being all-things-considered plainly requiring intelligence.

Almost every aspect of human behavior is evidence of innate sociality, as are some physiological characteristics – such as the prolongation of infancy and the whole psychological and physiological complex that produces continuous sexual receptiveness. Language is perhaps the best example – full-fledged language and not just signaling – together with its physiological basis, which presupposes a continuing, interacting society of other people to talk to and which would be inexplicable otherwise. And when there is sociality and language, there will necessarily be codes of morality.

III. MORALITY AND LANGUAGE

Are ritualized practices and punishments (and their attitudinal accompaniments) sufficient to constitute a morality? Practices necessary for the survival of late hominid cooperative groups most likely predate the evolution of language and therefore of moral words, although this depends on what counts as language and moral words. A clan could ostracize non-conformists and have what we call taboos without having language. Certainly, however, one may say, if they have a morality they must have moral concepts! But what is a moral concept? Furthermore, do moral concepts require moral words? And what are moral words? The criteria for having a moral concept should be a conclusion of our inquiry, not the data with which we begin. I suggested in the preceding section that there are empirically describable conditions under which moral words are appropriate, and hence conditions under which members of a society actually have moral beliefs, but that moral concepts, in a richer sense than that, do not exist.

Today there are people who do not use moral language, but instead use psychological jargon or profanity where the rest of us would use moral words. For

[16] This suggestion was made by Sober at a conference on evolutionary biology, The Ohio State University, December 1988.

[17] In pt. I, secs. I and II, of bk. III of Hume's *Treatise*. In sec. II he tells us that "The very feeling constitutes our praise or admiration.... We do not infer a character to be virtuous because it pleases: But in feeling that it pleases after such a particular manner, we in effect feel that it is virtuous." Of all the classical theories of the nature of moral beliefs and judgments, Hume's is most consonant with what I am proposing.

128 ANDREW OLDENQUIST

them, ordinary moral words may not be strong enough, or they may associate moral language with moral opinions they abhor, or they may be conscientious philosophers who think using moral language implies moral properties – and since they think there aren't any moral properties, they therefore ought not use moral language. But if everything else is the same, withholding moral language doesn't make their moral beliefs cease to be what they are. People who consider themselves moral nihilists can have moral beliefs even if they deny they do, and other people may fail to have a moral belief when they claim to have one. One can mistakenly think, for example, that one believes using profanity is immoral, that cheating large corporations is morally wrong, or that buying and selling stocks is immoral. It is tempting to say that if I believe I believe M, I believe M. This may be true of simple propositional beliefs (e.g., that the cat is out) but not of moral beliefs, if having a moral belief implies having certain attitudes, a readiness to offer reasons of a certain kind, and a willingness to make certain logical moves. Having a moral belief is like having an ulcer: it is a fact about oneself, though with vague boundaries, and one can be mistaken about whether that fact obtains, perhaps even more obviously than one can be mistaken about whether one loves a person.[18]

A bridge theory describes the niche occupied by moral words; it therefore can tell us when other words (with compatible emotional auras) are in that niche and doing the same job. People who won't call actions wrong or people wicked but under the same conditions[19] instead call them, respectively, "dysfunctional" and "rats" have moral beliefs and "moral concepts," even when they deny it. This is a desirable implication of the theory, since if there actually are moral beliefs and they have the kind of structure I have suggested, we should expect there to be various grounds for lack of self-knowledge about them.

It is not an embarrassment that the theory allows one to derive Mafia morality as well as more widely-agreed-upon social morality, as long as it is clear that what follows is that a particular group has moral beliefs, and not that these moral beliefs are true or justified. A bridge theory, by itself, is neutral about the latter claims. Sometimes people aver that those with whom they strongly disagree do not have a moral belief at all, not even a wrong or false one. A bridge theory allows us to distinguish with greater precision between a liking or hate and a moral belief, and grounds the distinction sufficiently for us to determine whether the Mafia or Charles Manson lack a morality at all, as distinct from having a morality we reject. Because someone can believe right what I believe wrong, there can be such a thing as Nazi morality or Mafia morality – but one's attitudes slide off into mere hates and likings when they insufficiently satisfy the conditions for being a moral belief, and not because I or most people find the belief morally odious. It is likely that if Charles Manson said he and his followers had a system of morality, the theory

[18] One might think that I have ignored the "performative" role of moral utterances. I think that "S said 'I promise'" is a special case and that "S believes lying is always wrong" is sufficiently like "S believes he has an ulcer" that S can be mistaken about each. The grain of truth in the idea of the creative power of moral words, however, is that *in the appropriate circumstances* "I believe that lying is always wrong" can be self-justifying – that is, my saying it will make it true that I believe that.

[19] That is, the conditions that satisfy a bridge theory and under which they would, were it not for their quirk about moral language, call them wrong and wicked.

would show him to be mistaken. But it probably would not show that the Mafia or Naga head hunters lacked codes of morality.

We should distinguish the question of whether morality requires moral language from the question of whether it requires language at all. I think that contemporary substitutes for moral words are parasitic on preexisting ones, and for this reason (and other reasons I shall give), language is necessary for morality. Moreover, a society with a language seems to constitute not only a necessary but also a sufficient condition for there to be a morality: a society with a language would almost certainly have the occasions and the intelligence to satisfy the criteria I listed for aversions becoming moral beliefs, and then the society surely would have words to distinguish them from aversions that do not meet the criteria. Moral language is whatever words are used to mark the distinctions I have attempted to describe by means of the bridge theory.

What about hominids without language, or those just beginning to acquire one – hominids who, instead of calling someone a rat, shriek or bite? Why does morality require language at all? It does if the social practices, feelings, and reasoning that constitute the marks of the moral themselves could not exist without language. Can we imagine a troop of social hominids who did everything a group with a morality did except use language, and in place of language shriek, push and grab, shun, and so on, in order to reinforce or proscribe behavior? But how would they appeal to reasons and universalize? Are there sufficiently close behavioral analogues to the list of eight characteristics I offered – for example, using signals and gestures, screaming and pushing – such that a prelinguistic troop could have a morality? I am inclined to think not; what seems most plausible is that premoral social control and cooperation develop gradually into morality along with the development of language, with no bright line to mark the boundary.

It is reasonable that item 7, the disposition to use moral words, be on the list of moral-belief-making characteristics. If one is expressing one's dislike for something and most of the other conditions apply, and the expression "But it's wrong" flies from one's mouth, it may then be a moral belief instead of a dislike, just because the word flew out. Most of the time we do not deliberate whether we confront a moral issue; we just find ourselves using the words. As with any of these conditions, moral language is not a necessary condition, but its presence or absence in the right circumstances can nonetheless make the difference between a moral belief and a mere attitude. What this suggests is that there is no uniquely moral idea, object, cognition, or perception – no moral essence (no moral homunculus, as it were) hidden in the center of the complex that is an action, its circumstances, and its apprehension. Circumstances and features approach certain configurations, and then we feel that "immoral" or "wrong" is the right word – or, more commonly, we just find ourselves using them or find ourselves wondering whether the act is right or wrong.

IV. TRUTH AND JUSTIFICATION

What is the relation between explaining why we have the rules and values we have and justifying them? There is no valid logical inference from an explanation to a justification. In general, however, the explanation of why a rule evolved in a society is that it contributed to its survival or flourishing. Cultural as well as biological explanations of why we have rules prohibiting incest, dishonesty, theft, disloyalty, and so on are almost invariably explanations of the rules' utility in the sense of their causal contribution to individual or societal survival. In general, evolved characteristics are useful; insofar as the evolutionary mechanism is cultural or biological adaptation, the characteristic by definition is (or was) useful. (Of course, the rule can outlive its usefulness for the society in which it evolved.) So it is unquestionable that most evolved features, including emotional and behavioral dispositions as well as rules and practices, have individual utility and often group utility.

The products of cultural evolution – including, with special obviousness, moral values and rules – are in general, useful. In the case of cultural evolution, group selection (by which is meant natural selection for characteristics that benefit the group as a collectivity) does not confront the same objections it confronts in biological evolution: there can be selection for socialization into and enforcement of moral values and rules that benefit the group at some relative cost to the individual.[20] In the case of innately social animals, moral rules have individual as well as group utility, because what preserves the society also preserves the individuals who cannot live without a society. Thus a utilitarian can make a utilitarian argument for the social morality that evolved from wants and needs, at least for the time of its evolution. It should be emphasized that I offer it as a fact that most moral rules evolved from wants and fears in roughly the way I have suggested, and that they therefore have utility. I am not attempting to prove that anything is good because it has utility, but merely that both biological and cultural evolution ensure that most of social morality does, in fact, have utility. Since what we explain is the benefit of having the rule or practice, even though particular occasions of its use may not be beneficial, the kind of utility demonstrated is rule-utilitarian or rule-consequentialist.

This utility is qualified in at least two additional ways. First, although a rule is (or was) utile, our moral motives are only sometimes expectations of personal or general utility. Second, the utility the rules and practices produce is not that of "everyone" (whatever that means) but a trade-off or compromise between the survivability of an individual's DNA and the survivability of the clan or society in which the individual lives and upon which his or her own survivability is dependent. Any *evolutionary explanation* of morality, whether it emphasizes biological or cultural evolution, is bound to imply a correlative *utilitarian argument* for the rules, for things evolve by natural selection because they are useful.[21]

The theory does not refute claims about moral facts and moral properties, but it does show such claims to be unnecessary and therefore proper targets for Occam's razor. The claims I have in mind include those of contemporary moral realists such

---

[20] That is, a Prisoners' Dilemma matrix for cooperative, exploitative, and mixed societies shows that in the best society (as defined by summed utilities) the individual is second best off, and is best off as the benefiting party in an exploitative relationship.

[21] Not all biological evolution is by natural selection. Some of it instead results from chance combinations of genes, harmless mutation, or genetic drift. There are equally non-adaptive reasons for much of cultural evolution. Moreover, some products of natural selection may have been useful at the time, but no longer are today. I shall consider this last point in more detail when I come to Richard Alexander's views about the evolution of morality.

as Thomas Nagel, Nicholas Sturgeon, and David O. Brink.[22] These also include "error theories" such as that of John Mackie[23] – who agrees with the realists that folk morality implies moral facts but goes on to deny that moral facts exist – and moral fiction theories such as Simon Blackburn's.[24] The theory is consistent with secondary senses of moral truth and falsity – theories of moral truth as endorsement or emphasis – but I find these of dubious philosophical significance.

The proposed "naturalistic" explanation of morality leads neither to moral nihilism nor moral skepticism, for, as I argued earlier, actual moral reasoning is untouched by these theoretical issues. We actually can make a persuasive case for some moral principles and virtues, given some facts about our social nature. Consider the easy proof that courage is a virtue. Without courage, one will be fearful and intimidated by everything – by officials, examinations, new opportunities, an attractive man or woman one wants to meet, difficult tasks, overbearing people, and various dangers. To the extent that people lack courage, they tend to quit, decline, and back away; if they completely lack it, they will have no chance to get the things they want and be happy. We do not need to talk about moral truths or moral facts to complete this argument. The conditional justification of the moral rules and contemporary virtues minimally necessary for cooperative social living is demonstrable in much the same way that the virtue of courage is. Without socializing the young to be honest, fair, and respectful of other people's bodies and property, a society will have no chance to flourish, protect its members, and perpetuate itself – and without society, individuals have little chance to survive. But the premises – that happiness, life, and human social living are good – are not things I try to prove.

We call robbery morally wrong because we fear and hate it, and the bridge theory conditions obtain; there is no need and little sense in postulating wrongness as something in addition to the fear and the hatred and the satisfaction of these empirical and logical conditions. The rejection of moral objectivism or realism should be seen as the next stage in the "Copernican revolution." The earth is not the center of the universe, the universe was not made for us, it is not the way it appears to our unaided senses, and values are not facts or properties in addition to our needs and aversions. It has long been a mystery to me how someone can accept the "Copernican" viewpoint in every aspect of nature except ethics. The evolution of language eventually included what we would call moral words. But what the moral words applied to were the objects of wants and aversions when overlaid by new characteristics listed in the bridge theories, some of these new characteristics themselves being dependent on the evolution of language. The new characteristics

---

[22] See, for example, Nagel's arguments about the badness of pain in *The View From Nowhere* (New York: Oxford University Press, 1986); Sturgeon's attempt, in "Moral Explanations," eds. D. Copp and D. Zimmerman, *Morality, Reason and Truth* (Rowman and Allanheld, 1984), to refute Gilbert Harman's ethical relativism; and Brink's criticisms, in "Moral Realism and the Sceptical Arguments from Disagreement and Queerness," *Australasian Journal of Philosophy*, 62 (1984), pp. 111–25, of John Mackie's arguments in *Ethics: Inventing Right and Wrong* (New York: Viking Penguin, Inc., 1985) against the existence of moral facts.
[23] As presented in Mackie's *Ethics; Inventing Right and Wrong*.
[24] See Blackburn's *Spreading the Word: Groundings in the Philosophy of Language* (New York: Oxford University Press, 1984).

no more imply moral facts than do the original, prenormative needs and aversions. Thus we have a naturalistic explanation of morality, by which I mean an explanation of the existence of moral beliefs and judgments that does not require moral ontology or moral epistemology.

V. THE CONTENT OF MORALITY

A philosophical anthropology can admit types of morality amenable to distinct explanations instead of trying to find a single essence. The search for such an essence never yielded a satisfying theory, and often excluded from "genuine morality" elements most people would want to include, such as loyalty and retribution. Moral beliefs are what most people call moral beliefs, and people are disposed to call a sentiment a moral belief when it satisfies bridge theory conditions. But the conditions are arrived at in the first place by noting usage: that is, that they modify sentiments about which most people use moral words. The list of conditions replaces a definition and allows, as categories of moral belief, sexual morality and loyalties as well as fairness, rights, virtues, ideals, prohibitions, and retributive justice. A fully worked-out philosophical anthropology would aim to give equally robust evolutionary explanations of each of these types; but we ought not always expect significant biological explanations, some types of morality probably being better explained in terms of cultural evolution.

Jeffrie Murphy[25] has offered two reasons why philosophers should care about the causal origins of moral principles. First, philosophers can help scientists develop causal theories of morality that are free of conceptual confusion. This is the familiar philosophers' self-portrayal as concept doctor, and which generally irritates scientists. Second, philosophical theories are defective if they make bad empirical assumptions, hence, we can learn from scientists. With this second point, I heartily agree.

Murphy has performed an important service by reminding philosophers of Charles Darwin's intelligent and sophisticated remarks about the nature and origins of morality in Chapters IV and V of *The Descent of Man*. Murphy points out that Darwin himself says (in Chapter IV) that any animal with social instincts would inevitably acquire a moral sense as soon as its intellectual powers become like those of humans. Murphy then correctly says that there remains a gulf, recognized by Darwin, between "social instincts" and a "moral sense" or moral beliefs. In *The Descent of Man*, Darwin offers a two-stage theory of the origin of morality. Murphy says that Darwin first explains as well as anyone has that natural selection would favor the sympathy and group regard that are necessary for society. Murphy points out, in elaboration, that shame is a social emotion[26] – we are distressed by how our fellows view us. Shame behavior, he says, is hiding behavior, as Darwin also said. Darwin falters, however, on the question of how these feelings and sentiments become moral beliefs. This gulf, of course, is what the theory I propose attempts to bridge.

Murphy suggests that the nonsocial parts of morality are less amenable to

[25] Jeffrie Murphy, *Evolution, Morality, and the Meaning of Life* (Totowa: Rowman and Littlefield, 1982).
[26] *ibid.*, p. 76.

biological explanation.[27] He says that *"rights, justice,* and *political liberty"* are not explainable by biology because they do not aim at social cohesion; on the contrary, they concern claims of individuals against the group. This whole domain of morality, he argues, results from "thinking about the oppressive nature of some collective claims."[28]

It is not obvious that the idea of fairness or treating equals equally and the rights of the individual against the state are at a greater remove from evolved needs and fears, or even that they conflict with collective morality. What I have in mind is this. If innately social beings have a strong need to belong to a group, outrage at not being treated equally or not being given full rights that others receive is understandable as terror at being treated as an outsider – as someone who is no longer a member of the moral community. My suggestion is that outrage at injustice derives from a terror of exile or clan exclusion, but the detailed development of this idea is not something I am prepared to do here.

There is a large category of moral beliefs caused by the requirements of child care. Many moral principles and felt obligations would be absent or different if we did not love, and at least two kinds of love belong to human nature because they are evolutionary products essential for child care. Sexual love (and a whole associated complex, including loss of estrus) evolved to keep parents together long enough to care for the infant and child through its most dependent years. Parental love makes us love and tend to our children, including, rather remarkably, when one thinks about it, infants: if aesthetics and convenience were our only consideration, it would surely be rational to strangle infants on sight.

Irenäus Eibl-Eibesfeldt, among others, argues that sexual morality developed in closely related ways in different cultures from a core of biologically evolved predispositions. The sexual bond, he says, developed for the care of infants and young children, and he adds that much ancillary affectionate sexual behavior is ritualized feeding and child care behavior.[29] Every culture has moral beliefs – codes, taboos, and requirements – that control or reinforce species-wide predispositions regarding philandering, sexual love, jealousy, parental love, incest aversion, and child rearing. Here is a domain of strong beliefs about right and wrong, rooted in ancestral likings and aversions that later turned into moral beliefs. (I surmise that love, jealousy, and other passions predate morals.) The specific forms these beliefs take in different societies result from different environments and chance happenings that anthropologists and ethologists will never be able to reconstruct. Nonetheless, many cultural differences whose causes are hidden – for example, why one culture defines incest as it does – are not that important to the philosophical enterprise. We still can explain a domain of morality concerning sex, child care, and love in terms of human nature, as long as our explanations remain on a level of generality that attends more to cultural similarities than differences.

Sexual and parental love are, I suggest, part of the ground of what are called "special obligations," that is, non-universalizable, non-selfish, loyalty-based obligations to loved ones and one's community that often compete with ideals and

[27] *ibid.,* p. 85.
[28] *ibid.,* p. 87.
[29] See various sections of Eibl-Eibesfeldt's *Love and Hate,* trans. Geoffrey Strachan (New York: Holt, Rinehart and Winston, 1972), especially pp. 155–65.

impersonal morality. The object of love is a particular, not a kind of thing, which makes obligations based on love irreducibly different from obligations based on the repeatable features of things. An adequate philosophical anthropology must account for both. A mother bonds to a particular, *her* baby, in order to tend her DNA, and not to any equally good baby in the clan. A parent loves his or her own child, and fears baby swapping, and a man (or woman) loves the mate who helps care for his (or her) DNA. Imprinting bonds one to a particular by noting a unique bundle of qualities.[30]

The situation actually is more complex. A gene, as a unit of selection, is a gene type – a kind of gene – and not a gene token. Kin selection altruism is the disposition to help anyone with (say) my kinds of genes, the amount of help proportional to the likelihood of a relative (sibling, cousin, etc.) actually having my genes. Inclusive fitness is the fitness of a scattered individual that is defined as the bearers of a given kind of gene. Yet, what the animal evolved to love and value is not a kind – a gene type of which it knows nothing – but a particular, an individual animal which is much more likely to share its gene types than other particulars in the neighborhood. Therefore one especially values an individual on a basis independent of the repeatable features in terms of which impersonal morality works.

On a higher level, one's family is a particular, valued more than other families which from the impersonal point of view are "just as good." The perfect "impartiality" of gene tokens toward members of their kind – a gene token's indifference to whether it or another of its kind survives[31] – and the fact that the gene as a unit of selection is a gene type do not give the animal impartial values: on the contrary, the animal bonds to a geographically determinate particular, its offspring, and to its mate.

This is what love has in common with self-love or egoism: in each case one values a particular, whose similarity to another thing does not make them of equal value. There is, then, a genetic explanation of the peculiarity of special obligations, ethical egoism, and loyalties: love, loyalty, and egoism are non-universalizable because they fix on the physical coordinates of where one's DNA types are likely to be located (or where protectors or caretakers of it are located). Love and self-love are the most important basis of felt obligations that are not impartial. Almost as important is the "bonding" an individual has to his or her own family, clan, or community. Here, too, its particularity derives from one's own particularity, which is the locus of one's DNA.[32]

[30] If group selection were true, the structure of morality probably would have been different; the varieties of altruism and sexual strategies would also have been different, and therefore sexual morality too. But there is no good evidence that it is true, with the exception of an ingenious model of group selection devised by David Sloan Wilson that actually works, but probably only for some of the social hymenoptera. See Wilson's "The Group Selection Controversy: History and Current Status," *Annual Review of Ecological Systems, 1983,* and a number of other papers by him.

[31] Evolutionary theorists commonly speak of genes as wanting, sacrificing themselves, and being selfish or altruistic. They feel comfortable speaking this way because they know they can unpack that talk into a much more cumbersome account of, say, a gene's selfishness as its disposition to cause its animal host to behave in ways that tend to get the gene-type replicated in the next generation, and so on.

[32] A good example of possible technology upsetting concepts is the science fiction case of replicating an object of love: we evolved to love our own child, but what if the machine makes ten, exactly alike? We just get confused, for reasons not unlike our confusion about personal identity in the face of thought experiments about replication of the self.

Eibl-Eibesfeldt has suggested two reasons why humans kill conspecifics much more than other animals do. First, weapons allow us to kill quickly and at a distance, allowing no time for the submissive gestures that otherwise terminate conflict.[33] I would add that killing at a distance hides the face and the signs of commonality in one's adversary. Michael Walzer, while discussing this matter, relates George Orwell's experience in the Spanish Civil War, when Orwell would not shoot an enemy soldier held in his sights on the opposing trench because the soldier was walking along holding up his pants with two hands.[34] Second, Eibl-Eibesfeldt suggests that culture causes "pseudo-speciation," a condition in which such a strong sense of insiders as distinct from outsiders is felt that outsiders are thought of like members of another species. "They're not really human," say slaveholders, indoctrinated soldiers, and Naga head hunters.[35] A culture necessarily separates people into members and outsiders, to whom we sometimes respond with the merciless murderousness that other animals show to members of other species.

Biologists who write about human nature and morality generally affirm universal selfishness as part of human nature – but they mean *biological* selfishness: that is, behavior that tends to get one's DNA passed on. Hence they count self-sacrifices for one's children and other close relatives as selfish. But they are also drawn to psychological egoism as strongly as are most social scientists. Richard Alexander is one of the more sophisticated of these biologists.[36] Alexander, along with most biologists who talk about moral psychology, is interested in what I call "behavioral selfishness": the behavior, on average, enhances one's likelihood of survival and reproductive success, but its motive could be altruistic, selfish, or neither. Robert Trivers's theory of reciprocal altruism[37] is a good example of a theory of behavioral selfishness; it is an evolved disposition to help only other helpers, thereby (the theory goes) making one better off than either egoists or promiscuous altruists. I should add that our hominid ancestors among whom the tendency for reciprocal altruism supposedly evolved could hardly know that it paid off better than egoism or indiscriminate altruism; we hence have no grounds for assuming that their motives were selfish.[38]

For Alexander, the basic mechanism of morality is indirect reciprocity, which allows him, he argues, to reconcile morality with biological selfishness, current or historical. The crux of indirect reciprocity is that I do not need to help only helpers

[33] Eibl-Eibesfeldt, *Love and Hate*, p. 98.

[34] Michael Walzer, *Just and Unjust Wars: A Moral Argument with Historical Illustrations* (New York: Basic Books, 1977), p. 140.

[35] The Nagas were (and apparently no longer are) head hunters from Northeastern India, and are described in detail by (among others) Christoph von füher-Haimendorf in *Morals and Merit* (Chicago: University of Chicago Press, 1967). It would be hard to find a better example of a determinate boundary to one's moral community. Within their villages, the Nagas observed civility, law, rules of social morality, and a sense of community; outside, the state of nature and heads.

[36] Richard Alexander, *The Biology of Moral Systems* (New York: Aldine de Gruyter, 1987), pp. 77–78. I have criticized Alexander's theory in a review of his book in *Mind*, June 1989.

[37] Robert Trivers, "The Evolution of Reciprocal Altruism," *Quarterly Review of Biology*, 1971.

[38] Indeed, no one knew this for sure until Robert Axelrod showed that the Prisoners' Dilemma strategy called Tit-for-Tat, which in form is nearly identical with reciprocal altruism, wins against all known competitors. See his *The Evolution of Cooperation* (New York: Basic Books, 1984), and also described by Douglas R. Hofstadter, "Metamagical Themas," *Scientific American* (May 1983).

if people disposed to help helpers are watching or will hear about me. It is a natural extension of how the disposition to help helpers can be in my interest: I am more likely to be helped if I gain a reputation as a helper; I do not need to depend for help on the recipient of my altruism. This also accounts for why we sometimes have an inclination, although a diminished one, to help non-helpers too (contrary to what Trivers's original version of reciprocal altruism predicts).

Alexander's indirect reciprocity is compatible, as is reciprocal altruism, with altruistically motivated action (the kind of altruism philosophers recognize), as well as with Butlerian particular passions.[39] Indirect reciprocity also is compatible with both phenotypic and genotypic self-sacrifice,[40] Alexander insisting only that in the ancient environments in which the altruistic predispositions evolved they were biologically advantageous. This grounding of indirect reciprocity in behavioral selfishness is indeed indirect, since Alexander only requires that, at some time in the past, the behavior was as a matter of fact beneficial to the agent's DNA. This circuitous and (sometimes) merely historical dependence on biological selfishness permits Alexander to explain a fairly impressive amount of moral and supererogatory behavior by indirect reciprocity. He gives generally plausible accounts of natural selection for following the rules, within the environments of early societies. "I am not assuming that all (or even most) apparently selfless acts are in fact reciprocated, but that such acts could not be performed unless, during evolutionary history, the rewards were on average greater than the costs."[41]

Alexander claims, without much argument, that morality arose to resolve conflicts of interest. This ignores a number of types of morality and value – such as the value of happiness, the badness of pain, and ideals of how to live one's life – which, in themselves, do not involve conflicts of interest. In his attempt to reconcile biological selfishness with morality as conflict resolution, Alexander suggests that the appearance of altruism is so beneficial that we deceive ourselves into believing we are not self-interested (whatever that means). It is in passages of this kind that he flirts with psychological egoism.

VI. DETERMINISM AND POLITICS

Implicit in what I have said is a loose kind of determinism; in particular, I have suggested that certain moral beliefs are genetically predisposed. Moreover, I proposed bridge theories which permit an inference from the nonmoral to the generically moral, which is a kind of reductionism. If the theory is correct, is morality less than it needs to be or illusory?

Nothing is wholly innate, nothing wholly learned; both causes are always necessary. We call behavior innate when its genetic causation is noteworthy, which usually is when it is easy to identify, the effect is significant, and it is difficult for us to find an environment in which the behavior doesn't occur. What this means is

---

[39] I mean particular passions as Bishop Butler explains them in *Sermon XI*, direct desires that aim only at their objects: to play, satisfy one's curiosity, rescue a person from the river, and so on.

[40] Phenotypic self-sacrifice puts the individual animal at risk; genotypic self-sacrifice is action that tends to diminish the representation of the animal's gene types (and not merely its gene tokens) in subsequent generations.

[41] Alexander, p. 160.

that causes we call "innate" are causes we wish to spotlight; so too, in certain circumstances, are causes we called "learned." These preliminaries out of the way, the question of whether a behavior is innate or learned, in this qualified sense, is perfectly coherent; in principle, it can be settled by deprivation experiments. As Conrad Lorenz showed,[42] if a bird raised in isolation sings its species-specific song, that capacity is innate. (However, it may be inadequate to the full effect – the song may be fragmentary or off key. Also, as I said, environmental causes are always necessary: the bird must be fed, etc.) So sometimes we can know when the interesting effect is innate or learned, as with the bird song. Almost as conclusive is universal or near-universal cross-cultural human behavior – such as smiling and the effect of smiling to reduce another's fear or hostility, staring, pair bonding, and the hundreds of behaviors ethologists are coming up with, most of them admittedly trivial for our purposes.

Nearly every behavioral trait that is predisposed by biological evolution is simultaneously a product of cultural evolution. Sex, pair bonding, incest and incest avoidance, child rearing, group loyalty, shaming, and ostracism are ceremonialized (for example, marriage, courtship rules, and parades) and have details that vary from culture to culture (for example, what counts as incest); these forms and ceremonies are taught by one generation to the next, indicating that what we presently see is a product of cultural transformation, or in other words, cultural evolution. It could not be otherwise for creatures that have a culture. Without culture, genetic predispositions show themselves in the same way from generation to generation (except for biological evolutionary change); culture shapes and elaborates what is important in our lives, including the effects of biological predispositions. Culture speeds up and diversifies evolution within the limits set by our genome. Culture itself is a means of transmission with variation, for example, by accidental changes, conquest, or social experiments.

The very idea of cultural transmission presupposes a genetic predisposition to conformity – what Boyd and Richerson whimsically call "the imitator gene." In *Culture and the Evolutionary Process*, Boyd and Richerson develop a detailed model of cultural evolution and its similarities to biological evolution. They argue that culture is an inheritance system and a system of evolution paralleling genetic evolution, and that therefore the full explanation of human behavior requires a study of natural selection and adaptation on the cultural level as well as on the biological one.[43] The fact that culture itself is a product of evolution does not rebut this claim, since such a general statement of origins doesn't tell us what a given culture will be like. They argue that some products of cultural evolution are not easily correlated with evolved predispositions. The relations between and relative inputs of biological and cultural evolution eventually must be examined in depth by any adequate philosophical anthropology.

There is no question that social evolution – cultural change – can affect biological evolution by changing the environment and hence the selective pressures

[42] See especially Lorenz's *King Solomon's Ring*, trans. Marjorie Kerr Wilson (New York: Crowell, 1952).

[43] It should be mentioned that Boyd and Richerson are interested in cultural evolution as often a superior basis for the explanation of cultural diversity, whereas my interest, and the general goal of a philosophical anthropology, focus on cultural universals (rather than differences) as clues to human nature.

we face. Therefore culture and our genetic makeup mutually effect one another. To begin with a whimsical example, if our automobile culture and drinking habits remain the same for 10,000 years, there will be natural selection for the ability of young people to drive cars safely while intoxicated. Since the advent of the industrial revolution, there probably has been some selection for the ability to tolerate new chemicals emitted into the environment, but industrial culture is too new for us to be able to detect actual changes. However, as long as culture has existed, there must have been selection for the ability to control one's passions – those who lacked this ability leaving behind fewer children because they more often were exiled, attacked, or not helped when they needed it. The environment created by culture and by the competition of cultures is an environment to which the individual must adapt; it produces biological selective pressures as do climate, disease, and predators. Cultural ephemera, such as automobiles, do not last long enough to affect evolution, but surely such developments as stone age group hunting and the adoption of agriculture did constitute strong selective forces.

Positions similar to those I have been defending have been severely criticized as "biological determinism," the criticism significantly inspired, I believe, by political ideology.[44] There are real problems here, and I shall try to separate them from ideological objections.

Causal determinism is not at issue, socialist critics of biological determinism such as Hilary Rose and Stephen Rose[45] offering no objection to the view that culture and the ruling classes determine moral beliefs. There ought not be controversy (although there is) over the view that we, like all animals, evolved to be conformers and (since we are intelligent creatures) are easily indoctrinated. Otherwise, a ruling class could not impose its values on us, and the numerous cultures around the world could not maintain their integrity from generation to generation. Biological, not cultural, determinism is the object of attack.

What is most objected to, in my opinion, are not pop sociobiological hypotheses with sexist or anti-socialist implications, such as Robert Audrey's suggestion that innate human territoriality dooms Soviet collective farms,[46] for then one need only refute, if one can, the offending hypotheses. Rather, what really rankles is the very idea of a human nature richer than the instinct of infants to suckle and to cry at loud noises. The crux of the matter is that social determinism allows philosophers who would be kings to dream of remaking humanity in the image of their ideology, whereas the idea of a non-trivial human nature is the idea of competition at the helm of history.

The thesis I defend is clearly reductionist: moral beliefs are complex kinds of desires and aversions, which in turn are naturally thought of as caused by biology and culture. If these desires and aversions are better explained by cultural than by biological evolution, as a host of social scientists claim, then my emphasis on the biological will have to be corrected, although the theory will be no less reductionistic. If human nature is more plastic than sociobiologists think, and more

---

[44] See *Not in Our Genes: Biology, Ideology, and Human Nature*, Richard C. Lewontin, Steven Rose, and Leon J. Kamin (New York: Pantheon Books, 1984), and much of the writing in the newsletter *Science for the People*.

[45] See the essays in *Ideology of/in the Natural Sciences*, eds. Hilary Rose and Steven Rose (Boston: G. K. Hall, 1980).

[46] Robert Audrey, *The Territorial Imperative* (New York: Atheneum, 1970), p. 102.

a product of culture than I think, an adjustment is called for; this ongoing argument about the proportional inputs of culture and biology, however, ought to excite only curiosity, not passion and ideologically motivated anger.

Consider a few genuine problems arising from plausible hypotheses about human nature concerning incest aversion and group loyalties. All cultures believe incest is wrong; the belief is explainable by a bridge theory and worldwide aversion to incest. The innateness of incest aversion is highly plausible: sexually re-producing animals have a few recessive genes that are lethal only when received from both parents, and hence have evolved incest avoidance mechanisms (a few species of moths and a few other organisms are illuminating exceptions) ranging from abandonment and kicking out of the nest to, among chimpanzees and humans, diminished sexual interest between siblings and others who grow up sharing their intimate social space.[47]

Incest, interestingly, was not part of the sexual revolution of the past three decades, even though contraceptives make it genetically harmless. What ought a rational person to think about incest?[48] One answer is that the emotional costs imposed by the innate aversion mechanism make "safe" incest disutile. But this is not a satisfying answer; most people think incest is just wrong, a horror, rather than merely an imprudent practice for the sophisticated reason given above. Ought children and their parents who think they ought to want the joy of sex together simply seek therapy, or a pill, that suppresses the bad feeling, just as someone who feels (but no longer believes) that interracial sex is wrong ought to try to get rid of the fossil emotion? Another answer is simply to accept both the felt moral disapproval and the genetic-evolutionary explanation. I am tempted by but dissatisfied with that position. It raises large questions about why we are dissatisfied when we find there is a cause but not a reason for a moral belief, and about whether philosophers ought to hide the truth about the origins of moral beliefs from the masses.

The problem of the need for and dangers of group loyalties is more important. A consequence of innate sociality is that people are not essenceless, as existentialists and some Western Marxists think, but have social identities on which their sense of well-being depends. And the social units to which people belong – their families, institutions, communities, and nations – are of non-instrumental value; and they are objects of group loyalty, not merely of instrumental value, as the radical individualist and social contractarian tradition would have us believe. We should note the difference between saying it is natural (Aristotle, Cicero, Aquinas, and most of the ancients) and saying it is convenient and safer (Hobbes, Locke, the whole social contract tradition, and most American sociologists and social psychologists) to live in groups or society. The former has its roots in the communitarian nature of traditional societies, and fits the facts as human ethologists and evolutionary theorists are beginning to develop them. The latter is

[47] See Jane Goodall in *In the Shadow of Man* (Boston: Houghton Mifflin Co., 1971) on the incest avoidance of the otherwise promiscuous chimpanzee Flo, and Joseph Shepher, "Mate Selection Among Second Generation Kibbutz Adolescents and Adults: Incest Avoidance and Negative Imprinting," *Archives of Sexual Behavior, 1971*, on the lack of sexual liaisons among unrelated young people raised communally in Israeli kibbutzim.

[48] William Lycan first called my attention to this puzzle in a conversation a number of years ago.

the product of individualist ideology. Here is a clear instance of the relevance of human nature to social and political thought, requiring us at least to reappraise elements of the organic theory of society and, perhaps, find as much wisdom in de Tocqueville as in Rawls or Nozick.

But we cannot have the benefits of "community" without accepting a distinction between insiders and outsiders. This is what, in its extreme form, Alexander called pseudo-speciation, and is a source of racism and war-making nationalism. From the perspective of most of us, pure organicism destroys autonomy and leads to a kind of social black hole. Extreme individualism, on the other hand, brings with it alienation and loss of community. This is a problem I have discussed at length elsewhere,[49] but without complete satisfaction and to which it would be well if philosophers devoted more attention.

VII. CONCLUSION

I have sketched a theory that offers both a causal and an analytical explanation of morality, in such a way that the two support one another. The bridge theory is the analytical part: moral beliefs are desires and aversions, under certain conditions whose descriptions themselves do not require moral terms, and moral language refers to nothing *sui generis,* but evolved to label desires and aversions that satisfy enough of the conditions.

A philosophical anthropology explains the bridge theory conditions as what we should expect, given our present knowledge of human nature as a product of evolutionary history. It is a human nature that is utterly dependent on society, intelligent, individually and biologically selfish, group egoistic, and altruistic. An inquiry into deep needs that became values reveals a common cross-cultural content that concerns the requirements of child care, treatment that is fair or equal relative to other group members, and rules that prohibit predatory and other antisocial behavior. At a still deeper level, the need to protect one's DNA, as represented in children, explains why we have two levels of morality – loyalties and special obligations whose objects are particulars, and domains of impersonal, intra-societal, social morality.

Evolved fears and needs become moral beliefs, moral beliefs and society are necessary for each other, and society is necessary for human life. But these considerations do not "prove" any normative system; rather, if the theory is correct, traditional philosophical questions about proof and moral properties become irrelevant.

Morality is part of nature, not a surd or mystery that stands outside of our biological and cultural history. Morality is more real, not less so, because of this: not only is moral reasoning as available as under any other theory, morality makes sense. We can begin to understand its use, its diversity, its cross-cultural common content, and how it grew out of loves, and hates, and wants, and fears from a time when there was no such thing as morality.

Philosophy, The Ohio State University

[49] This is discussed in my *The Non-Suicidal Society* (Bloomington: Indiana University Press, 1986), chs. 2, 9, 10, and 18.

THE FEMINIST REVELATION

By Christina Sommers

In the *Proceedings of the American Philosophical Association* for the fall of 1988, we find the view that "the power of philosophy lies in its radicalness."[1] The author, Tom Foster Digby, tells us that in our own day "the radical potency of philosophy is particularly well-illustrated by contemporary feminist philosophy" in ways that "could eventually reorder human life."[2] The claim that philosophy is essentially radical has deep historical roots.

Aristotle and Plato each created a distinctive style of social philosophy. Following Ernest Barker, I shall call Aristotle's way of doing social philosophy "whiggish," having in mind that the O.E.D. characterizes 'whig' as "a word that says in one syllable what 'conservative liberal' says in seven." Later whigs shared with Aristotle the conviction that traditional arrangements have great moral weight, and that common opinion is a primary source of moral truth. The paradigm example of a whig moral philosopher is Henry Sidgwick, with his constant appeal to Common Sense and to "established morality."[3] On the more liberal side, we have philosophers like David Hume who cautions us to "adjust [political] innovations as much as possible to the ancient fabric," and William James who insists that the liberal philosopher must reject radicalism.[4]

In modern times, many social philosophers have followed the more radical example of Plato, who was convinced that common opinion was benighted and in need of much consciousness-raising. Looking on society as a Cave that distorted real values, Plato showed a great readiness to discount traditional arrangements. He was perhaps the first philosopher to construct an ideal of a society that reflected principles of justice, inspiring generations of utopian social philosophers.

Our A.P.A. author thus belongs to a long and distinguished Platonist tradition

---

[1] Tom Foster Digby, "Philosophy as Radicalism," *Proceedings and Addresses of the American Philosophical Association*, vol. 61, no. 5 (June 1988), p. 860.

[2] *ibid.*, pp. 860–61.

[3] See Ernest Barker's introduction to Aristotle's *Politics*, where he argues that Aristotle was "a Whig of the type of Locke or Burke." *Politics of Aristotle*, ed. and trans. Ernest Barker (Oxford: Oxford University Press, 1973).

[4] Both David Hume and William James warn against the hazards of social and political radicalism. Here is Hume on the subject of political experimentation: "To ... try experiments merely upon the credit of supposed argument and philosophy can never be the part of a wise magistrate, who will bear a reverence to what carries the mark of age; and though he may attempt some improvements for the public good, yet will he adjust his innovations as much as possible to the ancient fabric..." (*Essays on Moral and Political Subjects*, pt. II, essay XVI). William James saw the rejection of radicalism as central to the pragmatic method. "[Experience] has proved that the laws and usages of the land are what yield the maximum of satisfaction.... The presumption in cases of conflict must always be in favor of the conventionally recognized good. The philosopher must be a conservative..." ("The Moral Philosopher and the Moral Life," *Essays in Pragmatism* (New York: Hafner, 1948, p. 80)).

that views philosophy as an organon for radical social reform. The opposing Aristotelian/whiggish tradition is today far weaker and certainly less popular among social philosophers: most feminist philosophers repudiate it altogether. Dr. Digby has high praise for the feminist social critics who are exposing the contemporary Cave as sexist ("androcentric") and unjust; he predicts that "feminist philosophy will one day be seen as one of the pivotal developments in the history of philosophy."[5] Digby's assessment reflects the view of the feminists themselves, who are convinced that feminist philosophy is initiating an intellectual revolution of historical dimensions. My own view that this judgment is intemperate and altogether unwarranted will be made evident throughout the ensuing discussion.

I. FEMINISM AS A RADICAL PARADIGM

For the benefit of those who have not been edified by much reading in feminist philosophy, I shall cite some characteristic positions of some leading feminist philosophers. It is practically impossible to do justice to all the newest turns of feminist theory. Feminist literature is in constant ferment; there is a kind of feminism of the week, but keeping track of it would engage all one's time. I shall therefore outline Alison Jaggar's useful and influential typology of contemporary feminist theory.[6] Jaggar identifies four dominant feminist "frameworks": liberal, Marxist, radical, and socialist.

1. Liberal feminism, according to Jaggar, has its origins in the social contract theories of the sixteenth and seventeenth centuries. Liberal feminists demand that principles of liberty and equality be applied to women, and they actively work to remove laws and to reform institutions that restrict women's autonomy or range of opportunity. Historically, liberals have worked to accomplish the following for women: suffrage, the right to own property, the right to obtain a divorce, access to credit and educational opportunities, and other rights enjoyed by men. Liberals do not, however, challenge the basic assumptions of democratic capitalism. Mary Wollstonecraft and the later John Stuart Mill are cited by Jaggar as examples of liberal feminist theorists. But Jaggar also discusses a more radical and contemporary version of liberalism (which I shall call egalitarianism). Jaggar gives no examples, but the views of Susan Okin and Richard Wasserstrom come to mind.[7] Both deploy liberal principles in order to make the case for complete equality between men and women. Okin argues for a feminist reading of John Rawls. She believes that if the participants in the original position were ignorant of their sex, they would probably opt for a genderless society in which the family as we know it is abolished in favor of an egalitarian alternative.

---

[5] Digby, p. 860.

[6] Alison Jaggar, *Feminist Politics and Human Nature* (Totowa: Rowman and Allanheld, 1983). A similar typology is described by Rosemary Tong in "Feminism Philosophy: Standpoints and Differences," *American Philosophical Association Newsletter on Feminism and Philosophy* (April 1988), pp. 8–11.

[7] See Richard Wasserstrom, "Racism and Sexism," *Philosophy and Social Issues* (Notre Dame: University of Notre Dame Press, 1980), p. 26; Susan Moller Okin, *Justice, Gender and the Family* (New York: Basic Books, 1989).

> The family is the linchpin of gender, reproducing it from one
> generation to the next . . . [F]amily life as typically practiced in our society
> is not just, either to women or to children. Moreover, it is not conducive to
> the rearing of citizens with a strong sense of justice. . . . A just future would
> be one without gender.[8]

Okin doesn't specify the changes entailed by a sexually neutral social contract.
Richard Wasserstrom, on the other hand, gives a detailed account of an ideal
"sexually assimilated" society in which the gender system has been overthrown.

> [T]here would be no expectation that the family was composed of one
> adult male and one adult female, rather than, say, just two adults – if two
> adults seemed the appropriate number . . . [P]ersons would not be
> socialized so as to see or understand themselves or others as essentially or
> significantly who they were . . . because they were either male or female.
> . . . Bisexuality, not heterosexuality or homosexuality, would be the typical
> intimate sexual relationship in the ideal society that was assimilationist in
> respect to sex.[9]

2. Marxist feminists constitute the next major group in Jaggar's typology.
Following Frederick Engels, Marxist feminists hold that women's oppression will
be abolished in the classless society; the discriminatory aspect of the gender
difference will be overcome when the class struggle is won. There do not seem to be
many current feminist theorists writing under this banner, but Jaggar and others
discriminate the Marxist perspective since it has been a critical influence on radical
feminism and socialist feminism – the other two major categories in Jaggar's
typology.

3. Radical feminism emerged from the liberation movements of the 1960s. It sees
women as the most oppressed group in history, and denies that this oppression can
be removed merely by changing the economic system or even overthrowing the
class system. Women are oppressed by men; the recognition of this fact is the
starting point of radical feminist philosophy, and it gives it a confrontational and
highly controversial character.

Two of the contemporary theorists mentioned by Jaggar, Mary Daly and
Andrea Dworkin, have worked out an imaginative and elaborate view of the
"patriarchy" in which men are variously characterized as death-affirming rapists
and warmongers. Daly calls them "Necrophiliacs."[10] According to Andrea
Dworkin:

> Men love death. In everything they make they hollow out a central
> place for death . . . in male culture slow murder is the heart of eros, fast
> murder is the heart of action, and systemized murder is the heart of
> history.[11]

---

[8] Okin, pp. 170–71.
[9] Wasserstrom, p. 26.
[10] Mary Daly, *Gyn/Ecology: The Metaethics of Radical Feminism* (Boston: Beacon Press, 1978), p. 59.
[11] Andrea Dworkin, "Why So-Called Radical Men Love and Need Pornography," ed. Laura Lederer,
Take Back the Night: Women in Pornograpy (New York: William Morris, 1980), p. 139.

Women, by contrast, are life-affirming, caring, and nurturing. Radical feminists seek to give expression to women's experience in a new feminine epistemology while exposing the masculinist aspects of classical epistemology as denigrating and hostile to women's ways of knowing. The political character of the male point of view affects the most abstract disciplines. Here is how Catherine MacKinnon articulates this claim:

> [Feminism's] project is to uncover and claim as valid the experience of women ... This defines the task of feminism not only because male dominance is perhaps the most pervasive and tenacious system of power in history, but because it is metaphysically nearly perfect. ... Its force is exercised as consent, its authority as participation ...[12]

Virginia Held looks forward to the day when the "patriarchy is overthrown" and women do the "organizing."

> Instead of organizing human life in terms of expected male tendencies toward aggression, competition and efforts to overpower ... one might try to organize human life to nurture creativity, cooperation and imagination, with the point of view of those who give birth and nurture taken as primary.[13]

Some radical feminists follow de Beauvoir in abjuring motherhood itself as oppressive to women. In her "Motherhood: The Annihilation of Women," Jeffner Allen tells us what being a mother really means:

> A mother is she whose body is used as a resource to reproduce men and the world of men ... Motherhood is dangerous to women because it continues the structure within which females must be women and mothers, and, conversely, because it denies to females the creation of a subjectivity and world that is open and free.[14]

4. Socialist feminism is a synthesis of Marxism and radical feminism: its goal is to abolish both class and gender. "Socialist feminism," says Jaggar, "seeks a society in which 'masculinity' and 'femininity' no longer exist."[15] After noting that the ideal society is not immediately realizable, Jaggar points to some things that socialist feminists believe can be done right away:

[12] Catherine MacKinnon, *Toward a Feminist Theory of the State* (Cambridge: Harvard University Press, 1989), pp. 116–17.
[13] Virginia Held, "Birth and Death," *Ethics*, vol. 99, no. 2 (January 1989), p. 388.
[14] Jeffner Allen, "Motherhood: The Annihilation of Woman," ed. Joyce Trebilcot, *Mothering, Essays in Feminist Theory* (Totowa: Rowman and Allanheld, 1984), p. 315.
[15] Alison Jaggar, p. 340.

One institution to which some socialist feminists are seeking immediate alternatives is the stereotypical 20th Century nuclear family ... [They] see this structure as a corner-stone of women's oppression: it enforces women's dependence on men, it enforces heterosexuality, and it imposes the prevailing masculine and feminine character structures on the next generation. In addition, the traditional nuclear family is a bulwark of the capitalist system ...[16]

Jaggar, who finds this version of feminism most plausible, notes that uninitiated women in the capitalist, patriarchal cave are subject to common illusions that serve to reinforce male dominance. "The ideology of romantic love has now become so pervasive that most women in contemporary capitalism probably believe they marry for love rather than for economic support."[17] The socialist feminist utopia includes technological as well as social transformations:

[W]e must remember that the ultimate transformation of human nature at which socialist feminists aim goes beyond the liberal conception of psychological androgyny, to a possible transformation of 'physical' human capacities, some of which, until now, have been seen as biologically limited to one sex.[18]

Socialist and radical feminists are divided on how the revolution will come to pass. Jaggar continues:

Socialist feminists, by contrast [to radical feminists], are sufficiently Marxist to be skeptical that the white male ruling class would give up its power without a violent revolution; however they are confident that such a struggle could be won by the overwhelming majority of the population whom they view as their potential allies.[19]

Jaggar mentions several other contemporary feminist sub-groups: lesbian separatists, anarcha-feminists, Freudian feminists, eco-feminists, radical women of color, and French "post-structuralist" feminists. They share a common goal of articulating the experiences of women that, for some, serve as the basis of a distinctively "feminist epistemology." All take characteristic pride in their revolutionary perspective on society and the family.

II. LIBERAL FEMINISM AND GENDER FEMINISM

Feminist thinkers of a liberal (that is, Millian) persuasion are not at the core of contemporary feminist philosophy, and they are not among those Digby praises. Jaggar harks back to the nineteenth century for examples of influential liberal

[16] *ibid.*, p. 336.
[17] *ibid.*, p. 219.
[18] *ibid.*, p. 132.
[19] *ibid.*, p. 340 (part of this passage was misprinted in the first edition; see the 1988 edition for correct text).

feminists. Liberal feminism is a significant force outside the academy.[20] But it is not the favored standpoint among academic feminists; in particular, liberal feminism does not inspire contemporary feminist philosophers.

Liberal feminists are content to achieve equality of opportunity and full legal equality; they are not, in principle, at war with the "gendered family" or with other aspects of society that place value on masculine and feminine differences. As Jaggar correctly, if somewhat disparagingly, says:

> For the liberal feminist ... the roots of women's oppression lie in women's lack of equal civil rights and equal educational opportunities. There is little attempt at historical speculation as to why such a lack should exist. Because the roots are so easily visible, women's oppression can be tackled immediately by a direct attack on sexist discrimination. When this discrimination has been eliminated, women will have been liberated.[21]

Liberal feminists are not out to second-guess women on what they really prefer. On the whole, they follow John Stuart Mill in being attentive to the preferences, aspirations, and ideals of women – even when these include such "gendered" choices as conventional marriage and motherhood. In short, the liberal feminists are more liberal than feminist – or, rather, they are feminists in wanting for women what any liberal wants for anyone suffering from bias: namely, fair treatment.

The feminist schools Jaggar mentions – egalitarian, Marxist, radical, and socialist – all tend to see popular women's culture as something that needs to be "critiqued" and, perhaps, eliminated. These gender feminists, as I shall call them, view social reality in terms of the "sex-gender system." In Sandra Harding's words, this system is a

> system of male-dominance made possible by men's control of women's productive and reproductive labor, where 'reproduction' is broadly construed to include sexuality, family life, and kinship formations, as well as the birthing which biologically reproduces the species ... [The sex/gender system] appears to be a fundamental variable organizing social life throughout most recorded history and in every culture today.[22]

Leading contemporary feminist philosophers have adopted this perspective on history, society, and culture. In addition to demanding a radical restructuring of society, the gender feminist calls for an epistemological revolution that will expose masculinist bias and ultimately remove its mark from our cultural and social heritage. As a liberal feminist, I am saddened to see that the radical perspective has

---

[20] Sylvia Hewlett is a good example of a working liberal feminist. She left the academy when her academic sisters did not give her adequate support in her attempts to manage a family and an academic career. See her *A Lesser Life: The Myth of Women's Liberation in America* (New York: William Morrow, 1985).

[21] Alison Jaggar, eds. Alison Jaggar and Paula Rothenberg, *Feminist Frameworks* (New York: McGraw Hill, 1984), p. 85.

[22] Sandra Harding, "Why Has the Sex/Gender System become Visible Only Now?", eds. Sandra Harding and Merrill Hintikka, *Discovering Reality: Feminist Perspectives on Science* (Dordrecht: D. Reidel, 1983), p. 312.

proved so beguiling to the majority of feminist academics. In what follows, I shall examine some of the attitudes and assumptions of gender feminism and some of the consequences for philosophical feminism of adopting the gender perspective.

III. TRANSFORMING HUMAN NATURE

The gender feminist is radical in her Platonist confidence that a genderless ideal could be promoted by raising the consciousness of the dwellers in the patriarchal cave. Two assumptions, one negative and the other positive, are at the ground of her optimism. First, there is the negative thesis that there are no inherited human traits determining a sex/gender difference that would form a significant barrier to the realization of the egalitarian, assimilationist ideal. Here, perhaps, the feminists follow Simone de Beauvoir, who denied there was such a thing as a distinctive human nature. But American feminists are also convinced of Richard Rorty's dictum that "socialization goes all the way down," determining almost all the functions and practices that are specific to human beings.[23] This leaves room for the second assumption, which I call the thesis of corrigibility: the positive thesis that what we think of as human nature is plastic and corrigible, offering real possibilities for radical social change brought about by conscious manipulation of the beliefs and institutions that now largely define our social relations and mores.

On this view, human nature as we have hitherto understood it is, in large part, a myth invented by men to oppress women. For example, unlike the desire for food – which is biologically given, but not specifically human – the widespread desire for heterosexual relationships is thought to be sociologically determined. It is, in that sense, a gendered and not a sexual phenomenon. That is, it is determined by society, not by biology. More generally, a genderless society would in no way run up against any genetic or biological constraints.[24]

If acculturation is not the elaboration of any specifically human biological traits – if it is historical, social, accidental, or political – then it is essentially mutable. This doctrine, that human nature has no fixed essence, if added to the more positive doctrine that sociology goes all the way down, is then assumed to entail the thesis of corrigibility.

The feminists here make a common mistake: they conflate mutability with corrigibility. It is one thing to maintain (rightly or wrongly) that human nature is diverse and mutable, and that in each society it is the product of particular historical and social forces; it is quite another to claim that because human nature is changeable, it is politically corrigible. For it does not follow that we have either the knowledge or the ability to effect the kinds of changes adumbrated by the gender feminists. To assume that we can effectively and responsibly intervene to

---

[23] Richard Rorty, *Contingency, Irony, and Solidarity* (Cambridge: Cambridge University Press, 1989), p. 185.

[24] Many feminist philosophers are convinced that babies are born bisexual and are then transformed into "males" and "females" by their parents. See, for example, Ann Ferguson, "Androgyny as an Ideal for Human Development," eds. M. Vetterling-Braggin, F. Elliston, and J. English, *Feminism and Philosophy* (Totowa, NJ: Rowman and Littlefield, 1977), p. 61; Gayle Rubin, "The Traffic in Women: Notes on the 'Political Economy of Sex'," ed. Rayna R. Reita, *Toward an Anthropology of Women* (New York: Monthly Review Press, 1975), pp. 157–210; and Harding, p. 127.

change the mores that in fundamental ways define or determine us to be as we are – heterosexual, family-centered, genderized, and non-assimilationist – is to assume that we can take *full* charge of our social history. But nothing in history suggests that corrigibility goes all the way down.

My point is that the whig as well as the radical can embrace the idea that human nature is socially defined. But the whig is sensitive to the possibility that, in its own way, a particular social history may be as great a barrier to effective radical change as the "biological nature" that the feminists inveigh against. On the other hand, such evidence as we have argues for extreme modesty in assessing our abilities to bring about radical change without courting unforeseeable disasters.

Let me say that I do not wish to take any particular stand on the nature/nurture question. I plead ignorance and even some confusion as to how to set about talking about it.[25] I am saying that the feminist theorists do not appear to have a better grasp of the problem than anyone else, and that their confidence in the proposition that, say, a genderless society is achievable and a clearly worthwhile goal of moral education is quite unwarranted.

We are now aware that large-scale human intervention into natural systems can be disastrous. We know that natural history has its reasons and its wisdom, and that we are largely ignorant of both. For the present, at any rate, ecology is a modest science whose practical advice seems to be confined to telling us to *desist* from any large-scale intervention because of our appalling ignorance. I believe that much of this whiggish moral applies to the proponents of radical social reform. The sociological lessons are what the whig intuitively understands, but what the radical in her optimistic zeal is so willing to ignore.

It is ironically true that so many who are sensitive and considerate when it comes to issues of ecology are so intemperate when it comes to embracing an activist and radical social philosophy whose goal is to eliminate such things as the "gendered family." Perhaps we need a group of moral ecologists who would protect our fragile but vital social institutions (some of which have taken millennia to evolve) in the way ecologists help us to protect systems in nature.

Now I do not mean to say that we cannot look at utopian ideals for guidance in making needed changes; I simply mean that we cannot deploy any ideal in the wholesale utopian manner that the gender feminists do – as blueprints for the radical reform of preferences, values, aspirations, and prejudices. For those who do not like the word "conservative" I offer the more accurate and, perhaps, less tendentious term 'conservationist'. The careful and socially responsible philosopher – the Aristotelian whig – is a liberal and a conservationist; she wants reform, but she treads carefully in her dealings with such fundamental institutions as the family or the rearing of children. By contrast, the feminist who believes in the pervasiveness of the sex/gender system of male oppression is led to look upon the women she wants to liberate as a duped constituency whose actual preferences need not be taken seriously.

[25] But see Sarah Blaffer Hrdy, who persuades me that this confusion can be dissipated: *The Woman Who Never Evolved* (Cambridge: Harvard University Press, 1981). A persuasive case for biologically-based male and female differences is found in Donald Symons, *The Evolution of Human Sexuality* (Oxford: Oxford University Press, 1979).

IV. The Benighted Constituency

Feminists recognize that to make palatable such novelties as a genderless society, communal parenting, or bisexuality would require radical measures in "reeducating" both men and women. Many would restructure education to counter and ultimately to remove the widespread preference for heterosexual relationships. This is precisely reminiscent of Plato's call for a *new* consciousness that dispels the illusions of the Cave and a *new* mode of "socialization" that will inculcate the attitudes appropriate to the well-functioning just and genderless society. That any such socialization is implementable and workable is highly dubious. But whatever one may say of its feasibility, this feature of the feminist perspective on social criticism – its readiness to reeducate the benighted majority by "raising" its consciousness – is morally and politically unattractive. Here, the gender feminist – like other radical social philosophers – shows her illiberal colors. Where the liberal attends to the actual professed aspirations of those she wants to help, the radical is impatient with them. The goal of restructuring human beings and human society by changing what the average person professedly wants in favor of what he or she "ought to want" is an essential feature of gender feminism. In this fundamental respect, gender feminism is crudely illiberal and undemocratic.

It is indeed the case that most American women are not in sympathy with some of the fundamental assumptions of gender feminism. But that has not inhibited feminist theorists from claiming to be positioned at the "standpoint of women," whence they report on the insights afforded them by "the woman's perspective." Some interesting answers to the question 'Why aren't all women feminists?' are cited by Jaggar:

> Within radical feminism, two main lines of reasoning are offered to explain women's submission to domination. One line stresses the lack of objective options for women, portraying them as almost totally trapped by the patriarchy ... submitting to men in order to survive. The other line ... sees women as deluded, tricked or bewildered by the patriarchal culture, patriarchal science, and even the language of the patriarchy.[26]

Jaggar herself speaks of "perhaps ... developing a feminist version of false consciousness," and cites psychoanalytic and Marxist explanations of why so many contemporary women have the wrong kinds of preferences and the inability to grasp their own true interests.[27] Catherine MacKinnon's theory about why so many women failed to support the Equal Rights Amendment is characteristically condescending:

[26] Jaggar, p. 149.

[27] Jaggar says: "Most of the current socialist feminist accounts depend on a psychoanalytic theory of character formation, arguing, for instance, that the mother-rearing of children, in a sexist and heterosexist social context, results in psychologically passive girls ... and aggressive boys ... [But] given its materialist presuppositions socialist feminism recognizes that a psychological theory alone could never constitute a complete explanation ... [Socialist feminists] are claiming merely that certain forms of praxis generate psychological predispositions to perpetuate those forms of praxis." *ibid.*, pp. 150–51.

I think that these women . . . feared the meaning of sex equality in their lives, because sex inequality gave them what little they had, so little that they felt they couldn't afford to lose it. They hung on to their crumbs, as if that was all they were ever going to get.[28]

It is not hard to see that such accounts of why so many women are not feminists leave the feminist theorists quite free to discount all grass-roots opposition to feminism. Non-feminist sentiment is conveniently seen as the product of a socialization that has educated women to their subordinate roles. It therefore need not be taken seriously except as an obstacle in the path of realizing the genderless ideal.

The problem of how to communicate with a constituency so ill-prepared to accept the feminist message is naturally receiving keen attention. Thus Mary Anne Warren, confronting the difficulty that her version of androgyny may not, as she puts it, "play in Peoria," argues for the "need to speak to them in language they will understand."[29] But Elizabeth Lane Beardsley finds this too concessive.

[Warren believes] that people who are suffering from conceptual confusion must be spoken to 'in a language they will understand' . . . An alternative strategy for communication is to speak to them in a language they *will come to understand* . . . Let us cure conceptual disease by methods which are abrupt, but in the end more humane.[30]

Beardsley and Warren do not differ in one important respect: both agree that the people they want to help are "suffering from conceptual confusion" and both agree that humane measures should be taken to help them. They differ only on how best to proceed.

V. FEMINIST MISOGYNY

Women have been socialized to want the role of mother, to marry good providers, to like clothes that render them "sex objects." The feminist is depressed by all such symptoms of a craven femininity. What is to be done with the duped majority of women who choose conventional motherhood? Simone de Beauvoir's candor, as far as it goes, is refreshing:

No woman should be authorized to stay at home and raise her children . . . one should not have the choice precisely because if there is such a choice, too many women will make that one.[31]

28 Catherine MacKinnon, *Feminism Unmodified* (Cambridge: Harvard University Press, 1989), p. 226.
29 Mary Anne Warren, "Is Androgyny the Answer to Sexual Stereotyping?", in *"Femininity," "Masculinity," and "Androgyny,"* ed. Mary Vetterling-Braggin, p. 170.
30 Elizabeth Lane Beardsley, "On Curing Conceptual Confusion: A Response to Mary Anne Warren", in *"Femininity," "Masculinity," and "Androgyny,"* ed. Mary Vetterling-Braggin, p. 197.
31 From "Sex, Society, and the Female Dilemma: A Dialogue between Simone de Beauvoir and Betty Friedan," *Saturday Review* (June 14, 1975); quoted in Nicholas Davidson, *The Failure of Feminism* (Buffalo: Prometheus Books, 1988), p. 17.

However, de Beauvoir does not tell us anything about the kind of society in which Big Sister has the authority and power to prevent women from living the lives they may prefer.

Sylvia Hewlett, a moderate feminist who canvassed for the Equal Rights Amendment, is one of the few feminists who have been chastened by the knowledge that women are opposed to the current brand of feminism. Hewlett points out that the E.R.A, was not defeated by some combination of male chauvinist pigs, but by "women who were alienated from a feminist movement, the values of which seemed elitist and disconnected from the lives of ordinary people ... [and who] suspected feminists of being contemptuous of their values and aspirations — which centered on family life."[32] Compare *that* explanation for the failure of the Equal Rights Amendment with that of MacKinnon cited earlier.

Indeed, when one pays uncondescending attention to what women actually want and dream about, one realizes just how daunting the task is that de Beauvoir would face as a Philosopher Queen who is prepared to take authoritarian measures to *ensure* that her subjects take full advantage of their subjectivity. De Beauvoir has less confidence than Warren or Beardsley in the possibilities of persuading the women of Peoria to live in the light of the feminist enlightenment. For that is not what they want.

It is important to be aware of how the radical approach, which is so dismissive of established morality, has led the feminist to an undemocratic elitism that is so condescending to its claimed constituency. But it is equally important to understand that the roots of condescension are to be located in philosophical radicalism itself, which perverts the true task of moral philosophy and social criticism by its confident and principled disregard of traditional morality and common values. Radical philosophers characteristically believe themselves to have a clear perception of the "objective interests" of the people they want to help. Where liberal reformers are dependent on finding out about the ideals and preferences of those they help, radicals come to the task of social reform already equipped with a principled knowledge of what their constituents "really" want and need. Deploying their understanding of the "objective interests" of women, gender feminists tend to disregard the values of men and women who may like many aspects of *la différence*. The values of the uninitiated are "subjective" and must be discounted when they conflict with the genderless ideal. (Radical philosophers are not good at seeing themselves in ironical perspective. The irony of an egalitarian elite would not have been lost on Hegel.)

It seems clear (to me, at any rate) that the primary job of social philosophy is to make good theoretical sense of the moral world in which we live. Even as we grant that ideals of justice and equality are needed to guide us in repairing the moral imperfections of our institutions and social arrangements, we must be on guard against any deployment of these ideals that is illiberally insensitive to moral common sense. When the feminists advocate abolishing the family, or when political radicals advocate the undermining of a democratic government, they

---

[32] Hewlett, p. 211.

violate our preanalytic commitments to common-sense morality. Plato believed that the morality of the Cave was largely illusory "appearance." But a reasonable moral theory aims generally at saving appearances and making sense of them, and not at a wholesale dismissal of established morality as an illusion. And good social criticism should be based on a reasonable moral theory.[33]

VI. REVOLUTION OR REVELATION?

The effort to dispel the male world view and to replace it by a new feminist perspective has been broadly characterized as an effort to develop a new feminist epistemology. In a recent survey article entitled "Feminism and Epistemology" which, aptly, was published, not in a professional journal devoted to classical epistemological issues, but in *Philosophy and Public Affairs*, Virginia Held reports on the feminist conviction that they are the initiators of a historical revolution comparable to those of "Copernicus, Darwin, and Freud."[34] Indeed, as Held points out, "some feminists think the latest revolution will be even more profound." According to Held, the "sex/gender system" is the controlling insight of this feminist revolution. Elizabeth Minnich declares the revolution in these words:

> What we [feminists] are doing, is comparable to Copernicus shattering our geo-centricity, Darwin shattering our species-centricity. We are shattering andro-centricity, and the change is as fundamental, as dangerous, as exciting.[35]

Held describes the "intellectually gripping" and revolutionary effect of the sex/gender system on feminist research. "Now that the sex/gender system has become visible to us, we can see it everywhere."[36]

A claim of this revolutionary magnitude, enabling some to see a social mechanism – hitherto unnoticed – that affects "most of the social interactions that have ever occurred between humans" – is something that philosophers tend to view with considerable skepticism.[37] I have dubbed the feminists who accept this perspective on history and society "gender feminists." The gender feminists are radical in their belief that they are in the forefront of an intellectual and political revolution. They are radical in believing themselves to be in possession of a privileged perspective on social reality that provides a crucial key for political understanding and political action. And they are radical because nothing less than

---

[33] For a fuller account, the reader may wish to see my "Filial Morality" in the *Journal of Philosophy*, no. 8 (August 1986), and "Philosophers Against the Family," eds. Hugh La Follette and George Graham, *Person to Person* (Philadelphia: Temple University Press, 1988).

[34] Virginia Held, "Feminism and Epistemology: Recent Work on the Connection between Gender and Knowledge," *Philosophy and Public Affairs*, vol. 14, no. 3 (Summer 1985), pp. 296–307.

[35] Elizabeth Minnich, "Friends and Critics: The Feminist Academy" (keynote address), *Proceedings of the Fifth Annual GLCA Women's Studies Conference* (November 1979). Quoted in Gloria Bowles and Renate Duelli Klein, *Theories of Women's Studies* (London: Routledge and Kegan Paul, 1983), p. 4.

[36] Virginia Held, p. 297.

[37] That philosophers are reluctant to bring the full weight of analytic criticism to bear on the large feminist claims is partly due to the correct perception that, for their part, many feminists treat adverse criticism as an attack on women.

the elimination of the sex/gender system itself is acceptable as a solution to the ills and injustices for which it is responsible. While she does not question its objectivity, the gender feminist is nevertheless moved to ask: "Why has the sex/gender system become visible only *now*?" But one may also ask: Why is it still *in*visible to so many?

The gender feminist is inviting us to share in the fruits of an intellectual revolution of historic dimensions, one that is as fundamental and as far-reaching as those of Copernicus and Darwin. And, indeed, the discoveries of a Darwin or Copernicus have the common feature she is pointing to: by giving us a new way of seeing what was there *all the time*, they changed the course of intellectual history. Once made, such discoveries are repeatedly confirmed – not only in their original form, but in the way they structure and explain new observations providing new understanding about the way things are and the way they work. Pasteur's discovery of the cause of human disease also comes to mind. We now "see" that micro-organisms are the casual agents of disease "everywhere." Moreover, we understand fully *why* what Pasteur saw had *not* been seen before – for example, why Galen did not and could not see what Pasteur showed us.

The kind of revolutionary discovery that fundamentally changes our perspective on a wide range of phenomena, and that we associate with the likes of Pasteur, Copernicus, or Darwin, also had its analogue in prescientific days. One may think of Zoroaster preaching his doctrine of malicious evil forces doing battle with the forces of good, teaching his disciples to see their life struggle in a new light by viewing it as part of the battle between Ahura Mazda and the lying Druj. One imagines how Zoroaster changed the perspective of the farmer who henceforth saw himself fighting alongside Ahura Mazda and against the evil Spirit who threatened his crops. These insights of Zoroaster did radically change the lives of millions of people, shaping their reality by shaping their perspectives; henceforth, the world could never be the same for them. Indeed we may hear the disciples saying "Now that the forces of the Druj have been exposed, we can see these forces at work everywhere."

It is fair to say that what Zoroaster revealed and preached was no less revolutionary than the revelations of Darwin, Copernicus, or Pasteur. All the same, we should hardly describe it as a scientific revolution. Indeed, that is precisely the question that is posed to us in assessing the claim being made by the contemporary feminist when she declares that she is initiating a profound perspectival revolution. Is the feminist "discovery" of the sex/gender system of male domination more like the insights of Zoroaster or of Louis Pasteur?

It is important to see that this question arises because of the particular claims being made by the gender feminists. No such claims have been put forth by liberal feminists, whose aim is to eliminate discrimination and mitigate the sufferings of women who are socially and politically disadvantaged. The liberal feminist agenda is political and moral; a feminist theory of history or of knowledge plays no discernible role in the ongoing effort to initiate reforms that would ameliorate the lot of women. It takes no epistemological revolution to see what a liberal feminist like John Stuart Mill or Mary Wollstonecraft sees in the plight of women. It takes no uncovering of "new ways of knowing" to understand that women are politically and socially disadvantaged. Thus what the gender feminist is hailing is not a newfound ability to see that women are unfairly treated, but a perspectival, scientific revolution that identifies the underlying causes of injustice by exposing the pervasive sex/gender system that subordinates women and holds them in thrall.

Of course the difference between the liberal and gender feminist is not merely one of perspective. It is practical as well. Liberals want reform; for example, they want women to have equal academic opportunities for education. Having achieved parity, or near parity in certain schools of law or medicine, or in undergraduate enrollments, they move on to apply their efforts in other schools. Not so the gender feminists. For them, knowledge itself is essentially androcentric and what is being taught in the universities is "masculinist"; that women have achieved parity in enrollment and treatment is hardly relevant; the system itself must be changed. The gender feminist is thus embarked on a program of radical reform that would eventually "transform the academy."[38]

Consider again the insights of Pasteur and Zoroaster. They differ radically in content, but they share the revolutionary perspectival feature under consideration: both discoveries changed the way we see things; both affected the course of intellectual history; both are comprehensive theories encompassing a wide range of phenomena. Of course, Pasteur's discoveries have several familiar features that render them scientific rather than religious. First, we have been given a straightforward explanation for our earlier ignorance. Where Pasteur could point to the recent refinements in optical instruments, and to other new technological advances that made his discoveries possible, Zoroaster could only point to his private encounter with the angel Voho Manah (literally "good thought") for the source of *his* insights. Second, Pasteur gives excellent directions to those who have not seen what he saw, so that they can set up the conditions for seeing just what he saw. Third, Pasteur's insights have been empirically confirmed by myriads of critical experiments.

Our question, admittedly crude but hardly unfair, remains: is the insight of the feminist more aptly comparable to the kind of insight afforded us by Pasteur's discoveries? Or is it the kind of insight one may get from a powerful religion, a religion that does indeed persuade its adherents and changes their lives, but that cannot be counted as a scientific discovery?

I hope it is clear that the question is not meant to cast aspersions on any religion. I think it is probable that many a Zoroastrian farmer derived great benefits from his religious perspective. Nevertheless, the distinction between a scientific and a religious perspective is not to be slighted. And it is abundantly clear that the gender feminist is claiming closer affinity to Pasteur than to Zoroaster. The feminist talk is of research, advances, and new discoveries (a new Enlightenment!) which will correct the errors of the male sciences and arts.

[38] See, for example, Marilyn R. Schuster and Susan R. VanDyne, "Curricular Changes for the Twenty-First Century: Why Women?", in *Woman's Place in the Academy: Transforming the Liberal Arts Curriculum* (Totowa: Rowman and Allanheld, 1985), p. 18; and Margaret McIntosh, "Seeing Our Way Clear: Feminist Revision of the Academy" (keynote address), *Proceedings of the Eighth Annual Greater Lakes College Association Women's Studies Conference* (November 5-7, 1982), p. 13.

Held tells us how the "sex-gender system" is now being seen everywhere by scholars engaged in feminist research. What sort of sightings are being reported? To be fair to feminist claims, we should make some attempt to accept the invitation to look upon familiar phenomena through the prism of the sex/gender hypothesis. Deploying this twentieth century perspectival instrument and training it on familiar natural and social phenomena, we should find that nature and society stand revealed in a new light.

It turns out, however, that the sightings being reported are, broadly, of two kinds. We find, when we examine the first kind, that what is revealed is not so new after all; it is known to anyone who knows a bit about life. Such reports are gratuitously presented through the scope of the sex/gender system, for one needs no scope to see them. Upon examination of the second kind, where the feminist does report something really new, we find ourselves in the embarrassing position of not being able to see what she is so enthusiastically pointing out. Of course, it may be that this happens because we are unaccustomed to looking at things through the prism of the sex/gender system, but it is hard not to suspect that what these feminists are seeing is a vision not so much revealed as caused by the prism itself.

An example of the first kind of sighting is the report that women dress for men, or that women are paid less than men. Some of these sightings are questionable. (The wayward course of women's fashions surely resists a simple "dress for men" explanation.) But, in any case, the phenomena being reported are certainly not new and can hardly be said to be the fruits of a perspectival revolution into the dynamics of social reality. We do not need a feminist Copernicus to tell us about women's fashions or male bias.

An example of the second kind of sighting is the report of radical feminists like MacKinnon that most married women, unbeknownst to themselves, are prostituting themselves to their husbands.[39] Now this sighting is truly new; indeed, if shock value conferred truth value, it would alone be sufficient to suggest that the feminists are in possession of a new way of knowing the world. But we soon rightly suspect that these feminists are not reporting on the *Welt* but on their own *Weltanschauung*.

It has recently become clear to those who are properly fitted with the sex/gender prism that all of the special disciplines of knowledge must now be "reconceptualized" in light of the insights thereby revealed. For example, Sandra Harding reports that the scientist looks upon nature as the rapist looks upon the victim he wants to "penetrate."[40] One does not know what to make of this insight. It does not seem to carry the ring of truth, but on the other hand one is reluctant to call it false – and it seems ungenerous to call it nonsensical. This kind of epistemic deliverance of the sex/gender world view is, unfortunately, not atypical.

Other reported sightings are equally hard to credit as objective findings. Looking at the history of philosophy, the feminist philosopher may invite us to see how Descartes's analytical approach is androcentric and uncongenial to "woman ways

---

[39] MacKinnon, *Feminism Unmodified*, p. 59.
[40] Sandra Harding, *The Science Question in Feminism* (Ithaca: Cornell University Press, 1986), p. 116.

of knowing."[41] Looking at ethics, she highlights the masculinist bias in favor of rights and duties over care and responsibility.[42]

Secure in their conviction that they occupy a vanguard position that affords them special insight into all branches of knowledge, the gender feminists are turning to the task of "Transforming the Academy." We are, say Marilyn Schuster and Susan Van Dyne, "impatient with a curriculum that is predominantly white male, Western and heterosexist in its assumptions."[43] Much feminist literature is concerned with "reconceptualizing" the special disciplines. The feminist "critique" of the physical sciences is one of the busiest areas of feminist research. And again, if we look at science through the gender feminist's prism, the findings are (to say the least) intriguing. Here is Harding's concluding sentence in her influential book *The Science Question in Feminism*, telling us of the results of her investigations into the nature of the natural sciences.

> When we began theorizing our experiences . . . we knew our task would be a difficult though exciting one. But I doubt that in our wildest dreams we ever imagined we would have to reinvent both science and theorizing itself in order to make sense of women's social experience.[44]

It is not that the feminists have loose standards for what counts as good science. On the contrary, their standards are so exceptionally austere that the "male" sciences simply don't come up to snuff. For example, most of us naively believe that physics is by and large correct. But Held summarizes the conclusions of recent feminist researches into the foundations of science by telling us "from a feminist standpoint even the reliability of the physical sciences and of all that has been thought to be most objective and immune to distortion can be doubted."[45] We are asked to entertain the possibility that "our standard views of reality itself are masculinist and perhaps a feminist standpoint would give us a quite different understanding of even physical reality." Perhaps it would. But after being invited to entertain these austere doubts, it is pardonable to expect to be shown some concrete fruits of the more adequate feminist "theorizing." But we are not given a single

---

[41] See, for example, Linda Gardner, "Can this Discipline be Saved? Feminist Theory Challenges Mainstream Philosophy," Working Paper 118, Wellesley College, Center for Research on Women.

[42] This complex finding has objective merit, but it is hardly new; ethics has always moved between the poles of justice and mercy, or rights and responsibilities. It is much too early to say whether or not men and women have significantly different styles of moral reasoning. Recent studies strongly suggest they do not. See, for example, L. Walker, "Sex Differences in the Development of Moral Reasoning: A Critical Review," *Child Development*, vol. 55 (1984), pp. 677–91.

[43] Schuster and VanDyne, p. 5.

[44] Sandra Harding, p. 16.

[45] Virginia Held, p. 299. Held's survey of the progress of the feminist critique of science and other forms of masculine ways of knowing includes no reports of skeptical criticism. The (self-)congratulatory mood characteristically dominates discussion, extending even to "exhaustive" bibliographies. In a recent issue of the *American Philosophical Association Newsletter on Feminism and Philosophy* devoted to the feminist critique of the sciences, many critical articles were not cited. This led one of the neglected critics, Alan Soble, to complain in a letter to the editor: "Actually I was a bit surprised that other pieces critical of the project were not included in the bibliography, since taking into account what all sides have to say seems to be a necessary condition for philosophical discourse on a topic." See the *Newsletter*, vol. 88, no. 1, p. 19.

example of a scientific discovery inspired by the new perspective. We are not, in Margarita Levin's words, told "how feminist airplanes will stay airborne in the new world of feminist science."[46]

I submit that the global and intellectually incautious nature of gender feminist theorizing about nature and social reality strongly suggests that the vaunted revolutionary "discoveries" are essentially perspectival and doctrinal, being far closer to that of Zoroaster than to that of Pasteur. The suggestion is supported by the consideration that the feminist's insight, however intriguing and suggestive, remains esoteric and unconvincing to anyone who does not share her political ideology. I, for one, do not share the insight into the masculinist nature of the physical sciences. Nor has it been vouchsafed to me to exercise a particularly feminist "way of knowing" that affords me a moral or epistemic vantage that is unavailable to the average male. (Nor do I accept the unstated sexist proposition that men have *their* "way of knowing.") Instead, I find the declaration of a feminist Intellectual Revolution merely embarrassing.

If it is right to say that the discovery of the sex/gender system and its wholesale deployment to explain nature and society is basically religious, then that would help to explain why so few of us are vouchsafed the revelations that so exercise the feminist apostles. The inability to see what is revealed afflicts most people when a revelation is nonscientific and perspectival. Catherine MacKinnon looks on a married woman and sees her as a prostitute. To ask why MacKinnon sees what I do not see may be like asking why Ahura Mazda waited until the tenth century B.C. before revealing himself to Zoroaster, and why Zoroaster's revelation is still not accessible to most people.

Some feminists do acknowledge that their conversion to feminist epistemology is religious in nature.[47] If that were generally and frankly acknowledged, the feminist would still face the question of whether her particular faith is a cult that harms its devotees. But at this point in our discussion, that intriguing pragmatic question is not before us. For, in the main, the feminist philosopher indignantly resists the imputation that her doctrines are more religious than scientific. Indeed, as we have seen, she is prepared to give an "empirical" explanation for why so few women actually share her insights. Briefly and crudely, her answer is that those who persist in not seeing the powerful and pervasive effects of the sex/gender system are resisting that insight because of the stake they have in defending a system that has distorted their values.[48] But this sort of answer is a stock answer of many believers. Ask the Zoroastrian believer why so few people see the world as she sees it, and she too may tell you that most people are in thrall to the forces of evil.

[46] Margarita Levin, "Caring New World: Feminism and Science," *The American Scholar* (January, 1988).

[47] Janice Raymond, "Women's Studies: A Knowledge of One's Own," *Gendered Subjects: The Dynamics of Feminist Teaching* (Boston: Routledge and Kegan Paul, 1985), p. 55.

[48] In this vein, MacKinnon argues that women have learned to join the conspiracy that denied the violent and humiliating nature of the sex act and to believe they actually want sex as it is now practiced. She characterizes the willingness of women to have intercourse as a "complicitous collapse into 'I chose it'" that is part of a "strategy for survival." "Sexuality, Pornography, and Method: Pleasure under Patriarchy," *Ethics*, vol. 99, no. 2 (January 1989), p. 340.

VII. FEMINISM UNCRITICIZED

Now it may be said that declaring a new Renaissance or Enlightenment is a harmless and amusing thing to do. Why bother to puncture it? I believe that those who uncritically indulge the excesses of the gender feminists in this way are guilty of the kind of sexism that is truly disrespectful of women. For they are saying that intellectual women should not be held up to the same standards as men. The gender feminists are "critiquing" everyone; many of their arguments are literally *ad hominem*. There is an outpouring of books on feminist epistemology. Each book is reviewed by one or more fellow (so to speak) gender feminists who find it "powerful" and "convincing" and "passionate." There is an appalling dearth of cool, critical analysis of this literature.

This may be due to a pardonable desire not to get embroiled in controversy or to a distaste for a muddled and often boring literature. But whatever the reason, the intellectual cost of critical inattention is becoming very high. As long as professional philosophers allow free reign to the intellectual excesses of feminist philosophy, philosophy itself suffers.

While critical philosophy takes a holiday, we find some refreshingly straightforward criticism being voiced by nonphilosophers, some of whom are genuinely perplexed by the outsize claims of feminist philosophy – and not a little suspicious of its standing and coherence. When Elizabeth Fox-Keller claims that "the emancipation of science from its 'masculinist' heritage [requires] a transformation of the very categories, male and female, and correspondingly, of mind and nature,"[49] Joseph Adelson, who is not a philosopher but a psychologist, says "I have no idea what that means."[50] Presumbly, philosophers do know what it means. If we *too* do not know, we ought to say so. If we *do* understand Fox-Keller but find her wrong, we ought to say so. And, of course, if we both understand what she means and find her right, then what could be more exciting than the goal that awaits us: we should embark at once on the exhilarating voyage of intellectual discovery that leads to the emancipation of science and to the transformation of the very categories, male and female, mind and nature …

The feminist critique of the sex/gender system is part of a more general critique of society by social philosophers who would use one or another form of consciousness-raising to dispel the darkness of the Cave and to institute their ideal of a just social order. More often than not, the radical philosopher is innocuously utopian and socially irrelevant. The gender feminist would be so as well were it not that, in America, her influence on education is growing apace.

Philosophy, Clark University

---

[49] Elizabeth Fox-Keller, "Women Scientists and Feminist Critics of Science," ed. Jill Conway, Susan Bourque, and Joan Scott, "Learning about Women: Gender, Politics and Power," *Daedalus*, vol. 116, no. 4 (Fall 1987), p. 89.

[50] Joseph Adelson, "An Academy of One's Own," *The Public Interest* (Spring 1988).

HUMAN NATURE, SOCIAL ENGINEERING, AND THE REEMERGENCE OF CIVIL SOCIETY*

By Zbigniew Rau

INTRODUCTION

There is not much disagreement that the recent spectacular establishment of parliamentary democracies and market economies in Eastern Europe and the even more breathtaking events in most Soviet republics – which should culminate in the reemergence of the Baltic nations as independent states – may be convincingly conceived of as the triumph of civil society over the Marxist-Leninist system.[1] Both the collapse of the Marxist-Leninist system and the reemergence of civil society may be discussed in terms of theories which deal with the relationship between human nature and sociopolitical systems.

In the content of Soviet and East European experiences, I will argue in this essay that theories which base sociopolitical systems upon *potential* features of human nature rather than upon *actual* ones are ill-founded. First, I will discuss the difference between two kinds of theories of the relation between human nature and sociopolitical systems, as well as the criteria of the feasibility of those theories. Second, I will outline the effort to conceptualize and create the so-called new man in the first decades of the Soviet state. Third, I will discuss the achievements and failures of the Marxist-Leninist system in creating the new man in the light of work

* This paper was originally presented at a workshop, "The Reemergence of Civil Society in Eastern Europe and Certain Soviet Republics," conducted at the University of Texas at Austin and sponsored by the Center for Soviet & East European Studies at the University of Texas at Austin and the Soros Foundation. I would like to express my gratitude to Jamila Abdelghani for her comprehensive discussion of the paper at all stages of its writing; Wayne Allensworth for his suggestions concerning various issues related to its second section; Sidney Monas and Roger Scruton for their vigorous criticism at the workshop; and to Ellen Frankel Paul for her detailed written comments. Responsibility for the interpretation and any errors is, of course, my own.

[1] By civil society in this context, I mean various groups and movements which were established outside the structure and independent of the Soviet-type system. I will elaborate on this point in the last section of this essay. For different conceptual and ideological approaches to the phenomenon of the reemergence of civil society in Eastern Europe, see Ivan Szelenyi, "Socialist Opposition: Dilemmas and Prospects," ed. Rudolf L. Tokes, *Opposition in Eastern Europe* (London: Macmillan, 1979), pp. 187–208; Andrew Arato," Civil Society Against the State: Poland 1980–81," *Telos*, vol. 50 (1981), pp. 23–47; Zbigniew Rau, "Some Thoughts on Civil Society in Eastern Europe and the Lockean Contractarian Approach," *Political Studies*, XXXV (1987), pp. 573–92; and Zbigniew A. Pelczynski, "Solidarity and 'The Rebirth of Civil Society' in Poland 1976–81," ed. John Keane, *Civil Society and the State* (London: Verso, 1988), pp. 361–80. For attempts at an analysis of civil society in the USSR, see Gail W. Lapidus, "State and Society: Toward Emergence of Civil Society in Russia," ed. Seweryn Bialer, *Politics, Society, and Nationality inside Gorbachev's Russia* (Westview Press: Boulder & London, 1989), pp. 121–47, and John Gray, "Totalitarianism, Reform, and Civil Society," ed. Ellen Frankel Paul, *Totalitarianism at the Crossroads* (New Brunswick: Transaction Books, 1990). See also Richard Sakwa, *The State and Civil Society in the USSR* (Cambridge: Cambridge University Press, forthcoming). For a discussion of civil society as the force overcoming the Marxist-Leninist system, see Zbigniew Rau, "Four Stages of One Path Out of Socialism," in *Totalitarianism at the Crossroads*.

by Alexander Zinoviev, Czeslaw Milosz, and the Czechoslovak school of independent political writers. Finally, I will conclude that the reemergence of civil society in the region demonstrates the Marxist-Leninist system's failure in creating the new man – and, further, that this failure illuminates the flaw in theories which base sociopolitical systems upon potential features of human nature.

I. THEORIES OF ACTUAL AND POTENTIAL HUMAN NATURE, AND THE CRITERIA OF THEIR FEASIBILITY

Although it is difficult to establish what kind of an object of inquiry human nature might be, a search for a political theory which contained no explicit or implicit assumption concerning the nature, meaning, and purpose of human life at its core would be fruitless. All political theories embrace the relationship between human nature, however it is conceived, and the nature of political authority. Indeed, such theories embrace claims about basic truths of the whole of human life by asserting something about the nature of all men, by stating diagnoses of what is right and what is wrong with human nature, and by recommending on that basis programs or courses of action to be taken in public life.[2]

The fundamental difference between political theories is that some assume a view of human nature using men as they actually or normally are, while others imply an idea of human nature using men as they potentially might be – that is, as it is believed they could be.[3]

The first group of theories usually discusses human nature in terms of standards or definitions (for example, what it is to be God's creation, or to be a rational being) as well as in terms of interests, needs, and drives (biological, social, or cultural). For example, the more common Christian understanding of human nature stresses the notion of free will and man's ability to love, which reflects the image of God himself.[4] The Christian diagnosis of what is wrong with man is that he has misused his God-given free will, chosen evil rather than good, and therefore disrupted his relation with God. This diagnosis is followed by two prescriptions: first, the notion of salvation – that is, the regeneration of man by the mercy, forgiveness, and love of God (which occurs in the afterlife); second, the necessity of institutions, secular as well as ecclesiastical, to restrain or repress fallen man. Another example of a theory based on actual human nature is that of Hobbes, where the concept of human nature is based upon the fear of sudden death and the drive of self-preservation. The Hobbesian diagnosis of what is wrong with human nature is that man follows his natural, unsocialized drives which lead to the war of everyone against everyone.[5] The Hobbesian prescription for this state of affairs is the act of social contract and the creation of a sovereign who will force his subjects to follow the adopted standards of social life.[6]

---

[2] Compare the argument structure of Leslie Stevenson, *Seven Theories of Human Nature* (Oxford: Clarendon Press, 1974).

[3] I owe the following discussion to Graeme Duncan's "Political Theory and Human Nature," ed. Ian Forbes and Steve Smith, *Politics and Human Nature* (London: Frances Printer, 1983), pp. 5–19.

[4] Genesis 1:26.

[5] Thomas Hobbes, *Leviathan*, ed. C.B. Macpherson (London: Penguin Books, 1968), ch. XIII.

[6] Hobbes, *Leviathan*, ch. XVIII.

In such theories, observation of the past and present offers a useful tool for the evaluation of human nature, since it reflects what human beings essentially are. This is the case regardless of whether the author of the theory is conservative, and prefers a more static concept of human nature (as, for example, Burke) or liberal, and tends to see human nature as constantly evolving (as, for example, Mill).

In theories of actual human nature, the end of social engineering is not to change human nature but rather to create conditions to take advantage of it. A good example of this is the belief of many economists that cutting the capital gains tax will result in increased tax revenues. The calculation behind this belief is that reducing the taxes on profits would induce people – who are naturally self-interested – to invest and profit more from business ventures. This would in turn stimulate the economy; with more people prospering, the government would indirectly increase its tax revenues. Such a calculation is rooted in the assumption that profit-seeking is a part of actual human nature and that the task of the social engineer, that is, the government, is – while accepting human nature as it is – to improve the conditions in which an individual must live among others.

Theories of potential human nature usually discuss human nature in terms of capacities and possibilities. These theories are based on the assumption that human beings have significant and unrealized potentialities which could be developed under encouraging circumstances. The essence of such theories is that this development could lead to a categorically different type of man from that actually observed; the actual nature of man is deformed and mutilated by the contingent processes or arrangements that now exist. For example, in Marx, the most distinctive aspect of his conception of human nature is its social character: "the real nature of man is the totality of social relations."[7] There is no such thing as individual human nature, since all human activity is socially learned and determined by the kind of society that people live in. Marx's diagnosis of what is wrong with human nature is therefore, a diagnosis of what is wrong with society – that is, capitalist society. The social evil of capitalism is expressed in the notion of alienation, of man from himself and from nature.[8] Provided that, for Marx, nature means the social world, people who are alienated from it are not what they should or could be. Marx's prescription to abolish alienation is straightforward: "if man is formed by circumstances, these circumstances must be humanly formed."[9] If alienation is a social problem caused by the capitalist system, then the solution is to abolish the system and replace it with another by revolution.

In theories of potential human nature, observation of the past and present does not offer a tool for evaluation of human nature. Rather, the past and present reflect a systematic suppression or violation of potential human nature. Culture, private property, and institutional arrangements are seen as forces which make people what they are but not as they should or could be: that is, as they *truly* are.

[7] *Karl Marx: Selected Writings in Sociology and Social Philosophy*, ed. T.B. Bottomore (London: Penguin Books, 1963), p. 83. I refer to Marx as the representative of these theories, since I will go on analyzing Marxism-Leninism as the theory of potential human nature which was implemented in political practice. Of course, Marx was not the only representative of such theories; Rousseau before him and Marcuse after also fit into this rubric.
[8] *Karl Marx: Selected Writings*, p. 177.
[9] *ibid.*, p. 249.

In such theories, the end of social engineering is to change human nature itself. For example, many Marxist revolutionaries believe that the nationalization of most or all means of production will result in the transformation of human nature. The theory that underlies such a belief is that abolishing private property would, in the long term, lead to the cessation of both the self-interest of property owners and the alienation of the previously unpropertied, eventually leading to the appreciation of collective values. Such a calculation is deeply rooted in the assumption that those collective values constitute the essence of potential human nature, and that the task of the social engineer – that is, the revolutionary regime – is to bring them out.

Accordingly, the difference between theories of actual and potential human nature is not whether human nature is changeable, since both usually assume that it is (putting aside extremely conservative theorists). Rather, the difference between the two theory types is expressed in the answer each offers to the question of who can change it. In theories of actual human nature, human nature can indeed be changed – but by the individuals themselves (usually in an evolutionary process). In theories of potential human nature, human nature is changed by a social engineer (usually in a revolutionary process).

Theories of actual and potential human nature can be submitted to the critical scrutiny of normative, analytical, and empirical tests.[10] A theory passes the normative test if, after implementing the prescribed program, the rules of behavior discovered in the diagnosis and treated as a negative deviation of human nature are successfully replaced by standards of conduct which are seen as the essence of the concept of human nature. Accordingly, the standards of conduct which were originally ascribed to human nature come to rule people's individual and social behavior. In other words, a theory passes the normative test when it accurately predicts how human beings will behave once the theorist's predictions are adopted in practice. For instance, the Christian theory of human nature passes its normative test when "Christian love" determines the conduct of each and every Christian soul after salvation in the heavenly community; the Hobbesian theory passes it when each and every Hobbesian man adopts the standards of behavior enforced by his sovereign, and the Marxian theory passes it when each and every Marxian man overcomes his alienation and behaves according to the collective rules ascribed to his nature in communist society.

A theory of human nature passes the analytical test when its prescription against what is wrong with human nature offers a consistent solution in terms of the relation between individual human beings and their social environment. The solution is consistent when harmony is reached between individual human beings and the social wholes to which they belong. This is possible in turn only when there is no tension between the public and private spheres of an individual's life, which would result in a dual personality reflecting each of the two spheres. In other words, the harmony under discussion is achieved when each and every man who follows the rules of social behavior enjoys inner integrity. For example, Christian souls

[10] For a very similar argument structure, see Duncan's "Political Theory and Human Nature," p. 15. I extend his argument, substituting my own terminology ('normative', 'analytical', 'empirical') for his ('moral', 'logical', 'sociological').

achieve such integrity in the heavenly community after not partially but fully overcoming original sin; Hobbesian men achieve it under the rule of their sovereign after not partially but fully overcoming their unsocial conduct; and Marxian men in communist society find integrity, again, after not partially but fully overcoming their previous alienation.

In turn, a theory of human nature passes the empirical test when the program offered in its prescription can be brought to fruition in the world, and it works as the theorist thought that it would. For instance, the Christian, Hobbesian, and Marxian theories pass this test when the salvation of man by God, Hobbesian polity, and Marxian communist society are each empirically verifiable realities.

II. THE EFFORTS TO CREATE THE NEW MAN IN THE THEORY AND PRACTICE OF THE SOVIET STATE

The most persistent (and, indeed, spectacular) attempts at building sociopolitical systems upon the premises of theories of potential human nature are to be found in the revolutionary activity of Marxist-Leninist movements. The common feature of all these attempts, whether undertaken in Russia, Vietnam, or Mozambique, was to liberate human beings from their actual nature by the creation of a new man.[11] The most complex theoretical considerations concerning the project of the creation of the new man, as well as the longest efforts made by a state institution to put this project into practice, were launched in the Soviet Union. Moreover, the Soviet experience was commonly used for reference when undertaking the same task in other Marxist-Leninist systems. I will therefore use the Soviet attempts at the creation of the new man as a case study.

The notion of the new man is older than the Marxist-Leninist system. It was introduced by Russian revolutionary political thinkers and writers in the 1860s – such as N.G. Chernyshevsky, author of *What Is to Be Done? Stories about the New Men and Women* (1862), P.N. Tkachev, author of *The People of the Future* (1868), and S. Nechaev, who probably had his hand in the secret *Catechism of a Revolutionary* (1871). The notion which emerged from these works – that of the new man as committed revolutionary – had an enormous impact upon the intellectual formation of the Russian intelligentsia in the following decades and was ultimately accommodated in the Bolshevik ranks.

The best example of this is Chernyshevsky's influence upon Lenin – who, at seventeen years of age, studied Chernyshevsky's writings. On one hand, it was from Chernyshevsky that Lenin derived his understanding of dialectic, materialism, and political economy, since Chernyshevsky introduced him to Marx, Feuerbach, and Mill.[12] On the other hand, Chernyshevsky's novel *What Is to Be Done?* introduced Lenin to the concept of the new man. The influence of the latter upon Lenin was so strong that in 1902 he wrote – in conscious deference to Chernyshevsky – his own *What Is to Be Done?*, the essay which stated the basic principles of a centralized, disciplined revolutionary party. Indeed, in spite of Lenin's later criticism of populism, the link between Chernyshevsky's new men and women and those of Lenin is striking.

---

[11] See Mikhail Heller, *Cogs in the Wheel: The Formation of Soviet Man* (New York: Alfred A. Knopf, Inc., 1988), p. 7. Heller's book offers the best possible introduction to this subject.

[12] See Leonard Schapiro, "Lenin's Intellectual Formation and the Russian Revolutionary Background," in *Russian Studies*, ed. Ellen Dahrendorf (Harmondsworth: Penguin Books, 1986), pp. 188–252.

Chernyshevsky's characters – Lopukhov, Pavlovna, and Rakhmetov – conform their physical needs, feelings, and property to the revolutionary cause. They give up all their links with the present civil order, the prevailing morality, the conventional wisdom, and the recognized intellectual authorities. Lenin visibly echoed Chernyshevsky in his description of the revolutionary's life which

> demands the highest degree of endurance and self-denial: it demands of him that he should dedicate all his powers to work which is monotonous, which provides no visible results, which cuts a man off from all companionship with his friends; it is the kind of work that subjects the whole life of the revolutionary to dry, strict *réglementation*.[13]

Lenin made it very clear that this *réglementation* is the key to the success of the cause when he stated the operational principles of the Bolshevik party. He wrote:

> In order that the Center should be able not only to advise, persuade and argue (as has happened up till now) but really conduct the orchestra, it is essential that it should be known precisely who is playing what fiddle, and where, where each player learnt to play and what particular instrument he studied and is studying, who is playing the wrong notes and where, and for what reason (when the music begins to grate on one's ear) and whom it is necessary to transfer and in what manner and what place, in order to put an end to discord, and so forth.[14]

When the Bolsheviks came to power, there was a clear consensus among them on two points. First, as the leading Bolshevik intellectuals and economists – Bukharin and Preobrazhensky – wrote, the Communist society "must be an organized society."[15] Second, it was understood that the Communist society could be established only by the creation of the new man. As Lenin's wife, Krupskaia, put it: "Socialism will be possible only when the psychology of people is radically changed."[16] In turn, the Bolsheviks considered two options concerning the ways in which the new man could be created: by indirect or direct social engineering.

The first option was promoted by Lenin in some of his works; he announced it before the October revolution in his *State and Revolution*, the most utopian of all his writings. He further developed this option in his last set of articles in 1923. Lenin assumed that after the destruction of the bourgeois state and the ending of class antagonisms, the coercive functions of the state would gradually wither away. This would be possible since human beings, as soon as they become free from capitalist exploitation, would start changing their patterns of behavior. Lenin seemed to believe that

[13] Quoted in Schapiro, "Lenin's Intellectual Formation," p. 196. *Réglementation*, a French term, means "strict regulation by system."
[14] Quoted in Schapiro, "Lenin's Intellectual Formation," p. 241.
[15] N. Bukharin and E. Preobrazhensky, *The ABCs of Communism* (Baltimore: Penguin Books, 1969), p. 113.
[16] Nadezhda Krupskaia, *Pedagogicheskie sochineniia v desati tomach.* (Moscow, 1959), vol. VII, p. 12.

People will gradually become accustomed to the observance of elementary rules of living together – rules known for centuries and repeated for thousands of years in all codes of behavior – to their observance without force, without compulsion, without subordination, without that special apparatus for compulsion which is called the state.[17]

Lenin expressed a similar belief while discussing the prospect of collectivization. If the state managed to provide the peasants with some model cooperatives, the peasants would change their previous patterns of behavior, favor the new collective way of life and work, and voluntarily join them. Indeed,

there is 'only' one more thing that we have to do, and that is to make our population so 'civilized' and to understand the advantages of the whole population taking part in the work of the co-operatives, and to organize this participation. 'Only' this. And we need no other devices to enable us to pass to Socialism.[18]

In both cases, Lenin's concept of the creation of the new man by indirect social engineering was as follows: political power (the revolutionary Bolshevik party or the Soviet state) changed socioeconomic conditions (by eliminating capitalist exploitation or by launching model co-operatives), which in turn led to profound changes in the consciousness of the population and therefore in their patterns of behavior. The bottom line to this concept was that political power stopped short of forcing changes in human consciousness and behavior, leaving individuals to decide when to adjust to the conditions.

Of course, this is not to claim that Lenin rejected the concept of direct engineering, which indeed was carried out in the form of revolutionary terror. This resulted in the liquidation of the old upper class and the non-compliant members of the middle class, as well as the elite of the ethnic minorities throughout the Russian empire as the Bolsheviks reconquered their homelands. However, the most advanced effort to create the new man in the process of direct social engineering was undertaken not by Lenin but rather by his followers, who attempted to change the human psyche by using Pavlov's science of conditioned reflexes.[19]

The choice of the Pavlovian school as the scientific basis for social engineering was not an easy one.[20] Pavlov was repeatedly criticized by Soviet Marxist psychologists in the 1920s and early 1930s for his one-sided insistence that a knowledge of physiology was all that was necessary to understand human behavior.

---

[17] V.I. Lenin, *State and Revolution* (New York: International Publishers, 1932), p. 74.

[18] V.I. Lenin, *Selected Works* (London: Lawrence & Wishart Ltd., 1946), vol. 9, p. 148.

[19] In a now classic experiment, Pavlov trained a hungry dog to salivate at the sound of a bell, which had previously been associated with the sight of food. He developed a similar conceptual approach, emphasizing the importance of conditioning, in his pioneering studies relating human behavior to the nervous system. See *Encyclopedia Britannica* 1990, vol. 9, p. 215.

[20] I owe the discussion of this issue to David Jovorsky, "The Construction of the Stalinist Psyche," ed. Sheila Fitzpatrick, *Cultural Revolution in Russia, 1928–1931* (Bloomington: Indiana University Press, 1984), pp. 105–28, esp. 120–27.

Indeed, Pavlov's ideas were at odds with the Marxist conception of humans as historically determined social beings.[21] Moreover, he considered himself an idealist and vigorously denied that his concepts were materialist. Nevertheless, this did not prevent some Communist ideologists from finding Pavlov's ideas profoundly materialist and even, as Bukharin put it, "the iron arsenal of materialist ideology."[22] Following Pavlov's experimental psychology, Bukharin could assume, as in his widely quoted metaphor, that a human being was nothing more than "a sausage skin stuffed by environmental influences."[23] Such an interpretation of Pavlov's science of conditioned reflexes not only supported materialist philosophy, but also promised the success of direct social engineering.

Indeed, the main center of Pavlov's school, the Institute of Experimental Medicine in Leningrad, attracted the special interest of the renowned writer Maxym Gorky. On October 7, 1932, Gorky hosted a meeting between Stalin, Molotov, and Voroshilov and a group of scientists from the Institute, undoubtedly including its director, L. N. Fedorov. The result of the meeting was that the Council of People's Commissars granted the Institute the All-Union status as the nationwide center for "all around study of man." A little later Gorky hosted another meeting, this time between Stalin and a number of writers, at which Stalin bestowed upon them his now famous cliché: "engineers of human souls." The framework for the common effort of scientists and writers to carry out the task of direct social engineering was established.

From the above events, the notion of creating the new man by direct social engineering can be understood as follows: using all available scientific methods, the Center (the party/state apparatus) was to train the population to react in a common manner to the impulses sent by it. Those impulses were to replace the individual reflection of human beings and lead to those patterns of their behavior expected of them by the Center.

In summing up the presentation of the concept of the new man as stated by both Bolshevik (before the October revolution) and Communist (after the October revolution) ideologists, it is necessary to stress that the various ways of creating him did not alter the fundamental features of the end product. Indeed, there were three very different ways of creating the new man. The first new man, Lenin's revolutionary, was a product of his own critical reflection about the outside world. The second new man, Lenin's member of exploited classes who had been liberated by the revolution, was a product of indirect social engineering by the successful revolutionary political power. The third new man, say, Bukharin's Soviet citizen, was the product of direct social engineering launched by the party/state apparatus armed with the Pavlovian science of conditioned reflexes. What all new men had in common, whichever way they were created, was the replacement of their previous reactionary capitalist consciousness and patterns of behavior with new,

[21] Jovorsky, "The Construction of the Stalinist Psyche," pp. 124–25. Compare Jozeph Brozek and Dan Slobin, *Psychology in the USSR: An Historical Perspective* (New York: White Plains, 1972).

[22] This phrase originally stems from Bukharin's reply to Pavlov's criticism of Marxism in *Krasnaia Nov* (1924), nos. 1 and 2, quoted by Jovorsky, "The Construction of the Stalinist Psyche," p. 125.

[23] Quoted by I.D. Sapir, *Vysshaia nervnaia deiatel 'nost' cheloveka* (Moscow, 1925), p. 156. I owe this quotation to Jovorsky, "The Construction of the Stalinist Psyche," p. 125.

progressive socialist or communist ones. The essence of this change was the rejection of the individual's thoughts, values, desires, and actions and the adoption of collective ones. Conforming every sphere of the individual's life to the collective was possible only because the previously unrevealed collective potential of human nature would be liberated.

Accompanying the intensive discussion outlined above were efforts by the Soviet state to implement the program of social transformation in the belief that it would bring about the new man. In the first decade after the October Revolution, despite the period of worker control of industy, War Communism, and nationalization, the achievement in changing the patterns of behavior and the way of life of the masses of Soviet society was very modest indeed. As we know from the files of the Smolensk Archives,[24] the average Party activists at that time did not resemble iron-willed new men, revolutionaries sacrificing everything for the cause as described by Chernyshevsky and Lenin. Their obligations to the Party did not undermine their loyalty to families and neighbors. The workers lacked the proletarian collective consciousness; they maintained connections and sympathies binding them to the countryside from which they stemmed. Similarly, the peasants preserved village solidarity against the Soviet authorities and the new ways of life which were prescribed.

However, in the late 1920s and early 1930s, the unprecedented intensification of indirect and direct social engineering changed this state of affairs. Indirect social engineering changed the way of life of the minority of Soviet society – that is, the beneficiaries of the new system who sought advancement in its structures, especially during the period of collectivization and industrialization (for example, the Soviet-trained technical intelligentsia). Direct social engineering managed to change the way of life of the majority of society – that is, the peasants.

The point is, however, that both indirect and direct social engineering proved efficient in changing Soviet ways of life for reasons that had not been originally assumed by the Bolshevik and Communist ideologists. Indirect social engineering was efficient since upward social mobility was found attractive by a considerable part of society. This was the case not because of any obvious superiority of the collective way of life and work, as Lenin seemed to predict, but rather because of the opportunities to pursue individual political or professional careers and a new incentive system which rewarded those who complied with the new rulers. Similarly, collectivization as the pattern of direct social engineering worked – not because of an application of the Pavlovian science of conditioned reflexes – but rather because of the use of terror. Millions of peasants were killed, either by shooting, deportation, imprisonment, or mass starvation caused by the state confiscation of grain. This paralyzed what remained of the peasant community and destroyed its previous solidarity.

---

[24] The files of the Party headquarters in Smolensk concerning the socioeconomic and political life of the Smolensk *guberiya* and Smolensk *oblast* from 1917 to 1938. During the Nazi occupation, German intelligence discovered the collection and brought it to Germany for examination. At the end of the war, it fell into American hands. For discussion of the collection's contents see Merle Faison, *Smolensk under Soviet Rule* (Cambridge: Harvard University Press, 1958).

Nevertheless, whatever the gap between the theoretical concepts and political practice of social engineering, the task of transforming Soviet society was accomplished in the late 1930s. The individual found himself in a system which genuinely resembled the orchestra Lenin had written about decades before. At the top of the system was the Center, the party/state leadership. This combined three mutually interacting branches: the political (control of the secret police and army); the economic (planning and control of economic activity and distribution); and the ideological (imposing the officially established ideology and control of the channels of mass communication). The Center was in a position to implement its policy towards the individual, who was now required to identify himself with and promote the single system of official morality by his membership, participation, and activity in the political institutions and economic structures established and supervised by the Center.

II. The Marxist-Leninist System and the New Man: Achievements and Failures

The fundamental question which arises from the above discussion is how far the Soviet system succeeded in creating the new man. In other words, it asks how new this man was and how much he differed from his predecessor. The answers to this question differ profoundly since they depend upon the particular Communist system's stage of development, its natural variation, and the individual experience of the analyst himself. In order to understand the achievements and failures of the Marxist-Leninist system in creating the new man, it is necessary to review a representative spectrum of perceptions. I will therefore discuss the concepts of the following authors: Russian émigré scholar and writer Alexander Zinoviev, whose perceptions are based upon the Soviet experience in the 1960s and 1970s; Czeslaw Milosz, a Polish émigré writer, who refers to his observations in Poland in the late 1940s; and the dissident political thinkers of Czechoslovakia, who analyze their own situation in the 1970s.

Zinoviev and homo sovieticus

Zinoviev assumes that in the system under discussion, social engineering is so successful that the new man really does display all the features the Center expected of him. There is no distinction between the collective public and individual private spheres of his life, since his consciousness and behavior are, in both spheres, equally shaped by and subordinated to the social engineer. Indeed, *homo sovieticus*, as Zinoviev calls the new man

> ... has been trained to live in pretty dreadful conditions. He is ready to face hardships. He continually expects something even worse. He is humble before the dispositions of the powers-that-be ... [He] always tries to put a spoke in the wheels of anyone disrupting the customary forms of behavior ... He totally supports his leadership because he possesses the standardized consciousness formed by the ideology, a feeling of responsibility for the country as a whole, a readiness for sacrifice and a readiness to sacrifice others.[25]

[25] Alexander Zinoviev, *Homo Sovieticus* (Boston, New York: The Atlantic Monthly Press, 1985), p. 197.

Zinoviev assumes that his *homo sovieticus* has acquired "the minimum of vital goods, an uncomplicated life and minimum guarantees for the future ... at a price of losing his personal independence, the price of subjection to a primary collective, the price of communal enslavement."[26]

Indeed, Zinoviev's new man is not capable of rational and moral agency. On the one hand, he bears a striking resemblance to the Pavlovian dog, since he does not act according to his own calculation. Rather, he displays only "a more or less stable reaction to everything [he] bumps up against: a behavioral stereotype." On the other hand, he does not have any convictions, that is, any "*a priori* guides to how [he] should behave in a concrete situation."[27] Rather, he is "deprived of any social or moral foundation and ready for any abomination that circumstances might demand."[28]

The system *homo sovieticus* lives in is not predominantly based upon the terror of the Center; therefore, coercion from above is not a constitutive part of it. Rather, coercion arises from the new social structure itself, from the collective in which he lives and works.[29] Given that this social structure is unchangeable, the system reproduces itself. In this situation, the new man cannot overcome his status and emancipate himself from the collective.

In sum, in Zinoviev's analysis the Marxist-Leninist system fully succeeded in creating the new man.

Milosz and the captive mind

Milosz admits that, in the process of building the new system and the new man, the social engineer relies upon terror. Terror is required to further the phenomenon as a whole.[30] Indeed, the majority of the population (due to their strong Catholic beliefs which preclude conversion) is immunized against the "New Faith" from which the social engineer derives his legitimacy; therefore, their participation in creating the new system and the new man has to be forced. Nevertheless, Milosz does not consider the problem in "terms of might and coercion,"[31] since he does not analyze the situation of the average individual in the system under discussion. Rather, he deals with the state of mind of a member of the intellectual elite, the writer or philosopher who is a leftist or at least a sympathizer of the left, who as such is open to "the pressure of the argument" of the system.

The system portrays itself as the expression of the objective historical process; it offers participation in creating a new, better world. To this argument, the leftist intellectual – the captive mind, as Milosz calls him – cannot remain indifferent. Suffering from isolation and the lack of public recognition for the significance of

[26] Alexander Zinoviev, *The Reality of Communism* (London: Victor Gollancz Ltd, 1984), p. 125.
[27] Zinoviev, *Homo Sovieticus*, p. 11.
[28] Zinoviev, *The Reality of Communism*, p. 129.
[29] *ibid.*, p. 47.
[30] Czeslaw Milosz, *Native Realm* (London, Manchester: Sidgewick and Jackson/Carcanet New Press, 1981), p. 281.
[31] Czeslaw Milosz, *The Captive Mind* (New York: Vintage Books, 1953), p. 6.

his work, he longs for "an active and positive life" and its "social usefulness."[32] As a humanist, he desires to serve mankind. "Not mankind as it is," however, since they do not accept his work, "but mankind as it should be," that is, full of appreciation for his service.[33] Therefore, the captive mind understands the prospect of cooperation with the system as an opportunity to fulfill his longing and desire "in harmony with historical laws and the dynamics of reality."[34]

Desiring to cooperate with the system, the captive mind takes upon himself the task of the social engineer and changes his consciousness and behavior on his own. The essence of this process is to eliminate (or at least diminish) the distinction between the public and private spheres of his life, and to conform both of them to the expectations of the Center. There are two options open to Milosz's captive mind. First, he can entirely conform himself to the system. This requires the complete renunciation of all his previous religious and patriotic feelings, as well as all ethical beliefs which the Center finds unacceptable. Milosz compares this renunciation to swallowing the "Murti-Bing pill" (from a novel of fantasy by Polish writer S.I. Witkiewicz), which provided the patient with an organic world view.[35] The cure is painful, causing fundamental inner conflict and a temporary crisis of personality. Nevertheless, it leads to full unity with the system, which in turn brings a feeling of inner peace, harmony, and relief. The division between the public and private sphere of his life is over.

The second option Milosz's captive mind can choose is to publicly manifest his commitment to the system but simultaneously to defend his own identity against that system by taking "refuge in an inner sanctuary."[36] There he tries to preserve and cultivate his old, individual consciousness. He plays a game with the system which Milosz compares to Ketman, a sophisticated strategy worked out by Moslems in the Middle East who had tried to save their identities against the claims of powerful orthodox mullahs.[37] Success in the game "in defence of one's thoughts and feelings" becomes a source of satisfaction.[38] Nevertheless, the game itself brings about a fundamental division between the public and private sphere of the life of the player. The public sphere conforms to the demands of the social engineer, while the private does not.

Milosz's captive mind usually prefers to play Ketman rather than swallow the Murti-Bing pill. As a player, he remains capable of both rational and moral agency. Indeed, he is a rational agent who calculates the extent of his profitable concessions to the system, as well as the extent of the safe sphere of his privacy. Every day he makes choices which are aimed at retaining balance between the public and private spheres of his life. He is also a moral agent who undertakes this game in the name of his own normative concepts, which he considers superior to

[32] Czeslaw Milosz, *The Captive Mind* (New York: Vintage Books, 1953), p. 6, 12.
[33] *ibid.*, p. 11.
[34] *ibid.*, p. 11.
[35] *ibid.*, p. 3–23.
[36] *ibid.*, p. 54.
[37] *ibid.*, p. 54–57.
[38] *ibid.*, p. 53.

those imposed by the Center. He defends the possibility of acting according to those concepts in privacy.

Regardless of whether Milosz's captive mind decides to swallow the Murti-Bing pill or to play Ketman, he suffers from "the Hegelian bite" – that is, the belief that the system is a historical necessity. Therefore, as far as fundamentals are concerned, the captive mind is in agreement with the system; he accepts its philosophical legitimacy. In this situation, playing Ketman as "a means of self-realization" against the system becomes a game without any prospect of long-term success. Indeed, in the long run, the distinction between the captive mind and the system will disappear.

> After long acquaintance with his role, a man grows into it so closely that he can no longer differentiate his true self from the self he simulates, so that even the most imaginative of individuals speak to each other in Party slogans.[39]

Sooner or later the captive mind will become the new man. As Milosz assumes:

> Forty or fifty years of this education ... must create a new and irretrievable species of mankind. The 'new man' is not merely a postulate. He is beginning to become a reality.[40]

Milosz concludes that although the Marxist-Leninist system had not yet succeeded in creating the new man, it would undoubtedly succeed in the future.[41]

The Czechoslovak school and the reemergence of civil society[42]

The point of departure in the Czechoslovak analysis of the individual's condition under the Marxist-Leninist system is his relation to the official ideology. Indeed, it is the ideology that determines the place of any individual in the system and the way he should behave. As Vaclav Havel puts it, ideology is "a bridge between the system and the individual as individual."[43] It requires certain behavior from the individual which is in agreement with the ritual of communication prevailing in the system, such as taking part in the May Day rally, voting for Communist Party candidates, raising hands at meetings, and signing resolutions. The crucial point is that this kind of conduct is expected of everyone, regardless of his personal attitude

---

[39] Czeslaw Milosz, *The Captive Mind* (New York: Vintage Books, 1953), p. 52.

[40] *ibid.*, p. 73.

[41] Commenting on this issue, Andrzej Walicki writes: "*The Captive Mind* ... is a book about surrendering to 'mental captivity', not about defending oneself against it," Andrzej Walicki, "The 'Captive Mind' Revisited: Intellectuals and the Communist Totalitarianism in Poland," in *Totalitarianism at the Crossroads*, p. 67.

[42] Much of the material in the following discussion is taken from my paper, "The State of Enslavement: The East European Substitute for the State of Nature" forthcoming, in *Political Studies*.

ZBIGNIEW RAU

toward the official ideology. In other words, it is expected of believers and non-believers alike.

The explanation of this state of affairs is fairly straightforward. In order to implement the social engineer's prescription, conduct consistent with the ideology is required and enforced by the prospect of economic or administrative harassment of those who refuse to follow the established rules.

In order to understand this, a short discussion of the typical Soviet or Eastern European mechanism of consumer society is necessary. In the Soviet system, even in a period of maximum economic growth such as in the 1960s and 1970s, high consumer demand is continually accompanied by shortages on the market. A shortage on the market means that more is required than that the consumer have the necessary money in order to meet his entire demand. He also needs some advantage over other consumers who likewise have enough money. In principle, this advantage may be gained in either of two ways: the privileges gained through higher official status, or the position of the individual in unofficial economic structures. The first way applies to party and state bureaucrats and police and army officers, whose position implies access to special organizational measures, ranging from the allocation of housing and trips abroad to special stores for the sale of goods that are in short supply. The second way means that the individual is involved in the so-called second economy. This is not officially recognized, but is tolerated by the state and combines the elements of black markets, speculation, corruption, and private entrepreneurship. The enjoyment of a consumer society of the Soviet type must embrace access to the shortage-plagued market and at least one of these two additional sources.[44]

Anyone who violates the rules set up by the official ideology risks immediate expulsion from the circle of those who share these enjoyments. His job assignment, together with that of his family and even the prospect of a university education for his children, will be so low that he will be unable to ensure even the statistical average standard of living on the official market. Moreover, he will be cut off not only from the privileges enjoyed by the higher strata (if he belongs to them) but also from access to the second economy, since everything that is silently tolerated in others will be regarded as a criminal offence in his case.

Therefore, the individual does conform to the rules of ritual conduct as set up by the official ideology out of fear of the prospect of economic (and, eventually, administrative) harassment. It is fear that makes the ideology so successful that harassment becomes unnecessary.

In order to perform this function, fear has to take on a wider dimension than is generally ascribed to it. As Miroslav Kusy, a dissident scholar, points out, fear is usually treated as an occasional psychological reaction to a certain specific

[43] Vaclav Havel, "The Power of the Powerless," ed. John Keane, *The Power of the Powerless: Citizens against the State in Central Europe* (New York: M.E. Share Inc., 1985), p. 31.

[44] I owe this discussion to Wlodzimierz Brus' illuminating outline of the Soviet and East European economies in the 1960s and 1970s; see his "'Normalization' Processes in Soviet-dominated Central Europe," ed. Zdenek Mlynar, *Relative Stabilization of the Soviet Systems in the 1970s*, Study No. 2 (Koln, 1983).

situation.[45] In public life, fear is displayed as a reaction to particular predicaments involving risk (for example, an industrial action). Yet when fear ceases to be an occasional reaction to specific situations and becomes part of everyday experience, it turns into a lasting attitude.

When fear becomes such a lasting attitude, its consequences are not limited merely to the conformity manifested in public life. Fear of this kind affects the human personality itself. Indeed, it deprives a human being of the capability of detached reflection and rational action which follows this reflection. To put it another way, constant fear undermines the individual's status as a rational being.

As has been indicated above, individuals are supposed to behave according to the requirements of the official ideology, regardless of their personal attitude towards it. Therefore, they need not believe in it; as Havel stresses, though, "they must behave as though they did."[46] This in turn brings about no practical distinction between willing and unwilling or conscious and unconscious supporters of the system. Moreover, there is no distinction between its victims and its instruments, since "each helps the other to be obedient."[47] Hence, everyone is an integral part of the system.

Yet being part of the system implies a conflict between the identity of the individual and the identity of the system. Given the unchallengeable principle that "the center of power is identical with the center of truth," which "offers a ready answer to any question whatsoever,"[48] the identity of the system does not leave much room for the identity of the individual in public life. In this situation, the opportunity for the individual to develop his own personality is limited to the sphere of his private life. Usually, the power of the state does not overstep the line into private life; the way the individual enjoys himself in this limited sphere is up to him. He may spend his money, acquired in the first and second economy, on building houses, chalets, and cabins, growing unusual fruit and vegetables in his garden, and even traveling abroad. Moreover, he may express anti-system feelings. Indeed, as Milan Simecka, the scholar and often-prosecuted dissident, points out, people

> may curse, revile, and rail against allies, and profane all the Soviet sacraments. So long as they keep it for their private life and display their adapted faces in public and so long as no spiteful person reports them, the State makes no attempt to save their adapted souls. [It] is happy to allow this safety valve since private anti-communism, like the proverbial dog's bark, will not reach celestial ears.[49]

[45] For a discussion of bravery and fear understood as psychological categories and courage and cowardice treated as moral categories, and their application in the analysis of the position of the individual in the Marxist-Leninist system, see Miroslav Kusy, "On Civic Courage," *International Journal of Politics*, vol. ix, 1 (Spring 1981), pp. 39–51.

[46] Havel, *The Power of the Powerless*, p. 31.

[47] ibid., p. 36.

[48] ibid., p. 25.

[49] Milan Simecka, *The Restoration of Order* (London: Verso, 1984), p. 144.

Therefore, the conflict between public and private life takes place, to different extents, in every individual. The presence of two different competing identities, one part of the system and the other shaped by individual values, destroys the inner integrity of the individual. The destruction of integrity undermines, in turn, his moral identity. Discussing this issue, Havel writes:

> In everyone there is some longing for humanity's rightful dignity, for moral integrity, for free expression of being and a sense of transcendence over the world of existences. Yet, at the same time, each person ... somehow succumbs to a profane trivialization of his inherent humanity, and to utilitarianism. In everyone there is some willingness to merge with the anonymous crowd and to flow comfortably along with it down the river of pseudo-life. This is much more than the simple conflict between identities. It is something far worse: it is a challange to the very notion of identity itself.[50]

Thus, undermining human identity, the system undermines the status of the individual as a moral being.

These two main features of the individual's condition under this system – first, the undermining, due to constant fear, of the status of the individual as a rational being; second, the undermining of his status as a moral being, which is due to the permanent disintegration of his identity in public and private life – lead to a third: the destruction of his ability to take responsibility for public affairs. As Vaclav Cerny, another dissident intellectual, states, "the inability to act according to your own reason and conscience and to give independent consideration to the matter of human rights, justice, and the welfare of the nation" brings about "the state of total abdication of personal responsibility."[51] Indeed, the individual who "has no roots in the order of being" has "no sense of responsibility for anything higher than his personal survival."[52]

It is necessary to stress once again that, in the analysis of the Czechoslovak school, the individual is not identified with the system. His activity is not entirely subsumed by the system, nor is his reflection exclusively shaped by the official ideology. However, there is no doubt that, given his constant fear and the disintegration of his identity in public and private life, the individual's ability to pass independent rational and moral judgment is greatly weakened; its recovery requires extraordinary efforts. Accordingly, his ability to conceptualize independently, for example, a notion of liberty or justice must also be difficult.

Yet, in the system under discussion, there is a complete lack of personal responsibility for the public good. Therefore, it is important to notice that there is no society understood as a community united around commonly accepted values and shared obligations for implementing them.

[50] Havel, *The Power of the Powerless*, p. 38.
[51] Vaclav Cerny, "On the Question of Chartism," in *The Power of the Powerless: Citizens against the State in Central Europe*, p. 131.
[52] Havel, *The Power of the Powerless*, p. 45.

Nevertheless, the individual is in a position to find a way out of his miserable condition. In spite of the obstacles discussed above, he can "discover the proper moral orientation."[53] As Simecka stresses, this act "matures in private, in silence, without witnesses ... in the oppressive atmosphere" where "one has to weigh carefully one's values and at least learn to give them a name."[54] This discovery provides the individual with a basis both for daily personal decisions and for public work since, to use Havel's words, "it takes him back to the solid ground of his own identity" and eventually helps him "regain control over his own sense of responsibility."[55]

It might be useful to reconstruct this process with reference to the main features of the system under discussion. The individual who manages to command the fear which rules his public life regains the capability for detached reflection and for the rational action which follows this reflection. As such, he fully recovers his status as a rational being. Therefore, his ability to pass independent, rational judgement is also recovered. Accordingly, he can choose between the moral values he believes in private and those he must support in public. Choosing the former and being determined to stand for them in public life, he restores his moral integrity and consequently fully regains his status as a moral being. In turn, as a rational and moral being he is capable of taking responsibiity in public affairs. This is the ability needed to become a citizen.

Nevertheless, given the character of the system of social engineering under discussion, he cannot act as a citizen within that system and at the same time preserve his newly regained status as a rational and moral being. He can, however, act as a citizen by establishing, along with others (to use the words of Jan Benda, a dissident activist), a "parallel polis"[56] – that is, social organizations created independently of the system and outside its structure. In the understanding of the Czechoslovak writers, this "parallel polis" constitutes a rebirth of civil society. This indicates the direction by which the system may be overcome and constitutes the institution which can replace it in the long term. As Jan Tesar, another independent scholar, claims:

> If it is to be the beginning of change, it must gradually become an irrepressible trend to civic emancipation that will assume for itself all basic democratic rights and create its own democratic structures as elements of civil society. ... In time the structure of civil society may be compelled to assume some of the functions of the state because the state apparatus of a totalitarian dictatorship in decline eventually becomes incapable of catering to the elementary needs of society.[57]

[53] Havel, *The Power of the Powerless*, p. 100.
[54] Milan Simecka, "Community of Fear," *International Journal of Politics*, vol. ix, 1 (Spring 1981), p. 34.
[55] Havel, *The Power of the Powerless*, pp. 44–45.
[56] See Jan Benda, "Parallel Polis," ed. H. Gordon Skilling, *Charter 77 and Human Rights in Czechoslovakia* (London: Allen & Unwin, 1981).
[57] Jan Tesar, "Totalitarian Dictatorships as a Phenomenon of the Twentieth Century and the Possibilities of Overcoming Them," *International Journal of Politics*, vol. ix, 1 (Spring 1981), p. 99.

In other words, civil society overcomes or, in time, even replaces the system if people reject their previous status in it, leave its structure, and create their own. The crucial point in the transition from the condition determined by the individual's status as a part of the system to that of a member of civil society is his strong moral motivation. Accordingly, the moral character of the individual's decision to leave the structure of the state gives the newly-emerged civil society its moral dimension. As S.J. Trojan, another representative of the Czechoslovak dissident school, points out, since "the foundations of external freedom are laid in the inner being of each person," civil society is "a free society, created by free people."[58]

The analysis of the Czechoslovak school concludes that the Marxist-Leninist system completely failed to create the new man.

IV. CONCLUSION

It is now possible to pass judgment on Marxism-Leninism (treated as a branch of Marxism) as a theory of potential human nature. In order to do so, I will do two things: first, I will examine whether the analyses of the implementation of this theory in political practice, as presented by Zinoviev, Milosz, and the Czechoslovak school, can pass the normative, analytical, and empirical tests discussed earlier; second, I will evaluate the results of those tests in the light of the most recent events in Eastern Europe and the Soviet Union.

In Zinoviev's analysis, Marxism-Leninism passes all three tests. It passes the normative test, since the standards of conduct imposed by the social engineer rule the individual and social behavior of *homo sovieticus*. It also passes the analytical test, since harmony has been reached between *homo sovieticus* and the collective to which he belongs. Accordingly, there is no tension between the public and private spheres of his life; he therefore enjoys inner integrity. Moreover, according to Zinoviev's testimony, Marxism-Leninism seems to pass the empirical test, since the system managed to change human nature and therefore make communism the reality.

In Milosz's analysis, Marxism-Leninism passes only the normative test. The captive mind does in fact conform to the rules of behavior set up by the Center. Nevertheless, it does not pass the analytical test. Playing Ketman, the captive mind has a dual personality – one in public, another in private life. Therefore, he cannot reach a harmony with his surroundings or an inner integrity. Similarly, in Milosz's account, the theory under discussion fails the empirical test because as long as this dual personality characterizes the captive mind, the system has not managed to change human nature and communism cannot become reality.

In the analysis of the Czechoslovak school, Marxism-Leninism fails all three tests. First, the theory does not pass the normative test, since the members of civil society do not follow the rules of conduct imposed by the Center. Second, it fails the analytical test, since there are fundamental tensions between the members of civil society and the system. Third, it fails the empirical test, since the system has not managed to change human nature and, therefore, communism has not been established.

[58] S.J. Trojan, "In Defense of Politics," *International Journal of Politics*, vol. ix, 1 (Spring 1981), p. 73.

The crucial point which emerges from these analyses is that Marxism-Leninism proves completely unsuccessful as a theory of potential human nature if civil society has managed to emerge under its rule.

This point had already been stressed by the thinkers of the Czechoslovak school in the late 1970s, and became an empirically verifiable fact in Eastern Europe and the Soviet Union in the late 1980s. Wherever independent movements appeared, all traces of the features which characterized the new man were overcome by the members of those movements. Substantiating this claim is the existence and character of organizations which constitute various segments of civil society there. Witness the nationalist Karabach Committee in Armenia, the capitalist Economic Society in Poland, and the "decadent" Jazz Section of the Czechoslovak Union of Musicians, as well as independent political organizations ranging from conservatives, Christian democrats, liberals, social democrats, and socialists to anarchists. The members of all such organizations have been profoundly old men – not new men.

However, the emergence of civil society answers more than just the question of whether Marxism-Leninism has failed as a theory of potential human nature; it also answers the question of why it has failed.

The reason for its failure is to be found in its basic assumption that human nature is not in agreement with the real world. It claims that in the world as it is, the potential of human nature cannot be liberated by the efforts of individual human beings themselves. This task can be carried out only by an outside force: that is, revolution. Therefore, the fundamental tenet of this theory is that human nature can (and ought to) be changed only by social engineering. However, as has been shown in the above discussion of the three analyses, the aim of social engineering in implementing a theory of human nature is to deprive human beings of their rational and moral agency. This is the only way human nature can be changed in the desired direction. Accordingly, Marxism-Leninism as a theory of potential human nature must imply that it is possible to deprive human beings of their rational and moral capacity. Indeed, the very calculation of the successful implementation of this theory must be based upon this premise.

The fundamental differences in the evaluation of the system's efficiency in creating the new man in the analyses of Ziniviev, Milosz, and the Czechoslovak school result from their different perceptions of the relationship between the social engineer and the individual. Zinoviev and Milosz are in agreement with the Communist social engineer that it is possible to deprive human beings of their rational and moral capacity. Zinoviev claims that his *homo sovieticus* has already ceased to be a rational and moral agent. Milosz assumes that, though this has not yet happened, it will happen since his captive mind – regardless of his apparent success as a player of Ketman – will follow in the footsteps of Zinoviev's *homo sovieticus* in the future. The reasons for this similarity of analyses by Zinoviev and Milosz are to be found in their deep anthropological pessimism expressed in an important assumption concerning human nature. This is that the outer pressure of a social engineer always proves stronger than the inner strength of an individual.

The writers of the Czechoslovak school assume exactly the opposite. The outer pressure of a social engineer – regardless of how strong it may be – always proves weaker than the inner strength of an individual. Therefore, the social engineer can only *undermine* human beings' rational and moral capacity, not *deprive* them of it. Accordingly, a revindication of full rational and moral agency by individuals under the Marxist-Leninist system is possible. This revindication becomes widespread and complete only through civil society.

Civil society – as can be conceptualized from the works of the Czechoslovak writers – means a voluntary association of individuals (and eventually groups of individuals) whose strong sense of autonomy and independence from the system allows them to undertake their own activity in public life alongside the system's structure. Civil society is an association of rational agents who decide for themselves whether to join it and how to act in it. It is also an association of moral agents who promote their own concepts (for example, of liberty or justice) by which they want to replace the system. Therefore, the creation of and participation in civil society is caused by and further promotes the reassertion of its members as fully rational and moral agents.

The reemergence of civil society so understood unequivocally indicates why Marxism-Leninism as a theory of potential human nature is ill-founded: it implies that it is possible to deprive human beings of their rational and moral capacity. This miscalculation led to the collapse of the Marxist-Leninist system in Eastern Europe; it is leading it in the same direction in the Soviet Union.

It is justifiable to claim that any other political system which attempts to base itself upon other theories of potential human nature will share the fate of the Soviet empire. The reason for this is quite clear. Any theory of potential human nature is ill-founded, since it implies the same miscalculation that crippled Marxism-Leninism. It implies a change of human nature by social engineering: namely, the deprivation of the rational and moral agency of human beings. This does not mean, of course, that all theories of actual human nature are well-founded; they too may fail the normative, analytical, and empirical tests. However, the reason for their failure is fundamentally different. Theories of actual human nature may prove ill-founded only because of their false reading of human nature. Those of potential human nature are bound to prove untenable because of their assumption that a social engineer can deprive man of his rational and moral capacity. As I have argued in this paper, using as an example the most sophisticated attempt to change human nature, such attempts prove fruitless. Human nature, however difficult to define, is clearly resilient to forced alteration by social engineering.

Optimistically, the recent changes in Eastern Europe and the Soviet Union have also led the people of the region to this understanding. A Polish magazine recently published an article entitled, "What Has Been Gained?" In it, a 91-year-old Communist was interviewed (referred to only as "Comrade Guta" to protect her anonymity), a resident of "The Senior Citizen Home for Veterans of the Working Class Movement." Reminiscing over the years of her life given to dedicated service in the Party apparatus and secret police, she was disenchanted with humanity, and bitterly claimed that the reason for the collapse of Marxism-Leninism was that

> The idea was too great, too magnificent. People did not grow up to it. They could not cope with it. This is clear.[59]

---

[59] "Ile jest zdobyczy," *Polityka* (February 10, 1990).

That theories of potential human nature and the sociopolitical systems based upon them are fundamentally flawed is becoming conventional wisdom in the region where they had been implemented, even among the system's praetorian guard. If this wisdom, reflecting the ends which such theories have wrought in reality, can be reflected in the world of ideas, then the enormous costs of such an experiment will not be entirely in vain.

Government, University of Texas at Austin

HUMAN NATURE TECHNOLOGICALLY REVISITED*

By H. Tristram Engelhardt, Jr.

This essay is meant as a form of philosophical exorcism. The goal is to dispel the view that there are general secular grounds[1] for holding human germline genetic engineering to be intrinsically wrong, a *malum in se,* or a morally culpable violation of human nature. The essay endorses the view that major obligations of prudence and care attend the development of this technology. However, these justifiable moral concerns can be seen more clearly when one has dispelled what must, from a secular perspective, be regarded as pseudo-issues.

I. Unnatural Acts and Germline Genetic Engineering

There are moral controversies that loom large in contemporary political and religious debates, about which philosophers have shown scant interest. In many instances, the reason for this lack of interest is clear: the debates are substantially wedded to particular religious or cultural world views. One might think of the debate concerning the naturalness of contraception and sterilization, which has taken place within a world view that often did not give high priority to medical interventions, and that saw nature as a normative guide for conduct. This led to a disposition to accept the trials of this life and, as a result, to eschew novel technological interventions.[2] When combined with the neo-Aristotelianism of St. Thomas Aquinas, it led to condemning these interventions on the grounds that they perverted the intrinsic goals of nature.[3]

In condemning contraception, for example, Pope Pius XI argued not on scriptural grounds alone, but in terms of a view of nature: "But no reason, however grave, may be put forward by which anything intrinsically against nature may

---

* I am grateful for the comments, suggestions, and critical remarks of George Khushf. Though the essay profited much from discussions with him, the author has in many ways remained an old mumpsimus.

[1] By general secular moral grounds for or against particular actions or policies, I mean grounds that should be recognized as having moral weight by moral agents without the presuppositions of particular religious or ideological premises.

[2] The Old Church Slavonic word "podvig," which identifies the spiritual value of accepting the trials of this life, has been advanced by Orthodox theologians in their discussion of new reproductive technologies as a ground for accepting infertility rather than striving to treat it. See, for example, the remarks of Bishop Vladika Makarios in *Orthodox Outreach,* vol. XII (October 1989), p. 13.

[3] St. Thomas Aquinas, for example, argued on natural law grounds that, all else being equal, masturbation – because it violates the natural law – was a more serious sin than fornication, which violates considerations of charity. *Summa Theologica* II–II, pp. 153–54. 5 Pius XI, "Casti connubii" (31 December 1930), *Five Great Encyclicals* (New York: Paulist Press, 1957), p. 92. This encyclical and statements like it are embedded within a philosophical tradition that has attempted to generate general rational arguments to establish the immorality of a range of actions on the grounds that they are immoral. In this regard, one might note the special papal endorsement of the philosophy of St. Thomas by Pope Leo XIII in his encyclical "Aeterni patris" (August 4, 1879).

become conformable to nature and morally good." Such arguments are generally interpreted as religious, even when the principal antagonists condemn such interventions on the basis of arguments embedded within philosophical understandings of human nature and of the obligations of persons regarding that nature.[4] These philosophical arguments are generally seen to be dependent on particular religious or cultural premises, even though their authors may consider the arguments to be philosophical, not religious.[5]

Despite the readiness of many to dismiss such philosophical arguments as irredeemably rooted in religious understandings[6], an allied controversy has loomed large: the morality of germline genetic engineering.[7] Germline genetic engineering is regarded by many as morally improper, because it involves artificially changing the human genetic inheritance.[8] There has been much public uncertainty about the moral propriety of genetic therapy. National Institutes of Health (NIH) guidelines, for example, only allow experiments involving somatic

[4] It is worth noting that religious understandings of nature have led to considering nature sacred and worthy of protection against unwarranted injury or intrusion. Thus, one finds an argument against environmental pollution and destruction by Alfred Russel Wallace, Darwin's co-author of *The Origin of Species*. "To pollute a spring or a river, to exterminate a bird or beast, should be treated as moral offences and as social crimes; while all who profess religion or sincerely *believe* in the Deity – the designer and maker of this world and of every living thing – should, one would have thought, have placed *this* among the first of their forbidden sins . . .." *The World of Life* (New York: Moffat, Yard, & Co., 1911), pp. 300–301. Such arguments from design seem to provide the foundations for some of the general objections against genetic engineering. For example, Jeremy Rifkin, in his 1983 resolution, presumes that "no individual, group of individuals, or institutions can legitimately claim the right or authority to make such decisions on behalf of the rest of the species alive today or for future generations . . .", and this assumes that the biological status quo is in and of itself for some reason preferable to a revised human biological state of affairs in which there would be less biologically-based disease and greater capacity to realize important personal goals. *Genetic Engineering News* (July–August 1983), p. 4. Aside from some design-based argument, his considerations are open to the riposte, "How may individuals or institutions, who affirm a commitment to diminishing human suffering, *not* employ germline genetic engineering whenever it becomes clear that it will achieve considerable benefits at little risk?"

[5] For a study of the intertwining of theological and philosophical arguments bearing on the condemnation of contraception as an unnatural or an immoral act, see John T. Noonan, Jr., *Contraception* (Cambridge: Belknap Press, 1966). A secular philosophical review of recent natural law arguments regarding contraception is provided by Carl Cohen, "Sex, Birth Control, and Human Life," *Ethics*, vol. 79 (July 1969), pp. 251–62.

[6] I will use "philosophical argument" to identify arguments that do not rest on divinely revealed truths, but on what can be established through the use of natural reason unaided by divine grace or revelation. I will use "religious argument" and "theological argument" to identify those arguments that rest on revealed truths or special culturally or traditionally established premises. I thus include natural theology under philosophy and identify religious arguments with revealed religion. I also would include, though it is not crucial for my discussions here, special cultural assumptions, which may not be religious in involving the endorsement of a transcendent or ultimate reality.

[7] By germline genetic engineering I mean an altering of the genetic material of those cells responsible for producing sperm or ova such that the changes can be passed on to future generations. In contrast, somatic cell therapy alters the genetic conformation in cells that do not produce sperm or ova so that the changes will not be passed on.

[8] I have addressed a number of these issues elsewhere. See, for example, H. T. Engelhardt, Jr., "Persons and Humans: Refashioning Ourselves in a Better Image and Likeness," *Zygon*, vol. 19 (September 1984), pp. 281–95; "Gentherapie an menschlichen Keimbahnzellen," in *Ethische und rechtliche Fragen der Gentechnologie und der Reproduktionsmedizin*, ed. V. Braun, D. Mieth, and K. Steigleder (Munich: Schweitzer Verlag, 1987), pp. 255–62; and *The Foundations of Bioethics* (New York: Oxford University Press, 1986), especially pp. 375–87. See also Bernard David and H.T. Engelhardt, Jr., "Genetic Engineering: Prospects and Recommendations," *Zygon*, vol. 19 (September 1984), pp. 277–80.

cell therapy, not germline therapy.[9] In a public opinion poll conducted by the Office of Technology Assessment of the United States Congress, 42 per cent of the respondents stated that they found the genetic alteration of the human germline to be morally wrong.[10] However, the survey also gives data suggesting that the wrongness is not perceived to be absolute, but only *prima facie*. A sufficient reason would render intervention morally proper: 76 percent approved of germline human gene therapy if it involved treating a genetic defect that could lead to a usually fatal disease, and only 11 per cent opposed such an intervention in all circumstances.[11]

Groups such as the World Council of Churches have been more condemnatory in asking "member churches to support a complete ban on experiments involving the genetic engineering of the human germline."[12] As early as 1982, the Council of Europe made similar (though much more vague) recommendations by requesting an "explicit recognition in the European Human Rights Convention of the right to a genetic inheritance which has not been interfered with, except in accordance with certain principles which are recognized as being fully compatible with respect for human rights."[13] More unambiguously stated condemnations have appeared through private groups, such as the theologians who joined Jeremy Rifkin, the American critic of technology, in publishing a resolution "That efforts to engineer specific genetic traits into the germline of the human species should not be attempted."[14] At best, one can say that there has been a general moral hesitation regarding the propriety of genetically altering human germ cells.

This hesitation constitutes both a practical and a philosophical problem. It is a practical problem because, in the near future, our capacities to alter the human germline genetically are likely to develop substantially. We will need to fashion public policy in this area. It is a philosophical problem because, in our society, public policy is usually provided with moral justifications. In a secular society such as ours, if philosophy is to discharge one of the traditional roles of the humanities (i.e., to assess the core ideas and images of the ambient culture critically), then either the theological concerns will need to be exorcized from secular discussions or a way must be sought to articulate them in general secular terms.

In any event, anticipatory public policy reflections are likely as technical progress in this area accelerates. With the completion of the Human Genome Project – the project of determining the position of each gene on the human chromosome – we will possess a map giving us the location of all human genes.[15]

[9] Barbara J. Culliton, "Gene Therapy Guidelines Revised," *Science*, vol. 228 (May 3, 1985), pp. 561–62.
[10] Office of Technology Assessment, *New Developments in Biotechnology* (Washington: USGPO, 1987), p. 71.
[11] *ibid.*, p. 74.
[12] Subunit on Church and Society, World Council of Churches, "Biotechnology: Its Challenges to the Churches and the World," adopted July 1989.
[13] Council of Europe Parliamentary Assembly, 23rd Ordinary Session, *Recommendation 934*, Strasbourg (1982). The statement as it stands is strategically ambiguous. On the one hand, it can be interpreted as condemning germline genetic engineering save for rather narrowly drawn exceptions (perhaps the cure of fatal hereditary disease). On the other hand, it can be interpreted as simply requiring informed consent and a positive benefit-harm ratio. Such ambiguity likely serves political ends.
[14] *Genetic Engineering News* (July–August 1983), p. 4.
[15] Office of Technology Assessment, *Mapping Our Genes* (Washington: USGPO, 1988).

The advances in the last 20 years, both with regard to our understanding of the human genome as well as our capacity to engineer changes genetically, suggest that the human genome will be up for thoughtful revision within the next century or two. But even beforehand, limited changes will likely be possible. In the not-too-distant future, our relationship to our biological nature will change from its being regarded as a constraint to its becoming an object of manipulation.

At first, we will likely only provide a gene to individuals who lack one necessary for the production of a required protein. This will be accomplished by inserting the gene into somatic cells. We will probably first address recessive traits due to the absence of a gene needed to produce a required protein. A promising initial model involves removing bone marrow or other blood cells, introducing the desired genetic material into those cells, and then replacing them in the body once the insertion of the gene appears to have succeeded.[16] With time, we will likely not only add genes, but also excise them. It may very well turn out that this will be possible only at the zygotic stage. But if one removes an undesired dominant gene at conception, not only will the resulting individual be cured, but all the individual's progeny will also be protected from the gene's effects. It will be inviting to use such technology for many recessive genes as well. After all, even if an individual has been cured by somatic cell gene therapy, the individual's offspring may continue to carry a deleterious gene. Treating only the individual likely commits one to treating some of the individual's descendants, should they reproduce with a carrier. In addition, germline genetic engineering may be abetted by progress in *in vitro* fertilization that will permit one to correct a genetic error in the zygote, allow the zygote to divide, extract one cell, freeze the rest of the zygote, and then test to see whether the attempt at genetic engineering has been successful.

Even if the technological abilities still lie somewhere in the future, the foreseeability of germline genetic engineering – the theoretical capacity to reengineer the genetic information in the human germline – is one of the most dramatic developments in human technology. We belong to the first generation able theoretically to envisage the biological redesigning of human nature. The dramatic possibilities that lie before us suggest that unique moral issues are at stake. But a claim of unique moral seriousness, I will argue, cannot be coherently defended in general secular terms. Here, philosophy serves the function of (if nothing else) letting the fly out of the bottle – of showing that no unique secular moral problem exists. Instead, there are well-tried and important issues of prudence. Concerns regarding the consent of individuals and about realizing more benefits than harms properly attend germline genetic engineering, as they do all human experimentation and clinical interventions. But the absence of a basis for special moral limits will mean that, in the best of all secular worlds, given the progress of science and the benefits that such interventions will allow, germline genetic engineering will become desirable and morally endorsable. That realization is in itself revolutionary: human nature, as we know it today, will inevitably – for good secular moral reasons – be technologically reshaped.

[16] Barbara J. Culliton, "Gene Therapy Guidlines Revised," *Science*, vol. 228 (May 3, 1985), pp. 561–62; "Gene Therapy OK'd," *Science*, vol. 242 (October 7, 1988), p. 21; Leslie Roberts, "Human Gene Transfer Test Approved," *Science*, vol. 243 (January 27, 1989), p. 473; "Human Gene Transfer Test," *Science*, vol. 241 (July 22, 1988), p. 419.

II. DEMYSTIFYING HUMAN NATURE

Contemporary secular philosophy cannot give a canonical moral account of human nature. It cannot show why human nature must remain as we find it. In order for the current design of human nature to be regarded as morally normative, one would need to show either (1) that the process of its design was such as to convey intrinsic moral significance to the design, or (2) that there are properties of the design that show the design to have an absolute moral claim on us. Neither of these demonstrations is possible, once human nature is accepted as the outcome of natural processes and natural processes are understood in the absence of transcendent teleological claims.[17]

After all, human nature as a biological structure, and as the biological substratum and basis for human psychological and sociological phenomena, is the result of random mutations, accidental events, the constraints of biochemistry, genetic drift, natural selection, and other natural forces. Insofar as natural selection has worked well, it has adapted us to past environments, environments in which we no longer live, though it is now in the process of adapting us to the environments in which we find ourselves. However, since natural selection rewards inclusive fitness (i.e., not necessarily individual fitness, but the reproductive success of one's kin), and inclusive fitness by itself has no special moral claim on us as an overriding moral goal, we are left with human biological nature as a mere given, which is more or less well adapted to our current environment, depending on the goals one has for adaptation (e.g., likely long-range survival of the species, given a broad range of possible environmental changes; likely long-range survival of the species, given a narrow range of possible environmental changes, etc.).[18]

The point is that an empirical account of the biological structures that constitute human nature reveals only a particular result of a particular history, not a normative structure. After all, humans as members of a particular biological species, as members of Homo sapiens, are included in the family Hominidae of the suborder Anthropoidea within the order of primates of the class mammalia because of particular physical features, which could have been somewhat different. Humans are obviously primates in having pentadactyl hands at the end of markedly long limbs, with large feet, etc. Humans are physically distinguishable as members of Anthropoidea because of the structure of their central nervous system and the tendency to walk upright. The latter biological characteristic surely underlies the

[17] I do not here raise the separate issue of functional explanations in biology or of the role of immanent teleological explanations in accounting for biological phenomena. See, for example, J.R. Kantor, *The Logic of Modern Science* (Bloomington: Principia Press, 1953), esp. ch. 11, "Events and Constructs in Biology." See also Larry Wright, "Functions," *Philosophical Review*, vol. 82 (1973), pp. 139–68; and Christopher Boorse, "Wright on Functions." *Philosophical Review*, vol. 85 (January 1976), pp. 70–86; See also Ernest Nagel, *Teleology Revisited and Other Essays in the Philosophy and History of Science* (New York: Columbia University Press, 1979), esp. ch. 12, "Teleology Revisited," pp. 275–316; and Francisco J. Ayala, "The Autonomy of Biology as a Natural Science," *Biology, History, and Natural Philosophy*, ed. Allen D. Breck and Wolfgang Yourgrau (New York: Plenum, 1972), pp. 1–16.

[18] Depending on how much individuals value the long-range survival of the species, they will need to take steps – at least until the advent of quickly and easily applicable genetic engineering – to preserve genes that do not provide adaptation in our current environment, but which would contribute to human survival in possible future environments (e.g., after a nuclear war, a collision with a large asteroid, radical environmental changes due to the loss of ozone, etc.).

capacity of Hominidae to engage in symbol-related or symbol-dependent behaviors and in tool-making. But there is no reason to believe that the particular biological structures are, exactly as we find them, necessary conditions (except in very general terms) for the intellectual and social capacities of humans. The particular shaping of limbs, the particular character of joints, and the particular constellation of emotional propensities that mark humans are unlikely to be necessary conditions for the very possibility of our lives as rational persons. These particular characteristics are rather likely in great measure to be the outcome of happenstance and natural selection.

If it is not feasible as a result to state in moral terms the importance of the contemporary design of human biological nature, because that design is the result of happenstance and other conditions, then particular characteristics will in principle be morally open to revision. Indeed, the contemporary biological organization of humans may not provide the best way to achieve the goals we may wish individually and collectively to realize through our bodies. As Sir Peter Medawar observes, "nature does not know best." Instead, nature creates a "tale of woe [including] anaphylactic shock, allergy, and hypersensitivity."[19] Another way to put the point is that evolution has not necessarily reached the best solution (from the point of view of individual humans or human societies) to the problems of human bioengineering. As a result, one can easily develop a short list of human characteristics seriously meriting revision at some time in the future when our capacities with germline genetic engineering are fully matured. These would include (1) presbyopia, the nearly universal difficulty experienced by humans over 40 in achieving a short focal length, as needed for reading; (2) menopause, with its concomitant osteoporosis (and the sequellae of collapsed vertebrae, broken hips, etc.) and senile vaginitis;[20] and (3) the shortened life expectancy of males (in 1985 males in the United States had a life expectancy of 71.2 years, as opposed to 78.2 years for women), which is in part due to genetically determined increased risks of diseases – such as myocardial infarction and cancer of the prostate.

Not only are there a number of species-typical infirmities that many men and women would be glad to set aside in most circumstances, both for themselves and for their children, but it will also be difficult to draw the line between curing those and conferring new positive benefits.[21] Consider, for example, the possibility of engineering into humans a resistance to the AIDS virus (a resistance which is possessed by some primates) or to other infectious diseases. Would such an

---

[19] Peter Brian Medawar, *The Future of Man* (London: Methuen, 1960), pp. 100ff.

[20] Some have written of menopause as a disease, indicating the perceived need to use disease language in order to authorize desired medical interventions. Robert W. Kistner, "The Menopause," *Clinical Obstetrics and Gynecology*, vol. 16 (December 1973), pp. 107–29.

[21] It is at best doubtful that one can discover without appeal to particular cultural and individual values what should count as states of disease or states of health. For some excerpts from the controversies regarding this issue, see Christopher Boorse, "On the Distinction Between Disease and Illness," *Philosophy and Public Affairs*, vol. 5 (Fall 1973), pp. 49–68, and "Health as a Theoretical Concept," *Philosophy and Public Affairs*, vol. 44 (December 1977), pp. 542–73, H. T. Engelhardt, *The Foundations of Bioethics* (New York: Oxford, 1986), pp. 157–201; William K. Goosens, "Values, Health, and Medicine," *Philosophy of Science*, vol. 47 (March 1980), pp. 100–115.

intervention involve curing (prophylactically) a disease or achieving a particular positive view of human capacities? The same can be said with regard to other interventions that may in the distant future become feasible: (1) altering the currently genetically-programmed loss of calcium from bones in elderly humans, (2) increasing the intelligence of humans, or (3) increasing the cardiorespiratory reserve of humans. If there is no normative design in nature disclosable in secular terms, then from a secular point of view there will be no moral difference in principle between curing a defect (i.e., restoring the *de facto* "design" of humans) and enhancing human capacities (i.e., altering the *de facto* "design" of humans in order to achieve better the goals persons have – which goals themselves are likely to change).

The plight of secular arguments aimed at forbidding germline genetic engineering in principle is that they require showing that human nature as it is found itself provides a moral ground for constraining those who would wish to alter or refashion it. In the absence of some natural theological argument to establish a Designer endorsing the current design of human or otherwise to confer moral significance on the given character of human biological structure, the character of human biological nature will, from a secular context, be open to thoughtful revision.

III. EDUCATING THE MORAL SENTIMENTS OR GENETICALLY ENHANCING THEM

Though the advent of germline genetic engineering will not introduce novel moral concerns stemming from an obligation not to alter human biological structures, such technology will add a new dimension to reflections on how one ought to protect the matrix of social relations needed for a peaceable commonwealth. Much of the history of political philosophy is focused on envisaging the social structures needed to accommodate, balance, direct, or contain the belligerent passions, inclinations, and dispositions of humans.[22] The constellation of human inclinations and dispositions has been taken to be a given, something with which human institutions must come to terms. Insofar as substantial change was envisaged, it was sought through education, which was to solve the problem of directing individuals to be moral, to be socially cooperative, and to avoid rending the fabric of a peaceable polity.

Plato, for example, observes "that education is, in fact, the drawing and leading of children to the rule which has been pronounced right by the voice of the law.... That the child's soul, then, may not learn the habit of feeling pleasure and pain in

---

[22] Political structures have generally been regarded as ways of containing or directing human impulses because of the view that in a state of nature, without political structures, "the life of man [would be] solitary, poore, nasty, brutish, and short." Thomas Hobbes, *Leviathan, or the Matter, Forms, & Power of a Commonwealth Ecclesiastical and Civill* (London: Andrew Crooke, 1651), pt. 1, ch. 13, p. 62. It is for such considerations that Immanuel Kant argues, for example, that it would be immoral to resolve to remain in the state of nature. "In general they act in the highest degree wrongly by wanting to be in and to remain in a state that is not juridical, that is, a state of affairs in which no one is secure in what belongs to him against deeds of violence." *The Metaphysical Elements of Justice* (Indianapolis: Bobbs-Merrill, 1965), p. 72, Akademieausgabe vol. 6, 307ff. I do not mean to suggest that genetic engineering could obviate the need for political structures, only that some particular forms of violence for which now the only remedy is police power may in fact be curable.

ways contrary to the law. . . ."[23] Education addresses the difficulty of motivating individuals to see their own good or happiness achieved through the realization of the general good or happiness. Thus, for instance, John Stuart Mill observes, "If the view adopted by the utilitarian philosophy of the nature of the moral sense be correct, this difficulty will always present itself until the influences which form moral character have taken the same hold of the principle which they have taken of some of the consequences – until, by the improvement of education, the feeling of unity with our fellow creatures shall be (what it cannot be denied that Christ intended it to be) as deeply rooted in our character, and to our own consciousness as completely a part of our nature, as the horror of crime is in an ordinarily well-brought-up young person."[24] Education is regarded as a most appropriate instrument for achieving a well-working, just society.

A widely endorsed view is that humans by nature possess positive social tendencies, which must be orchestrated in order to suppress the antisocial ones so as to achieve a well-ordered commonwealth. This appears to be a position endorsed by Hume. "Any artifice of politicians may assist nature in the producing of those sentiments, which she suggests to us, and may even on some occasions, produce alone an approbation or esteem for any particular action; but 'tis impossible it should be the sole cause of the distinction we make betwixt vice and virtue. For if nature did not aid us in this particular, 'twou'd be in vain for politicians to talk of *honourable* or *dishonourable, praiseworthy* or *blameworthy*."[25] But here, again, education is seen to play a cardinal role by developing moral sentiments. "As publick praise and blame encrease our esteem for justice; so private education and instruction contribute to the same effect."[26] Education, both through the correct social structures and through proper upbringing, is endorsed because it molds or draws out moral character.

Orthodox Marxists, in particular, have sought solutions to the problem of human antisocial tendencies through reshaping social structures. They have held that current difficulties with social organization derive from the alienation of individuals due to exploitative social structures. Once the social structures are appropriately altered, socialist man will emerge, able to live in a non-exploitative relation with others. This will come about because "The communist socio-economic system is marked by an unprecedentedly high level of development of the productive forces, capable of ensuring the production of the abundant material wealth required to meet all society's demands. . . . The state will wither away and be replaced by communist self-administration. Law will disappear together with the state."[27] The social structures of communism are seen to be sufficient to reform the corrupt nature of man. Difficulties have remained due to the "lag of people's

[23] *Laws* II, 659d, in *The Collected Dialogues of Plato*, ed. Edith Hamilton and Huntington Cairns, trans. A. E. Taylor (Princeton: Princeton University Press, 1969), p. 1256.

[24] *Utilitarianism*, ed. Oskar Piest (Indianopolis: Bobbs-Merrill, 1957), pp. 34–35.

[25] David Hume, *A Treatise of Human Nature*, ed. L. A. Selby-Bigge (Oxford: Clarendon Press, 1964), bk. III, "Of Morals," pt. 2, sec. 2, p. 500.

[26] ibid.

[27] A.P. Sheptulin, *Marxist-Leninist Philosophy* (Moscow: Progress, 1980), p. 488.

consciousness behind social being."[28] This lag (along with "other factors") has been used to explain "the anti-social behaviour on the part of some members of socialist society .... But these contradictions, first, concern only a few members of socialist society and, second, are successfully overcome in the course of building communism."[29] The emphasis is on securing desired social circumstances by changing social – rather than biological – structures.

When wide-ranging genetic germline engineering becomes possible, the challenge of the governance of a polity will need to be restated. It may indeed turn out that there is a range of human antisocial dispositions and inclinations that can be more easily modified through genetic engineering than through education or through coercive or instructive social structures. One will then need to ask what balance among the influences of social structures, education, and biological structures a community should find endorsable as means for ensuring the existence of a peaceable community. For the purpose of example and discussion, one might agree with the argument of some sociobiologists who have contended that the inclination of young males to kill other young males is biologically based and was established because of its contribution to inclusive fitness.[30] In contemporary environments, when young male belligerence is augmented not only by firearms but by nuclear weapons, their contribution to inclusive fitness may have been altered.[31] Should such problems be addressed only through education and the law (or other social structures), were a simple genetic solution more effective? Indeed, if it is determined that some syndromes of marked lack of impulse control and of violence have a significant genetic component,[32] it will likely be the case that many would-be parents would want their progeny "treated" because of both familial and social concerns.

In the light of our future biotechnological capacities, the achievement of ideal social institutions will need to be rethought in terms of the proper equilibrium in the achievement of a peaceable polity to be struck between biological constraints on the one hand and social and political constraints on the other. In a sense, this question of the efficacy and consequences of different approaches to nurturing the moral sentiments has been anticipated, insofar as the problem of the moral sentiments is understood to be an empirical one. Hume, for example, takes the position that the judgment ("the final sentence") by which characters and actions are judged "amiable or odious, praiseworthy or blamable ... depends on some

---

[28] ibid., p. 473.

[29] ibid.

[30] For an account of the sociobiological basis of male aggressiveness, see F.B. Livingstone, "The Effects of Warfare on the Biology of the Human Species," ed. M. Fried, M. Harris, and R. Murphy, War: The Anthropology of Armed Conflict and Aggression (Garden City: Natural History Press, 1967), pp. 3–15. See also Donald Symons, The Evolution of Human Sexuality (New York: Oxford University Press, 1979), pp. 144–58. For an ethnographic study of violence, see Napoleon A. Chagnon, Yanomano: The Fierce People (2nd ed.; New York: Holt, Rinehart and Winston, 1977).

[31] These prudential considerations regarding mass destruction would play a role in addition to other moral judgments that one would want to make regarding homicidal proclivities even under "natural" circumstances.

[32] For a description of some of the syndromes I have in mind, see Vernon H. Mark and Frank R. Ervin, Violence and the Brain (New York: Harper & Row, 1970). The authors indicate their view that some dispositions to extreme violence may have important genetic components.

internal sense or feeling, which nature has made universal in the whole species."[33] Hume then construes the foundations of ethics as empirically based and therefore open to empirical study.[34] It is just one step further to see the moral sentiments as open to technological recasting. This need not be regarded as an invitation for coercive treatment of individuals in order to secure societal goals. If the changes that will be achieved are sufficiently desirable so that they not only avoid social harms but also facilitate individual success in a high-technology, post-industrial society, then the genetic changes will be desired by individuals for their children. In short, one can separate problems of coercion and political tyranny from the issue of the positive enhancement of the human species through germline genetic engineering, including changes that will enhance the character of social life.

IV. Festina Lente

A. Micro-level concerns. If there are no reasons in principle that bar the use of germline genetic engineering, one will need to approach such prospects as one should any other technological innovation – with caution and prudence. One will be well advised to begin by providing germline genetic engineering first for those genetic defects involving lethal genes, so that any unforeseen harms will likely be less than what would result from the conditions if left untreated. Such genetic treatment may be especially morally attractive to individuals who are generally (but not absolutely) morally opposed to abortion and would therefore not find prenatal diagnosis and selective abortion to be the approach of choice in avoiding the birth of a defective child. Indeed, the optimum candidates for accepting germline genetic engineering will be parents who wish to avoid, in nearly all (but not all) circumstances, selective abortion or the discarding of early zygotes – but who will accept genetic manipulation along with selective discarding of zygotes or early abortion in the face of serious defects engendered by the process of the treatment itself.

In such circumstances, since couples have the legal right to reproduce even when they know that the children likely to result will be severely defective, the option of genetic engineering at the point of conception can be justified as offering a positive balance of benefits over harms. Since no one actually consents to being conceived or being born, the issue of respecting autonomy will have to be approached in terms of the hypothetical choice of a rational decision-maker under such circumstances. However, since the circumstances outlined would as a rule provide a positive balance of benefits over harms under almost all secular rankings of harms, this test would be met as well.[35] In addition, the test of respecting autonomy would be met with regard to the would-be parents through their actual authorization.

As a consequence, at the micro-level, the usual moral tests required for research involving human subjects would have been satisfied. One would have (1) respected

[33] David Hume, *Enquiries concerning the Human Understanding and concerning the Principles of Morals,* ed. L.A. Selby-Bigge (2nd ed; Oxford: Clarendon Press, 1957), pp. 172–73.

[34] *ibid.,* see pp. 174–75.

[35] There are serious difficulties with hypothetical choice theories, which I do not deny. Rather, insofar as such accounts can be reasonably held to succeed, the envisaged choice to use germline genetic engineering should meet the criteria set by such accounts.

the persons involved (i.e., by gaining consent from those with deliberative capacity and by acting in a way that would meet the interests that a subject would likely endorse, were the subject a rational decision-maker) and (2) acted beneficently (i.e., by engaging in an action that is, on balance, not harmful and is specifically directed to maximizing benefits and minimizing harms).[36] As a result, considering such interventions simply at the micro-level, unless the interventions themselves are intrinsically immoral, there will be no moral prohibitions against them once the usual canons of caution and prudence are satisfied.

B. Macro-level concerns. The prospect of ameliorating the problems of antisocial behavior through genetic engineering raises concerns because of the risks it may involve and because it allows a biological pursuit of perfection that can be characterized metaphorically as the pursuit of the superman. As to the first issue, it is indeed a scholium of the maxims of prudence that "the devil you know is more manageable than the devil you don't." Still, the risk of humans destroying themselves remains quite high. Prudence argues for the pursuit of a less belligerent, more resistant strain of humans rather than the eschewal in principle of germline genetic engineering aimed at the solution of human behavioral and biological problems understood in a social context. Moreover, the pursuit of the superman (or superwoman) is not in and of itself evil. Though moral concerns regarding the obligation to respect the autonomy of others and to protect individuals from harm will properly dictate procedural and substantive protection, these concerns cannot justify an absolute prohibition if there is nothing intrinsically wrong with the biological improvement of the human species. With societal goals in mind, the appropriate prudential concerns when employing germline genetic engineering will be more complex than when only individual or familial wishes and goals are at issue. But the address of societal issues will not in and of itself in principle bar germline genetic engineering in the absence of secular arguments that can establish the immorality of using biological means to improve the human status – arguments that have hitherto not been forthcoming.

V. PERSONS AND HUMAN NATURE: A CONCLUSION

Persons in self-consciousness make themselves their own objects; in self-consciousness, they judge themselves. They appraise the extent to which they can realize or have realized their goals. Persons turn to their nature, and often judge it flawed by heteronymous inclinations and biological shortcomings. In so doing, persons come to regard their bodies as objects to be manipulated. In everyday life, one experiences the body as something to be improved (e.g., by exercise and physical training). Medical technology has extended this sense of the body as manipulable (e.g., joints can be restored to function with artificial prostheses).[37] Moreover, technologically targeted psychoactive drugs have increased the sense of the mind being controllable through actions on the body (a sense already given in

[36] National Commission for the Protection of Human Subjects of Biomedical and Behavioral Research, *The Belmont Report* (Washington: USGPO, 1978).

[37] H.T. Engelhardt, Jr., *Mind-Body: A Categorial Relation* (The Hague: Martinus Nijhoff, 1973), pp. 130–39.

the use of alcohol and other traditional drugs). In short, in a number of circumstances, persons critically thematize their human nature and reflect on how it might optimally be revised.

Self-consciousness "naturally" engenders a Cartesian or Kantian contrast between persons as endorsers of goals and persons as embodied self-consciousness limited in action by the particularities of their embodiment.[38] Because persons can envisage goals apart from considerations of the actual limitations of their own biological embodiment, the particularities of their embodiment can then come to be regarded as limitations that stand surd and merely factual against the sphere of self-conscious reflection and aspiration. When particular elements of human biology take on the character of obstacles and technology offers the possibility of their removal, the revision of human biological nature (including the biological basis of unwanted impulses and emotional states) becomes a plausible task for persons.

In a sense, the technology of germline genetic engineering only underscores an old theme. Traditionally, the fallen character of human nature was seen to justify prayers for the reforming and illuminating grace of God. In a secular, scientific context, the shortcomings of human nature now occasion reflections about the feasibility of germline genetic engineering. In either case, human nature is recognized as fallen or inadequate. The reflective character of persons brings the merely given factual character of human biological nature to critical reappraisal. What is novel is not the wish, but the possibility of its fulfillment.

The future feasibility of germline genetic engineering adds the prospect of acting upon our self-critical judgments regarding the shortcomings of our human nature. Because of the critical, self-assessing character of persons, the practical moral judgments engendered by the prospect of such technological advances are unavoidable. They are tied to us as persons and to the likelihood of our expanding technological capacities. Since these prospects cannot in principle be denied on moral grounds, we should anticipate that, if the current indications of the possibility of scientific advances in the area of germline genetic engineering are reliable, we will in the future confront the unavoidable moral task of prudently using human germline genetic engineering. In the end, humans will revise human nature.

Center for Ethics, Medicine, and Public Issues Baylor College of Medicine

---

[38] By a Cartesian or Kantian contrast, I mean the contrast between that element of us that is known in self-conscious reflection (e.g., my plans, desires, etc.) and that element of us that is disclosable only through empirical study or observation (i.e., determining whether I have sufficient cardiorespiratory reserve to climb a particular mountain in two days). Thus, for Kant, morality becomes a matter of what is articulable in reason; the particularities of embodiment and the character of human inclinations become irrelevant. "But since moral laws should hold for every rational being as such, the principles must be derived from the universal concept of a rational being generally." Immanuel Kant, *Foundations of the Metaphysics of Morals*, trans. L.W. Beck (Indianapolis: Bobbs-Merrill, 1976), p. 28, Akademietextausgabe, vol. 4, p. 412.